Aspects ...

THE SOC...
OF MODERN BRITAIN

GENERAL EDITORS

John Barron Mays
Eleanor Rathbone Professor of Sociology
University of Liverpool
Maurice Craft
Professor of Education
University of Nottingham

ASPECTS OF MODERN SOCIOLOGY

General Editors

John Barron Mays Professor of Sociology, University of Liverpool
Maurice Craft Professor of Education, University of Nottingham

This Longman library of texts in modern sociology consists of three Series, and includes the following titles:

THE SOCIAL STRUCTURE OF MODERN BRITAIN

The family
Mary Farmer
University of Liverpool

The political structure
Grace Jones
Chester College of Higher Education

Population
Prof. R. K. Kelsall
University of Sheffield

Education
Ronald King
University of Exeter

The welfare state
Prof. David Marsh
University of Nottingham

Crime and its treatment
Prof. John Barron Mays
University of Liverpool

Patterns of urban life
Prof. R. E. Pahl
University of Kent

The working class
Kenneth Roberts
University of Liverpool

The middle class
John Raynor
The Open University
and *Roger King*
Huddersfield Polytechnic

Leisure
Kenneth Roberts
University of Liverpool

Adolescence
Cyril Smith
Social Science Research Council

The mass media
Peter Golding
University of Leicester

The legal structure
Michael Freeman
University of London

Rural life
Gwyn Jones
University of Reading

Religious institutions
Joan Brothers
University of London

Mental illness
Bernard Ineichen
University of Bristol

Forthcoming titles will include:

Minority groups
Eric Butterworth
University of York

The economic structure
Prof. Cedric Sandford
University of Bath

SOCIAL PROCESSES

Bureaucracy
Dennis Warwick
University of Leeds

Social control
C. Ken Watkins
University of Leeds

Communication
Prof. Denis McQuail
University of Amsterdam

Stratification
Prof. R. K. Kelsall
University of Sheffield
and
H. Kelsall

Industrialism
Barry Turner
University of Exeter

Social change
Anthony Smith
University of Reading

Socialisation
Graham White
University of Liverpool

Forthcoming titles will include:

Social conflict
Prof. John Rex
University of Warwick

Migration
Prof. J. A. Jackson
University of Dublin

SOCIAL RESEARCH

The limitations of social research
Prof. M. D. Shipman
University of Warwick

Social research design
Prof. E. Krausz
University of Newcastle
and
S. H. Miller
City University

Sources of official data
Kathleen Pickett
University of Liverpool

History of social research methods
Gary Easthope
University of East Anglia

Deciphering data
Jonathan Silvey
University of Nottingham

The philosophy of social research
John Hughes
University of Lancaster

Data collection in context
Stephen Ackroyd
and
John Hughes
University of Lancaster

The Middle Class

ROGER KING B.Sc.Econ., M.Sc.
Principal Lecturer in Sociology
Huddersfield Polytechnic
and
JOHN RAYNOR B.Sc.Econ., D.Phil
Dean, Faculty of Education Studies
The Open University
with
DALLAS CLIFF B.Tech., M.A.
GEOFFREY SPARKS B.Sc.(Soc.), M.Soc.Sc.
Department of Behavioural Sciences
Huddersfield Polytechnic

Second edition

Longman London and New York

Longman Group Limited,
Longman House,
Burnt Mill, Harlow, Essex, UK.

Published in the United States of America
by Longman Inc., New York

First published 1969
Second edition 1981

British Library Cataloguing in Publication Data

King, Roger
The Middle class. — 2nd ed. — (Aspects of modern sociology: the social structure of modern Britain).
1. Middle classes — Great Britain.
I. Title II. Raynor, John, *1929* III. Series
305.5′50941 HT690.G7 80–41196

ISBN 0-582-29525-4

Printed in Singapore by Four Strong Printing Co

CONTENTS

EDITORS' PREFACE

This series has been designed to meet the needs of students following a variety of academic and professional courses in universities, polytechnics, colleges of higher education, colleges of education, and colleges of further education. Although principally of interest to social scientists, the series does not attempt a comprehensive treatment of the whole field of sociology, but concentrates on the social structure of modern Britain which forms a central feature of most such tertiary level courses in this country. Its purpose is to offer an analysis of our contemporary society through the study of basic demographic, ideological and structural features, and the examination of such major social institutions as the family, education, the economic and political structure and religion. The aim has been to produce a series of introductory texts which will in combination form the basis for a sustained course of study, but each volume has been designed as a single whole and can be read in its own right.

We hope that the topics covered in the series will prove attractive to a wide reading public and that, in addition to students, others who wish to know more than is readily available about the nature and structure of their own society will find them of interest.

John Barron Mays
Maurice Craft

FOREWORD

This book is the result of cooperation, but each of us has been responsible for individual chapters. Roger King has written Chapters 1, 3, 4, 7 and 8, John Raynor Chapter 2, Dallas Cliff has written Chapter 5, and Geoffrey Sparks Chapter 6. Thanks, too, to Janice Wood and Jackie Hepworth for typing various drafts of the manuscript.

Roger King
John Raynor
Dallas Cliff
Geoffrey Sparks

For Helen, David and Helen Mary

1

CONCEPTS AND ISSUES

Middle-class 'invisibility'

Sociologists frequently complain that research into stratification in Britain tends to neglect the middle class. But this is not entirely accurate. Although the middle class still receives far less attention than the working class, the number of studies of middle-class occupations and organisations has steadily increased in recent years. The complaint, however, does indicate a more specific problem; investigations focus mainly on particular elements of the middle class, usually those found in bureaucratic situations, such as low-level non-manual employees. There are few detailed accounts of less 'marginal', more 'established' groups such as medium-sized businessmen or independent professionals, although the work of Newby et al. on capitalist farmers is a notable exception.[1]

The middle class is not so much ignored as taken for granted by many sociologists who regard it as less of a 'problem' for class analysis than the working class. There is an apparent assumption that 'we all know' that the middle class is substantially advantaged by the reward system in western industrial societies, that it dominates economic, political and cultural institutions, and that, understandably, it wishes to preserve these privileges. The important questions then centre around the working class: does it, might it, contest these disparities of reward? Investigations of the British class structure in the last two or three decades have been primarily concerned with such themes as the 'embourgeoisement' of affluent workers, the sources of variation in working-class images of society, the alienation of manual workers in large-scale factories, and, increasingly, the alleged decline of traditional cultural constraints on working-class material aspirations. The dynamics of social change have been looked for in the class with an apparently 'objective' interest in challenging the *status quo*.

In part these concerns reflect the influence of Marxism on theories of class structure. Many Marxists suggest the probability of an increasing class polarisation between the 'two great hostile camps' in capitalist society, the bourgeoisie and the working class, and even non-Marxists who strongly discount this eventuality still take as a central issue for class analysis the possibility of a revolutionary assault on the capitalist order by a socialist-oriented working class. Some, such as Dahrendorf, have argued that Marx's 'polarisation' thesis led him to neglect the likelihood of an expanded middle class in maturing capitalism and that Marxism consequently is less relevant for accounts of 'new' non-manual employees than it is for manual workers. Marxism, however, has provided one of the few coherent themes in studies of the middle class – the question of the actual or potential 'proletarianisation' of clerical and other routine non-manual employees. This provides a theoretical framework for non-Marxist scholars too. Lockwood's classical account of 'the black-coated worker', whilst recognising the increasing similarity of clerical and manual class positions, is concerned with testing the Marxist notion of 'false consciousness' to describe the clerk's traditional identification with his employer, an interpretation he rejects.[2]

A further explanation for the relative lack of sociological attention paid to the middle class in comparison with the working class may be the problem of accessibility to 'middle-class élites'. Systematic empirical analysis of élite activity is understandably difficult, although the study of élites may not tell us much about the middle class, most of whom do not occupy élite positions. Many sections of the middle class feel neglected by political leaders, more so, perhaps, than some manual workers. Small businessmen, for example, tend to regard the middle class as a small 'minority' group, 'compressed' between the 'corporatist' triumvirate of state, big business and the TUC. This serves to indicate that the middle class is no longer a unitary grouping, if it ever was, but is composed of different parts with some sections more powerful than others.

The sociological tendency to underplay the middle class has probably been reinforced in this country by the long-standing reluctance of the British middle class to organise itself as an autonomous, specific political force. There have been few middle-class associations outside the established parties along the lines of the Mittelstand in Germany or the Poujadistes in France and, as Bechhofer et al. note, the docile British middle class has generally been prepared to work within the Conservative Party.[3] This could be changing. King and Nugent have charted the development of a number of middle-class organisations since 1974 that have kept their distance from the Conservatives, such as the National Association of Ratepayers' Action Groups (NARAG) and the National Federation for the Self-Employed (NFSE).[4]

Middle-class political quiescence reflects the general middle-class reluctance to admit to being middle-class or even to accept that classes exist. Following a survey of an occupationally mixed area of Liverpool, Webb noted that respondents were less likely to describe themselves as either working-class or middle-class in characterising their positions in the social structure if they were not offered the choice of class categories by the interviewer. This was especially noticeable for non-manual respondents. They were more inclined to use job or status criteria and describe themselves as 'a professional' or 'an architect', for example, than rate themselves as middle-class.[5] Robert et al.'s survey of nearly 500 economically active males, also in Liverpool, came up with similar findings. Although 33 per cent of blue-collar workers explained their party preferences in 'class' terms, this dropped to 14 per cent for white-collar respondents.[6]

Denials of 'classness' find expression in the non-class, non-political stance of middle-class organisations such as NARAG, the Middle Class Association (MCA), formed in 1974 by John Gorst, M.P., and the Freedom Association (FA; known formerly as the National Association for Freedom). NARAG persistently disclaims that it is a middle-class organisation and the Freedom Association claims it is a 'broad alliance that appeals to people from all social backgrounds', although both organisations attract predominantly professional, non-manual employees. There is a concern among middle-class activists to emphasise the virtues of social units other than class, such as family, community or nation, which reinforces notions of common interest transcending class position. The Conservative Party, although it attracts the predominant share of middle-class votes in elections, rarely seeks support as a 'middle-class' party – this would be electoral suicide with approximately one-third of working-class votes normally required to win a general election – and, especially at local level, it prefers to leave its 'middle classness' unstated. This reticence is not always shared by those middle-class polemecists, such as John Gorst or Patrick Hutber, who strive for a more assertive defence of middle-class interests. In his book, *The Decline and Fall of the Middle Class and How it Can Fight Back*, Hutber maintains that 'the great question is whether the confidence of the middle class itself has been shattered beyond repair, or whether the vanished smugness and certitudes of former years can be replaced with a more rational belief in its own worth'.[7] The latter appears doubtful. Gorst's Middle Class Association lasted for less than two years, and one of the reasons for its relatively quick demise was the internal conflict generated by the name of the organisation. Members became disenchanted with what they considered to be a blatant class appeal.

Middle-class apologists preferring a strident proclamation of middle-class virtues tend to argue that this unwillingness to use class labels indicates a sense of guilt at class advantage which only lends emphasis to the perjorativeness of terms such as 'middle-class' or 'surburbanite'. Lewis and Maude, for example, trace this defensiveness to the spread of egalitarianism which weakens notions of hierarchy.[8] Hutber suggests that middle-class 'furtiveness', the reluctance publicly to defend hardwon rewards, is fed by a fear of arousing expectations in other groups which can neither be fulfilled, because of Britain's parlous economic situation, nor deserve to be, because they would be achieved collectively, through the exercise of organised power, rather than by individual effort. King notes, too, that the middle-class cause is not helped by the apparently increasing propensity of its better-educated offspring to voluntarily relinquish middle class status. Some middle-class students, recognising their class origins and disliking them, have found attractive 'anti-middle class' theories, such as Marxism (or sociology?), thus adding to the perplexity of their parents

We should be careful not to assume that emphatic denials of the relevance of class differences necessarily indicate the absence of class feelings or class identity. After all, middle-class support for the Conservatives is generally more 'solid' than working-class support for the Labour Party, while some parts of the middle class, such as Newby et al.'s capitalist farmers, and Bechhofer et al.'s small retailers, are overwhelmingly Tory. The middle class is best characterised as displaying, in Giddens's terms, 'class awareness' – the 'acceptance of similar attitudes and beliefs, linked to a common style of life, among members of a class'. Giddens is clear that 'class awareness' does not involve recognition of a particular class affiliation, 'or the recognition that there exist other classes, characterised by different attitudes, beliefs and styles of life'. When this occurs it is best characterised as 'class consciousness', which in turn could lead to 'revolutionary class consciousness' – the 'recognition of the possibility of an overall reorganisation in the institutional mediation of power, and a belief that such a reorganisation can be brought about by class action'.[9]

It is not especially surprising that the middle class display 'low-classness'. Sociologists too readily assume that classes concretely exist in the way that, for example, families, or firms, or badminton clubs do. Particular groups or organisations are 'bounded social forms', to use Giddens's description, whereas classes are not. We should be very careful in using terms like class 'consciousness' not to imply a misleading purposiveness, as found in individual processes. However, there are also material reasons for denials of middle-class consciousness. Protestations of 'individual independence' and 'non-partisanship', although genuinely held, may serve as shields for class advantage. Labelling the class principle as 'illegitimate' seeks to prevent the disadvantaged from using one of its major weapons – organisation – in political struggle. It serves to resist collective challenges to the existing distribution of rewards and, particularly at local level, preserves middle-class control of local councils by Conservatives,

'Rate-payers' and 'Independents'. Newby et al. describe how this happens in the predominantly agricultural county of Suffolk. Informality and personal contact by councillors in their dealings with constituents are the norm; council house allocations, for example, are based on personal recommendations made by councillors, which 'leads to positive encouragement and maintenance of ties of personal dependency and loyalty by disadvantaged groups'.[10] Such processes operate to dampen collective resistance to council policies, as any generalised opposition is labelled 'irresponsible' and is bedevilled by individual efforts to create a good impression with respective councillors.

Appeals to the notion of a harmonious 'community' and the labelling of class action as divisive and unnecessary also reinforce the local dominance of farmers, landowners and middle-class 'newcomers'. These groups happily combine to keep the 'blight' of urbanism, in the form of new industries, away from their locality, and are well supported by sympathetic councillors and planning officials. But the consequence of apparently innocuous appeals to conserve local communities is the maintenance of low-wage rural economies with farmers avoiding competition with new manufacturers for labour and the higher wages that usually result.

Middle-class dominance, economic and political, is thus maintained without recourse to explicit 'middle-class interests'. There is little need for this; besides, as we have noted, overt class appeals for 'solidarity' are very distasteful for most sections of the middle class. Yet we must not underestimate middle-class awareness. Not only does the middle class predominantly vote for the Conservative Party, but the majority of white-collar employees, for example, are prepared to assign themselves to the middle class when presented with a choice of class categories. Roberts et al. point out that sociologists' use of the working-/middle-class dichotomy is to a large extent merely following the public's own practice. There is at least a rough approximation between 'subjective class position', the category into which individuals place themselves, and 'objective class position' as distinguished by manual or non-manual employment. Furthermore, class perceptions are tied to real differences in socioeconomic, cultural and political circumstances.

Identifying the middle class

Is there one middle class or should we refer to the middle class-*es*? These are not easy questions to answer, and often they fail to be posed, but identification of the middle class is necessary before we proceed much further. Aron doubts whether the middle class properly constitutes a class at all. He suggests that 'classes' are rarely distinct groupings; they only assume historical importance as they exhibit 'consciousness', particularly in conflict with other classes. The middle class is such a heterogeneous, fragmented entity that it rarely displays this 'consciousness'.[11] Unlike Aron, however, we assert that it is possible to recognise certain objective circumstances shared by an economic group, even if these factors may not lead to it sharing a common subjective awareness, and which allows us to refer to it as a 'class'. What constitutes these objective circumstances tends to vary with the theoretical approach adopted. Two major theories of class are usually distinguished by sociologists – the Marxist and the Weberian. Not only do they employ, respectively, different criteria for defining the middle class, they often impute contrasting fates for it.

Marx's theory of the middle class

Marx's analysis of class focuses on the social relations of *production* in societies. In societies characterised by the capitalist mode of production one group, the proletariat, which does not own or control productive property, is forced to sell its only 'commodity', its labour power, to those that do. Owners control the work process and 'possess' or legally own all that is produced. Part of the time worked by the worker for his boss, however, is 'surplus' to the cost of production and is expropriated and turned into profit by the owner. Value is produced only by proletarian 'productive' labour, yet the creator of value receives only that which enables him to reproduce himself socially (to keep himself and his family reasonably fed and clothed, for example), the difference between his wage and the market price of the commodity going to the capitalist, non-productive, non-manual workers, or the agents of distribution and exchange, for example, shopkeepers, financiers.

This stark portrayal of the inherent conflict of interest between capital and labour and its agents, the bourgeoisie and the proletariat, as the primary basis of class relations is exemplified by what Giddens refers to as Marx's 'pure' or 'abstract' model of capitalism. The picture painted is of endemic class conflict arising from the need for owners constantly to accumulate capital, to maintain and improve profitability, and to keep costs (including wages) as low as possible. Such an analysis, it is often argued (but see below), leaves little room for a 'middle' class; the emphasis instead is on the increasing polarisation, the mass assembling, of the two major classes, the bourgeoisie and the proletariat.

Marx's account of capitalism is more complex than this. The capitalist mode of production coexists with other modes in actual, concrete societies, and in his empirical studies Marx recognises the existence of several 'intermediate classes' that either consist of 'fractions' of the two main classes, such as the petit-bourgeoisie which is part of the bourgeoisie proper and is characterised by its low level of property ownership, or 'transitional classes' representing elements of a superseded set of relations of production which persist in the new form of society, such as feudal classes. But there is a tendency for these transitional classes to 'decompose' with the development of the capitalist mode of production; perpetual economic crises close small firms and accelerate mergers and the development of large monopolies, thus leading to the 'proletarianisation' of large numbers of the petit-bourgeoisie and small capitalists.

Weber and the middle class

Weber follows Marx in identifying classes as groups with an economic base. However, while Marx locates classes within productive relationships, Weber situates them within the labour *market*. The owners and controllers of enterprises are characterised as 'buyers' of labour in a market where skills or qualifications, for example, push up the 'price' that an employer has to pay for different types of labour. Stress is thus laid on the *distribution* of rewards (e.g. income) and the inequalities of this distribution – skilled labour or labour in short supply receiving more than unskilled labour – rather than the expropriation of surplus labour by the capitalist in the production process, although the two can hardly be disassociated. 'Class' refers to a category of individuals similarly located in the labour market to the extent that they have roughly the same opportunities to acquire both material and non-material (e.g., status, leisure) rewards. They possess what Weber calls common 'life chances'. Individuals in the same 'class situation' may come to recognise and act upon an awareness of mutual interests, that is they become a 'social class', although Weber does not fully explore the factors that may be conducive to this.

A problem with Weber's approach is that it tends to lead to the identification of a multiplicity of classes; there are almost as many 'market' or 'class' positions as individuals, although the notion of 'social class' helps to delimit the number of 'acting' classes. Like Marx, however, Weber regards property and lack of property as the basic categories of all class situations. Thus he distinguishes between classes that are 'positively privileged' in that their members control forms of property which are usable for the realisation of income in the market, and 'negatively privileged' classes that lack property. Unlike Marx, Weber does not confine the category of 'property ownership' to those possessing industrial property; 'positively privileged' classes contain all those whose class situation is determined by the possession of any type of property that may be used to obtain material rewards, such as housing. Class conflict may arise in any market situation where there is differential access to property. He suggests, however, that even within the ranks of the propertyless, there are those who possess 'property' with a market value, such as the skills possessed by some manual workers. Yet while the skills possessed by manual workers remain important, with the development of bureaucracy, organisation and the rational legal state, the marketable skills of the 'middle class', predominantly the possession of educational qualifications, become more significant as a source of income.

Weber's notion of stratification possesses two further important elements: *status*, involving specific 'styles of life', which may bisect class relationships, and *party*, which is orientated towards the acquisition and maintenance of political leadership. Weber indicates that middle classes are not transitory but reflect the multidimensionality and persisting complexity of social stratification which renders inappropriate simple dichotomous conceptions of class relations.

Critics of Marx have argued that the expansion of the middle class in modern industrial societies poses major difficulties for his theory of class. Dahrendorf, for example, characterises 'post-capitalist' society as much more diversified than Marx envisaged; this is created by three key processes: (i) the decomposition of capital, namely the separation of owner and manager; (ii) the decomposition of labour, marked especially by divisions of interest based on skill levels; and (iii) the growth of the 'new' middle class. These developments, it is argued, are markedly at variance with Marx's claims for the increasing distinction between just two classes in capitalism.

Furthermore, Dahrendorf doubts whether even the new middle class constitutes a distinct class at all. It is a class 'born decomposed... there is no word in any modern language to describe this group that is no group, class that is no class, and stratum that is no stratum'.[12] Dahrendorf takes issue with two other competing theories about the position of the new middle class. One view, associated with Bendix, maintains that the new middle class is simply an extension of the old capitalist class. Most middle-class occupations, it is argued, have been structurally differentiated out of leading positions in industry, commerce and the state, and are characterised by the exercise of delegated authority. A second theory, put forward by Mills, for example, claims that the salaried employee is much closer to the proletariat than to the capitalist; they share a common situation of propertylessness, while traditional differences between them in income and status are declining.

Both theories are incorporated within Dahrendorf's proposition that the middle class is divided into one or other of the two major classes, and that a significant line can be drawn between salaried employees who occupy positions that are part of a bureaucratic hierarchy, and those non-manual workers that are outside the administrative chain of authority. The former shares ruling class authority while the latter, such as the office clerk or the salesperson, have a proletarian class situation and are more disposed towards trade unionism. For 'bureaucrats', however, 'the supreme social reality is their career that provides, at least in theory, a direct link between every one of them and the top positions which may be described as the ultimate seat of authority'.

Dahrendorf insists that classes are constituted by position in organisational hierarchies, which are characterised by the possession and non-possession of authority, rather than the ownership and non-ownership of productive property; property is simply a type of authority. Some parts of the new middle class have this authority and others do not. Within 'imperatively coordinated associations', such as the state or the firm, possession of, and exclusion from, authority generates opposing interests and recognition of these different interests may lead to class conflict, including that within the new middle class. In modern industrial societies, therefore, capitalist or socialist, class conflict arises from the clash of interest between those that command and those that obey.

One advantage of Dahrendorf's attempt to locate the middle class within a theory of conflict, as a class divided against itself, is that the dynamic of social relationships is retained, whereas situating the middle class within a scale of stratification, such as income or prestige, simply *creates* a middle class from the method employed. It is somewhat artificial to locate the middle class between, say, the very rich and the very poor, with little theoretical suggestion as to why the middle class *exists* as a distinct social category. The problem with Dahrendorf's analysis, however, as Giddens notes, is that there is something 'rather forced' in the assertion that some bureaucrats employed in government agencies constitute part of the ruling class simply because they are connected to political leaders through a chain of authority. Government administrators do not simply execute ruling class commands but are also subject to them, both as employees and as citizens.[13] Parkin complains that Dahrendorf's organisational conception of class is too narrow and ignores the wider social context. More important, Dahrendorf neglects the purpose of the authority structure within enterprises – the pursuit of profit (not obedience as such) – and the background role played by the state, particularly legal apparatuses, in ensuring the dominance of property relations. Thus, Parkin argues, 'class conflict between managers and managed is ultimately not containable or resolvable within the walls of the organisation'.[14]

Dahrendorf asserts that the growth of the new middle class, one section linked with the ruling class and another with the proletariat, contradicts Marx's claims for the development of a polarised class structure in capitalist societies, but it is not clear that it does. A number of Marxist writers argue that Marx did not neglect the rise of the new middle class, although they recognise that it raises problems for Marx's analysis. Urry suggests that this 'new' middle class fulfils two essential functions in capitalism; it provides a class that consumes more than it produces and is thus able to purchase the inevitable 'overproduction' of a system geared to production for profit rather than use, especially with the decline of feudal groups, which were essentially consumers; and, secondly, the new middle class expands with the growing requirement for efficient administration and control in a developing capitalist economy.[15]

However, the rise of white-collar groups enjoying often substantial material and non-material advantages over manual workers has posed awkward questions for Marxist class analysis, particularly the class polarisation thesis, and a number of attempts have been made to assess the ideological and political leanings of these intermediate strata and the likelihood of their coalescence with the working class. Considerable effort has been expended by Marxists in recent years in clarifying the boundaries between the middle class and other classes. This has been approached initially by seeking to define the working class and, following Parkin, we may identify three broad responses to this boundary problem – minimalist, maximalist and intermediate.[16]

The minimalist approach to defining the working class is exemplified by Poulantzas who argues that the large category 'wage labour' may be divided into 'productive labour', which produces surplus value, and 'non-productive labour' which is paid out of the capitalist's profit, such as administrative labour. The category of productive labour is further divided into mental and manual forms, the former referring to supervisory and professional occupations that are advantaged by authority over the workforce, which sets them off from the working class, despite their contribution to surplus value. Thus technicians and foremen, for example, along with all forms of 'non-productive' labour, comprise the new petit-bourgeoisie, or a large and expanding middle class, while the working class consists only of a small number of manual 'productive' employees.[17]

The maximalist position operates with a narrower conception of the middle class and hence a broader notion of the working class. Productive labour includes all employees who, although they may be paid out of profit, are still exploited and denied the full rewards of their effort. Baran, for example, suggests that many white-collar workers exploited in capitalist society will usefully function in a socialist and as such they constitute part of the exploited working class that is destined to carry through the revolutionary transformation of social relations. They are to be distinguished from the 'real' bourgeoisie, for example financiers, landlords and entrepreneurs, for whom there is no place in a post revolutionary society, and who only properly constitute the middle class.[18]

The boundary between proletariat and bourgeoisie in the intermediate approach, however, is drawn within the middle class itself and derives from its tendency to perform both the function of capital and that of labour. Carchedi, for example, in his economic identification of the new middle class in monopoly capitalism, suggests that it lacks both legal and 'real' (fully authoritative) ownership of the means of production. However, its members are capitalism's non-commissioned officers, undertaking the function of control and surveillance in the extraction of surplus value, but also performing as workers themselves. The industrial chemist, for example, executes quality control tests (the function of the worker), which produces surplus value and for which he receives 'wages', but he also exercises control over other workers (the function of the capitalist), for which he is paid 'extra' – out of profit. This dual function thus explains why historically members of the new middle class receive higher incomes than simple wage-labourers. However, Carchedi argues that the new middle class is becoming steadily proletarianised as it gradually loses its supervisory function and as its work tasks become progressively 'deskilled' and routinised. As it joins the ranks of exploited wage-labour more completely it loses income and status. The middle class is thus characterised by an increasing split between a few who predominantly operate as managers or capitalist functionaries and an expanding group of white collar workers whose position approximates to that of the proletariat.[19]

The contemporary identification of the middle class by Marxist scholars bears a remarkable resemblance to Dahrendorf's characterisation of the middle class as internally divided between those who control and those who obey in organisations. However, a major difference with Dahrendorf's position lies in the Marxist proposition that the new middle class is ceasing to exist as an identifiable category. While an expanding new middle class prevents a radical polarisation of the class structure in Dahrendorf's eyes, for Carchedi there is a tendency for some of the new middle class's positions to become explicitly capitalist, but for most to resemble that of the working class.[20]

The problem with Carchedi's approach lies in its empirical application. Firstly, the distinction between productive and unproductive work is difficult to maintain in complex industrial societies and rests on acceptance of the labour theory of value. Carchedi argues that some non-manual employees, such as those in technical, managerial, supervisory, and clerical grades, are 'productive' when they perform the technically necessary job of coordinating the labour process (i.e., they act as members of the working class) and this contrasts with their additional 'control and surveillance' role as extractors of surplus value from the proletariat (i.e. when they act as members of the middle class). However, the empirical problem remains of how 'coordination' is to be distinguished operationally from 'control and surveillance' in concrete work situations.

Poulantzas has remarked on these difficulties. Unlike Carchedi he maintains that foremen and supervisors do not have dual class membership; the place they occupy in the social division of labour is *always* marked by capitalist authority, for they 'control' the labour process and extract surplus value from the workers. They may work, provide surplus labour and be exploited, but in capitalist relations of production it becomes impossible to differentiate a 'worker role' from a 'subaltern' role as these inevitably are interwined. They thus emphatically belong to the new middle class.

Finally, the emphasis on *production* and the process of capital accumulation for an identification of the middle class need not necessarily imply a rejection of Weberian 'market' analysis. After all, competition between firms in the market place provides the impetus for capitalist enterprises to maintain and increase profitability and thus effects rates of exploitation within the process of production. One approach is to employ the concept 'work situation', including relations of control and exploitation, alongside notions of 'market situation' and 'status situation'. This has been the method adopted by Lockwood.

Lockwood also operates with the notion that the middle class is in a structurally ambivalent position. Lockwood's dislike of theories which explain clerical workers' refusal to identify with manual workers, despite the similarity of their incomes, in terms of 'false consciousness', led him to reject the view that 'propertylessness' was sufficient to categorise a class position as 'proletarian'. Three aspects of class situation are identified: market situation – 'the economic position narrowly conceived, consisting of source and size of income, degree of job security, and opportunity for upward occupational mobility'; work situation – 'the set of social relationships in which the individual is involved at work by virtue of his position in the division of labour'; and status situation – 'the position of the individual in the hierarchy of prestige in the society at large'.[21]

Lockwood concludes that the clerk enjoys a more powerful and prestigious position within the work situation than the manual worker. The black-coated worker's market situation may approximate to that of the manual worker (although he has never been strictly 'proletarian' in terms of income, job security and occupational mobility), but differential authority and physical separation from the manual employee within the work situation, and the traditional status superiority of non-manual work, are obstacles to common identification. It is the clerk's work situation that explains identification with the ruling class, not false consciousness.

Lockwood's typology is not without criticism – *why* do changes in these three dimensions occur? – but it offers a useful set of operational guidelines for examining differences *within* the middle class, for contrasting non-manual and manual employment, and for investigating the extent to which some middle class occupations are becoming 'proletarianised'. First, however, we need to consider the use of manual and non-manual categories.

Manual/non-manual distinctions

Sociologists have usually regarded the contrast between manual and non-manual work as revealing the fundamental structural 'fault' in stratification, and as corresponding to real, persisting differences in life chances. The use of the description 'non-manual' also indicates the sociological tendency to define the middle class in terms of what they are *not*, that is they are *not* manual workers. As Garrard et al. remark, 'the middle class is often negatively defined as the residual category which remains when the manual working class has been subtracted from the population'.[22] Thus a great variety of groups, some more powerful and rich than others, are collapsed into one non-manual category. But is this practice still justified in the light of the increasing fluidity and normative 'decomposition' of the class structure? Have the widening basis of recruitment to middle-class jobs, the routinisation and possible proletarianisation of many non-manual occupations, and the spread of middle-class unionism blurred the manual/non-manual cleavage and made it less central for an understanding of the stratification order? How are the terms 'manual' and 'non-manual' to be defined, and to what do they refer?

There are massive, probably insurmountable difficulties in employing the terms manual and non-manual in a *literal* sense; some non-manual jobs (shop assistant, teacher) involve a good deal of manual exertion, for example. Bain and Price outline three major approaches to defining manual and non-manual work: the brain–brawn, the functional and the eclectic,[23] and this provides a useful starting point for a consideration of manual/non-manual distinctions.

The brain–brawn approach

This approach stems from the period when manual work was nearly always highly physically demanding; manual jobs characteristically involved labour 'by hand' while non-manual jobs called for 'mental' or 'brain' work. The brain–brawn approach uses this distinction to explain the typically different mode of remuneration for manual and non-manual occupations; manual work, depending on physical effort, is easily quantifiable and its value is measurable in terms of hourly rates or wages, whereas the same considerations cannot apply to 'brainwork', which is thus rewarded by a fixed salary. The problem with this approach is that virtually every job involves a mixture of both intellectual and physical labour. A filing clerk ('non-manual') may expend more physical energy at work than, say, a highly skilled electrician ('manual'). Furthermore, claims to non-manual classification are frequently status claims – the ratcatcher as rodent operator, the plumber as sanitary engineer – and are primarily demands for the remuneration and fringe benefits that non-manual status implies rather than indicative of the physical content of the occupational tasks.

The functional approach

Non-manual employment is characterised for some by its 'indispensability', as fulfilling organisational tasks previously undertaken by the owner. In this scheme non-manual work performs four major functions: administration; design, analysis and planning; supervisory/managerial; and commercial. These are delegated by owners to white-collar workers as enterprises develop. The problem with this approach is that, if an actual historical process is being proposed, there are difficulties in providing firm evidence for the claim, and that which does exist would surely indicate that much manual work has also been delegated by owners. Nor is it clear how this notion of 'entrepreneurial delegation' to account for the growth of middle-class occupations applies to white collar employees in the public sector, where the state is employer, or how it explains the relative modern growth in scientific and technical tasks.

The eclectic approach

A third solution for defining manual and non-manual employment rests on the notion of differing 'work milieux'. It suggests that for manual workers the work environment is 'mechanical' and geared to 'menial tasks', for example a shopfloor in a factory. Non-manual employees, however, work 'in the place of the bourgeoisie' – the office – and their environment is described as 'bureaucratic'. Unfortunately, although this distinction may reflect the physical separation of office and factory in, say, a car assembly plant, it hardly serves otherwise. Manual workers are an essential part of service or bureaucratic work environments, even if the cleaners and other ancillary manual workers needed to maintain an office block or a university building are 'invisible' until their services are urgently required or they take industrial action. A further argument, found in post-industrial society theories, that non-manual work involves acting on people whereas manual workers operate on objects is, as Bain and Price remark, empirically suspect and disregards a range of 'person-oriented' manual workers such as ticket collectors, bus conductors and doormen.

Bain and Price maintain that the features of manual and non-manual work identified in these three theories may be regarded best as different external symbols of the possession of, or proximity to, authority, although they admit that the substance of authority is likely to be less than it appears. Non-manual employment is, they maintain, *popularly* identified with the exercise of managerial control over manual workers. Not every non-manual worker directly commands operatives; for example, banking or other commercial white-collar staff have few manual subordinates. But non-manual work is associated with 'authority' of a kind that differs from the straightforward job expertise of the worker; it lays claim to what Poulantzas has described as a 'special form of knowledge'.

Poulantzas goes further than Bain and Price in arguing that the distinction between 'mental' and 'manual' labour is directly bound up with 'the permanent exclusion of the subordinated, those who are deemed not to "know how"'. Thus 'mental' roles are legitimised, irrespective of the empirical or natural content of a form of work. Manual/non-manual distinctions may be regarded as part of the ideological and political subordination of 'productive' labour: the separation of the mental labour of engineers or technicians, for example, from manual labour, 'represents the exercise of political relations in the despotism of the factory', and involves an ideological monopolisation and 'secrecy' that maintains relations of domination and subordination.[24]

The attempts by Bain and Price, and Poulantzas, to identify manual/non-manual distinctions as part of the social division of authority are more satisfactory than fruitless definitions centred on the 'content' of types of job. But difficulties still remain. Some 'middle-class' positions are as much subject to managerial command as those occupied by manual workers. Nor is it easy to distinguish at certain levels where 'real control' lies; the formal 'authority' of a clerical worker may be scornfully disregarded by skilled, well-organised workers who turn to higher level management in times of dispute. Furthermore, as Garnsey remarks, 'the routinisation and feminisation of lower-level white-collar work calls into question the appropriateness of taking conventional distinctions between manual and non-manual as class demarcations'.[25]

Even more serious objections to the manual/non-manual model have been raised recently by Parkin. He notes that the claim that differences between manual and non-manual labour provide the basis of class conflict rests on the premiss that capitalist society is characterised as one large industrial firm. But while the divide between white-collar and blue-collar constitutes the contestants in the struggle over rewards and for control in the factory, the firm is a less reliable guide to wider class relations than it once was. A variety of non-manual groups has developed in the public sector 'that cannot in any real sense be thought of as the tail end of a broad managerial stratum aligned against the manual workforce'.[26] Not only do such groups often work in settings with few manual workers but they also lack the managerial relationship to them found in the private sector. Furthermore, public sector employees are increasingly subject to the expenditure-cutting strategies of an impersonal, bureaucratic employer, with whom they negotiate their pay and conditions through trade union representatives, usually without the individual sanction of the commercial employee of being able to move to another employer. Thus the non-manual category lacks the similarity of condition assumed by the manual/non-manual model which overlooks differences between private- and public-sector employment.

Parkin queries whether an approach that stresses *differentiation* in the division of labour is appropriate as a general conception of a society characterised by conflict and cleavage. Although manual and non-manual groups may be distinguished from each other in terms of differential life chances, they are less easily regarded 'as groups standing in a relationship of exploiter and exploited, of dominance and subordination, in the manner presumably required of a genuine conflict model'. The relationships between classes are thus inadequately considered by the model, not as 'aspects of the distribution of power' or as involving conflicts of interests, but as 'mere social differentiation'. These problems associated with the manual/non-manual dichotomy lead him to analyse class structure in terms of strategies of social closure, which we consider towards the end of this chapter. We now turn to a consideration of the data on inequality and social differences associated with types of occupation.

Inequality and the middle class

One of the central debates in the class analysis of modern Britain in the 1960s was over the so-called 'embourgeoisement thesis'. This was associated chiefly with Ferdinand Zweig's, *The Worker in an Affluent Society*, which claimed that the material affluence of the post-war years had effectively dispersed traditional class divisions. Specifically, Zweig argued that working-class income levels were approaching those of non-manual employees and this was symptomatic of general advances in 'life chances', especially improvements in work conditions, housing, health and education.[27] This account of the dissolving British class structure struck a popular chord in the 'never had it so good' years of the Macmillan era, and the theme was widely discussed in television programmes and newspaper articles. Goldthorpe and Lockwood's demolition of the thesis is too well known to require elaboration here, for it has become essential reading for sociology students. It is sufficient to reiterate that their investigations of affluent car assembly operatives in Luton revealed that even affluent skilled workers, whose relatively high levels of income depended substantially on overtime and shiftwork, neither emulated middle-class styles of life, nor mixed socially with non-manual neighbours.[28]

Variants of the 'we are all becoming middle class' thesis persist, and some have seen in the expansion of non-manual employment in 'post-capitalist societies' the hope of a new stabilising third force that will severely reduce class tensions. Zweig, too, has argued recently that the spread of home ownership, the extension of educational opportunity and social mobility, and increased work satisfaction, has resulted in a convergence of manual and non-manual employees around a new style of 'middleclassness' which is marked by collective striving for materialistic gains.[29] Certainly many non-manual workers feel that their class advantage is disappearing and that, particularly in pay, they are being overtaken by manual employees. Roberts et al., having asked their respondents to name the groups they considered had improved their income during recent years, found that 'nearly every white-collar interviewee named a manual group as having made the greatest gains. Dockers, car workers and miners were frequently mentioned'.[30]

These sentiments are hardly novel. The fear of 'proletarianisation' has existed for almost as long as the working class itself, especially amongst lower-grade non-manual workers. In addition there have always been sections of the working class earning more than non-manual workers, albeit for longer hours and in dirtier conditions. Should contemporary stories of Rover-driving miners and 'overpaid' car workers be regarded as part of a well-established middle-class mythology that requires its 'folk devils' to sustain and substantiate uneasy fears of working-class advance, but which bear little connection to the underlying reality of persisting class inequalities? To answer this question we turn to recent empirical data on inequality and stratification in Britain.

Data

Social scientists generally use occupation as the criterion of social class in their empirical studies. There are at least three reasons for this practice: occupational data is economical and easily collected; occupation has been consistently shown to be highly related to most other factors associated with social class, particularly income and education; and, not least, most people overwhelmingly choose occupational characteristics for *their* criterion of class (see Table 1).

TABLE 1 *Characteristics used to describe the middle class and the working class*

Middle class	per cent of responses	Working class	per cent of responses
Occupation	61	Occupation	74
Income/level of living	21	Income/level of living	10
Attitudes/hierarchical location	5	Manners and morals	7
Manners and morals	5	Attitudes/hierarchical location	5
Education/intelligence	5	Education/intelligence	3
Family background	1	Other	1
Political	1		
Other	1		

Source: Reid, 1977, op. cit., Ch. 1, n32.

Parkin suggests that the 'backbone of the reward system' can be represented as a hierarchy of broad occupational categories, which runs from 'high' professional, managerial and administrative employment to 'low' unskilled manual jobs.[31] The hierarchy outlined by Parkin is very similar to the classification employed by the Office of Population and Censuses in the collection of census material (see Table 2).[32]

TABLE 2 *Typical occupations by social class (R.G.1970)*

Social Class	Examples
I Professional	Accountant, doctor, lawyer.
II Intermediate	Aircraft pilot, fire-brigade officer, school-teacher.
III Skilled non-manual	Clerical worker, sales representative, draughtsman.
III Skilled manual	Electrician, carpenter, bricklayer.
IV Partly skilled	Bus conductor, postman, packer.
V Unskilled	Labourer, cleaner, porter.

NB. In 1970, 43 per cent of the working population were in non-manual occupations.

Source: Adapted from Reid, 1977, op. cit., Ch. 1, n32.

Although such classifications indicate that the flow of rewards down the social hierarchy takes the form of a graduated continuum, most sociologists recognise 'a significant break' between the manual and non-manual categories. This break corresponds to real differences in the terms and conditions of employment, involving not just income but advantage conferred by position in the social division of labour, including the possession of authority. The family is especially important in maintaining disparities over generations because, according to Parkin, it plays a crucial part in 'placing' individuals at various points in the class structure. Parkin remarks that 'there is a marked tendency for those who occupy relatively privileged positions to ensure that their own progeny are recruited to similar positions'.[33] Parkin has recently cautioned against exaggerating this, however, noting that the increasing reliance on educational qualifications in determining occupational positions imparts greater 'risk' for bourgeois families seeking to ensure that their offspring are as advantaged as themselves than the direct transmission of property.[34]

Income

Data on income appear to confirm the 'significant break' thesis. Some manual jobs may be better remunerated than some non-manual positions, but there is a marked tendency for non-manual workers to earn more than manual workers. In April 1978, for example, the average gross weekly earnings for men aged twenty-one and over in full-time employment was just over

TABLE 3 *Earnings and Hours: all industries and services*

	Average weekly earnings	**Average hours per week**
F.T. Men, 21 and over, April 1978		
Manual	£78.4	46.0
Non-manual	£99.9	38.7
F.T. Women, 18 and over,		
Manual	£48.0	39.6
Non-manual	£58.5	36.7

Source: *Employers' Gazette*, January 1979.

£78, while for those in non-manual employment it was almost £100. Female non-manual workers also generally earned more than female manual workers (£58.50 and £48.0 respectively). Furthermore, a larger proportion of manual workers' pay is for overtime, as figures for average hours worked testify (see Table 3).

A number of studies emphasise the stability of income differentials over many years, despite the efforts of Labour governments, the introduction and extension of the welfare state, and the ravages and dislocations of war and inflation. Routh's investigation of the relation between occupation and pay found that differences between occupations hardly changed between 1906 and 1960 (see table 4), a trend which has persisted since 1960 (see Table 5).[35]

TABLE 4 *Changes in relative earnings, 1913/1914–1960; made earners only. Indices of earnings–average expressed as a percentage of the average for all men in the same period.*

	1913/14	1922/4	1955/6	1960
All non-manual	142	158	152	145
All manual	88	83	85	82
All men	100	100	100	100

Source: Derived from Westergaard and Resler's 1976 adaptation of G. Routh, 1965, op. cit., Ch. 1, n36.

TABLE 5 *Average weekly earnings in all industries covered by Department of Employment Surveys*

	Non-manual males	Manual males	Non-manual females	Manual females	(F.T. only)
1960	£19.10	£14.53	£10.15	£ 7.42	
1965	£25.53	£19.59	£13.71	£ 9.60	
1970	£36.12	£28.05	£19.59	£13.99	
1977	£88.90	£72.89	£53.80	£44.31	

Source: 'Trend in earnings 1948–77', *Employment Gazette*, May 1978 (adapted).

These figures, however, do not reveal important changes that have occurred. Westergaard and Resler note two of particular interest. First, the 'lower professions', such as schoolteachers, librarians and draughtsmen, have dropped to a point on the earnings scale only a little way above the arithmetic average, which is the level of skilled manual workers. Secondly, clerks no longer enjoy a level of remuneration on a par with skilled manual workers but are now positioned at some point between the skilled and semi-skilled, which is well below the overall average. There is also evidence of a widening gap within the non-manual sector, between the income levels of 'established' professionals and managers on the one hand, and those in lower routine occupations on the other. For example, average earnings for clerical and related male employees in public sector work, insurance and banking rose by 72 per cent between 1960 and 1970, but average earnings for *all* administrative employees rose by 89 per cent.[36] Within the non-manual sector certain groups may also experience a loss in earnings in comparison with manual workers. Bechhofer et al.'s analysis of the Royal Commission on the Distribution of Income and Wealth's investigation of a nationalised industry reveals that after-tax comparisons of senior managerial salaries with manual workers show much smaller differentials than before the war. They note that pay freezes and flat-rate increases in the 1970s under governmental income policies also may have compressed differentials.[37]

The overall impression, however, is one of stolidity in income patterns. Periods of declining differentials for some non-manual groups have soon been followed by periods of compensation. There is evidence, for example, that middle managers have recovered some of the lost ground of the early 1970s. One survey shows that between December 1977 and December 1978 management salaries rose by an average of 16.7 per cent, clerical salaries went up by an average of 14.9 per cent but 'operatives' only increased their earnings by 9.1 per cent.[38] However, income is not the only indicator of contrasting 'life chances' for manual and non-manual employees. For a broader perspective we need to include conditions of work as well.

Working conditions

As well as disparities of income there exist notable differences in the conditions of manual and non-manual labour. Giddens emphasises that the division of labour is one of the most significant influences on the formation of social classes within the modern industrial order. He remarks that 'machine-minding in one form or another, regardless of whether it involves a high-level of manual skill, tends to create a working environment quite distinct from that of the administrative employee, and one which normally enforces a high degree of physical separation between the two groupings'.[39] Physical separation is reinforced both by differences in mobility chances, especially as expressed through non-manual expectations of a 'career', and different positions within the authority of the business enterprise. Administrative workers tend to be involved in implementing, occasionally formulating, rules to which manual workers are expected to comply.

Despite problems in applying this approach to the public sector, there is a substantial body of empirical material in support of these conclusions. Wedderburn and Craig, for example, analysed a number of official publications containing data on the conditions of employment of six grades of employee, from skilled operatives to senior managers. Non-manual employees not only generally perform tasks free of irksome work rules and experience relatively high levels of intrinsic job satisfaction but receive better fringe benefits in the form of pension, sick pay and holiday provisions. For example, clerical workers in 74 per cent of their firms were entitled to over fifteen paid holidays per year, but this applied to only 38 per cent of operatives.[40] More generally, official government statistics reveal that although holiday entitlements for manual workers increased substantially from the mid-1960s until 1974–5, more recently there have been only small increases as workers have tended to choose pay increases rather than improvement in holidays (see Table 6).

Manual workers remain disadvantaged compared with their white-collar colleagues in most aspects of company sick benefit schemes. Many manual schemes require a year's employment before workers qualify for benefit, a rare requirement for white-collar schemes. Sick payments are frequently based on basic rates and take no account of regular overtime or bonuses for manual workers. A survey of company sick benefit schemes in 100 public and private sector organisations published by the Labour Research Department in 1979 found that nearly 30 per

TABLE 6 *Paid holidays: manual workers (full-time)*

Percentage entitled to annual paid holidays of duration (week)	**1966**	**1973**	**1975**	**1976**	**1977**
Two weeks	63	1	1	—	—
Between two and three weeks	33	2	1	1	1
Three weeks	4	38	17	18	18
Between three and four weeks	—	52	51	47	47
Four weeks and over	—	7	30	34	34
	100	100	100	100	100

Source: *Social Trends*, Central Statistical Office, HMSO, 1979.

cent of manual schemes did not pay out maximum benefits until fifteen years of service were completed, although only 7 per cent of 'staff' schemes took so long.[41]

Roberts et al.'s survey in Liverpool also indicates that 'affluent' manual workers fare little better than other workers in extra benefits for 'even when their income levels reach the "middle class" bracket, manual workers become no more liable to receive white-collar fringe benefits'.[42] For some non-manual employees the 'perks' of the job may be greater than the above figures suggest and include use of a company car, entertainment allowances or paid education for children. Westergaard and Resler indicate, too, that incomes policies do not apply effectively to salaries and fees that are negotiated individually, and regular annual increments to salaries, a feature of most 'middle-class' positions, are normally exempt from income controls.

Finally, we may note that despite well-publicised examples of white-collar redundancy in recent years, non-manual workers are far less likely to be exposed to unemployment than manual workers. In September 1978, as Table 7 shows, out of the total unemployed, around 20 per cent were from non-manual occupations while over 66 per cent were either general labourers or from other manual occupations – a proportion clearly out of phase with the general distribution of manual and non-manual positions indicated above in Table 2.

TABLE 7 *Occupational analysis: numbers registered at employment offices in Great Britain (Males, September 1978).*

	Percentage of total number unemployed
Managers and Professional	8.4
Clerical and related	9.0
Other non-manual occupations	2.8
Craft and similar occupations	13.5
General labourers	42.4
Other manual	23.9
Total	100

Source: *Employment Gazette*, December 1978, Table 109.

Prestige and other differences

Contrasting 'life chances' for manual and non-manual employees are literally opportunities for life; they cover the range of social existence and are expressed in data on mortality, sickness and disability, educational provision and attainment, residence and diet.[43] It is not surprising, therefore, that occupational categories ranking high in material reward are usually highly ranked in status terms. There is a substantial measure of public agreement on varying levels of occupational prestige, broadly following the lines of the Office of Population and Censuses' hierarchy, from 'professional' down to 'unskilled manual'. But it is not altogether clear what people understand by 'occupational prestige', and a number of studies suggest that it is not easy for respondents to divorce consideration of a position's 'status' from its 'market capacity'. Runciman found that manual workers were less likely to acknowledge the prestige of non-manual occupations (many are considered to be unproductive compared with physical or skilled labour) than to recognise the material superiority of a non-manual class situation.[44] Goldthorpe and Hope suggest that individual assessments of occupational status may reflect more a factual grading of job income and conditions than imply a particular status perspective.[45]

Nonetheless, individuals generally place a high value on 'middle-class' occupations and Parkin proposes that this stems from a 'learning' of the appropriate criteria by which occupations are evaluated. Jobs with 'responsibility' or 'authority' are thus more highly regarded than those characterised by physical effort. Parkin argues that these distinctions are legitimated by those in dominant positions, that is, those with 'responsibility'. Strong material interests lie behind this legitimation, for if the distribution of honour was dissonant with the distribution of material advantages 'then the system of inequalities would be stripped of its normative support'.[46] This is not to suggest that official definitions of occupational status are necessarily static. There are signs that the state's attitude to the value of non-manual labour has changed with the expansion in non-manual positions, particularly in the public sector. The Prices and Incomes Board, for example, refused to accept that non-manual work intrinsically carries entitlement to a higher rate of pay, perhaps reflecting the 'feminisation' and declining 'market power' of much routine white-collar work, and the increasingly heavy financial demands on the government as a major employer of non-manual labour.

Property and personal wealth

So far we have followed common sociological practice and considered class inequalities as deriving from the division of labour, particularly that between manual and non-manual occupations. However, we must not neglect productive property as perhaps the major source of inequality in capitalist societies for, as Parkin remarks, 'the powers and privileges emanating from the ownership of productive property are of a very different order of things from those resulting from the division of labour'.[47] Similarly, Westergaard and Resler describe the private ownership of property as 'the key to class division in Britain as in other countries'. Capital accumulation and the search for profit provide the dynamic for capitalist systems; the possession of productive property affords direct access to economic power, despite the growth in managerial control and diffusion of share ownership, while property interests still maintain strong links with conservative and liberal parties in western industrial societies.

The distribution of personal wealth is also much more unequally distributed than income, mainly because of the significance of inherited wealth in the pattern of wealth holding. However, recent Inland Revenue Statistics, although subject to fairly large margins of error because they exclude non-marketable assets such as state and occupational pension rights and include dwellings and other physical assets, indicate a long-term trend towards greater equality (see Table 8).

TABLE 8 *Distribution of wealth among identified wealth owners*

Wealth owned by most wealthy (%)	**Great Britain**				**United Kingdom**	
	1961	**1966**	**1971**	**1974**	**1975**	**1976**
1	28	23	20	18	17	17
2	37	31	28	25	24	23
5	51	44	40	37	35	35
10	63	56	52	49	47	47
25	80	75	72	71	70	68
50	93	91	90	90	90	88

Source: *Social Trends*, Central Statistical Office, HMSO, 1979, Table 6.37.

The greater spread of wealth, however, has been confined mainly to the richest quarter of the population, which suggests recent property taxes such as Capital Transfer Tax and Capital Gains Tax may have stimulated a redistribution of wealth within the richest families. If we confine ourselves to 'small property', that mainly used for consumption rather than production, such as houses, cars, and savings in the form of life insurance or building society deposits, then the uneven distribution of wealth between the 'middle classes' and the working class is quite apparent. Roberts et al.'s investigations, for example, revealed that while 33 per cent of blue-collar respondents were owner-occupiers, this figure rose to 72 per cent for white collar employees.[48] In part this signifies the importance of inheritance in the accumulation of wealth, even when amounts are modest; Bell's work on middle-class families illustrates the greater ability of the better-off to financially assist their offspring in purchasing a first home and, at a later stage, passing on their property at death.[49]

The continuing importance of family inheritance for the accumulation or property for production as well as consumption should also be stressed. Newby et al.'s study of capitalist farmers demonstrates how difficult it is for individuals to earn sufficient from employment to start their own enterprise. Almost 70 per cent of their largest farmers (1,000 acres plus), and 56 per cent of the smallest, either inherited their farms or were partners with their fathers and would eventually own the business outright.[50] Newby et al. described how the emergence of a two-class structure of owner-occupying farmers and landless farmworkers, and the decline of the large, non-farming landowner, has placed most farmers within the ranks of a more general entrepreneurial class rather than a landowning, patrician upper class with its associated 'leisurely' style of life. This is reflected in attitudes to 'working property'. Property is regarded largely in economic terms – as possible collateral for loans, as providing investment 'freedom', and as valuable source of appreciating wealth – rather than a source of status. Attitudes to farming have become businesslike, matching the economic rationality of the farmer's entrepreneurial counterparts in industry and commerce.

Finally, the accumulation of great wealth without property ownership is extraordinarily difficult. Yet the ideology of property ownership is remarkably resistant to challenge. Despite attempts by workers to occupy factories and to start cooperatives, and measures by government to extend the notion of 'property rights' in jobs through employment protection legislation, such as the Employment Protection Act 1975, the attitude that the owner of an enterprise possesses productive property in the same inviolate way that an individual possesses his own home with virtually full rights of disposal has diminished little, especially amongst employees in smaller firms.

The middle class as a re-emerging sociological 'problem'

There are signs of a quickening of sociological interest in the middle class, especially the much-neglected entrepreneur. Capitalist farmers, small businessmen and political campaigns by 'respectable' but rebellious middle-class activists have all recently received detailed scrutiny. This partly reflects a wider resurgence of interest in class conflict by both mobilisers of middle-class opinion, such as Gorst and Hutber, as well as academics, possibly as the result of numerous industrial confrontations in Britain in the 1970s. It also illustrates a recognition by sociologists of the deepening perplexity amongst the middle class as to what constitutes 'middleclassness'.

During the period of relative affluence in the 1950s and 1960s, sociologists, like many others, assumed the existence of a recognisable middle-class way of life with a distinctive set of values. Goldthorpe and Lockwood's seminal investigations of 'the affluent worker', while locating important changes in working-class values, hardly explored middle-class existence but largely assumed a characteristic pattern of sociability and individualism against which working-class behaviour could be measured. For others, such as obvious sympathisers like Lewis and Maude, middle-class values – individualism, independence, leadership – were associated with a good education and a taste for 'high' culture, particularly the arts. This depended on a comfortable material base provided by a good, secure income and property ownership. Lewis and Maude believed that, thus equipped, the middle class provided an unproblematic cultural exemplar for other groups, particularly the working class.

If this was ever an accurate portrayal of the middle class, it is no longer. The 'new' middle class – mostly employees – has expanded in number while the small businessman and independent professional, who comprised the centre of Lewis and Maude's middle-class universe, have declined in the face of the developing power of the state and big business. Moreover, this new middle class joins trade unions and goes on strike; it does not provide a source of emulation for the working class but climbs into the ring with it and publicly competes for goods and rewards. How then should we now characterise the middle class? Is it still possible to identify a specific 'middle class culture'? At least three major reasons may be advanced for suggesting that such questions have acquired a new interest in recent years.

Middle-class discontent

A resurgence of 'middle-class' discontent occurred in Britain in the 1970s which found expression in associations outside the usual habitat provided by the Conservative Party. The 'ratepayers' revolt' of 1974–6 spearheaded by the militant National Association of Ratepayers' Action Groups (NARAG), the mushrooming of aggressive small business associations such as the National Federation for the Self-Employed (NFSE), and the formation of Gorst's Middle Class Association (MCA) during the same period, are examples of new-found 'middle class' assertiveness. Although these organisations were responding to specific grievances – large rates increases, an additional insurance levy on the self-employed, new property taxes such as Capital Transfer and Capital Gains Tax, the administrative burdens imposed by Value Added Tax, and legislation, notably the Employment Protection Act, which impedes small business control over labour forces, they were part of a generalised middle-class rage at the extension of state regulation, trade union power and the apparent inability of a 'collectivist' Conservative government under Edward Heath to prevent it.

Yet the so-called 'middle class revolt' of the 1970s was less an expression of a coherent middle-class consciousness than the sign of an internal battle within the middle class. Small business and ratepayers' activists scornfully contrasted the 'new' middle class with the 'old', the 'parasitic' government bureaucrat with the 'real producer' – the self-reliant, growth-created entrepreneur. As such, stirrings of middle-class discontent may be regarded as symptomatic of underlying changes in the composition and position of the middle class in British society.[51]

Changes in the middle class

Many of the most striking changes in Britain's occupational structure in the post-war period have occurred within the middle class. Alongside the diminution in the numbers of small businessmen and independent professionals we have witnessed the non-manual proportion of the labour force increasing substantially, rising from under 30 per cent in 1931 to 45 per cent in 1971. In the same period the percentage of white-collar employees (those outside professional, employer and managerial ranks) went up from 18.2 per cent to 30.3 per cent.[52] These figures conceal an even more dramatic change, the entry into employment of large numbers of married women. Four million more married women work today than did in 1951–2 (6.7 million from 2.7 million); between 1921 and 1961 the proportion of women in non-manual employment increased from 31.7 per cent to 53.5 per cent, with most of the expansion taking place in routine clerical positions which now provide over 70 per cent of female non-manual jobs (see Table 9).

TABLE 9 *Socio-economic group of earners: by sex (Great Britain)*

	1971 and 1972	**1976 and 1977**
Men		
Socio-economic group (percentages)		
Professional, employers, managers	20	21
Intermediate and junior non-manual	18	18
Total non-manual	38	39
Skilled manual and own account non-professional	43	41
Semi-skilled and unskilled manual, and personalised service workers	20	20
Total manual	62	61
Total sample size (= 100%) (numbers)	2,579	16,250
Women		
Socio-economic group (percentages)		
Professional, employers, managers	4	5
Intermediate and junior non-manual	55	51
Total non-manual	59	56
Skilled manual and own-account non-professional	8	8
Semi-skilled and unskilled manual, and personal service workers	33	36
Total manual	41	44
Total sample size (= 100%) (numbers)	8,188	11,144

Source: *Social Trends*, Central Statistical Office, HMSO, 1979, Table 5.10 (adapted).

Sociologists have yet systematically to appraise the consequences of increasing female employment for their theories of class. Some regard the 'female' category as irrelevant for class analysis. Giddens, for example, suggests that women workers are largely 'peripheral' to the class system as 'women still have to await their liberation from the family'.[53] But this marginality of female labour for class analysis is questionable; not only is the income a married woman brings into the household an increasingly vital part of a household's budget, but, as Garnsey notes, general wage-rates and employment conditions are influenced by the weak negotiating resources possessed by most women workers. The contribution of women's work to the resources of the family and the outlook of its members is obscured 'by the customary sociological practice of aligning the class position of the family with the male head of household'. Employing the categories used by the Registrar-General's Office in their classification of occupations. Garnsey shows that in 1971 over 50 per cent of women were classed in non-manual categories on the basis of their own occupation, but only one-third were so classed by their husband's occupation. She argues that 'this suggests an important disparity in the work experiences of many husbands and wives'.[54] This is a conclusion in line with the findings of *The Affluent Worker* authors, who maintain that 'family bridges' between manual and non-manual employments are more significant than affluence in encouraging the spread of middle class values.

The expansion of the non-manual sector has also provided increased opportunity for social mobility. A number of papers and a recent book emanating from a sample survey enquiry into occupational mobility carried out from Nuffield College, Oxford, in 1972, have found 'evidence of a general rising probability of the sons both of manual wage-workers and of men in our intermediate classes having gained access to higher-level occupations'.[55] Goldthorpe et al. conclude that the sharp expansion of non-manual positions and the steady contraction in the number of working-class jobs has increased the chances for the sons of manual workers to 'avoid' manual employment. However, although absolute mobility has increased, this has little affected rates of relative mobility: opportunities for intergenerational advancement for different classes have remained remarkably stable.

The Nuffield findings seriously question the proposition that a fundamental line of cleavage exists within the class structure between non-manual and manual occupations, with a 'buffer zone' preventing all but short-range mobility by 'affluent' workers and more routine white-collar employees. Although a general degree of limitation on long-range mobility out of the working class does exist, Goldthorpe et al. found little evidence that the chances of intergenerational mobility for the working class are heavily concentrated within the skilled manual category. Conversely, they discovered considerable amounts of both downward mobility and 'counter-mobility' (temporary downward mobility), and this creates a more complex picture of recruitment to middle-class positions than is often portrayed. Clearly the growth of non-manual employment since the war, along with other factors such as differential class rates of fertility, has 'forced' considerable mobility into the middle class and, as a consequence, added to its sense of perplexity.

Middle class as cultural leader

The middle class is no longer unquestionably regarded as providing a cultural model for other groups, nor does its economic 'worth' go without challenge. It is not only the young radical that scornfully contests the superiority of middle class values, but the political Right – a traditional friend of the middle class – also contests the 'usefulness' of many middle-class occupations. Conservatives, such as Joseph, Boyson and Ridley, see many non-manual positions as a burden on Britain's productive capacity, particularly those in the public sector, although the independent professional and businessman are still viewed as possessing virtues of independence and productiveness. These more jaundiced accounts of the middle class have been reinforced by the fact that much of the growth in non-manual employment since the war has occurred in the public sector. Public service jobs increased from 14 per cent to 17 per cent of the total between 1961 and 1971 while manufacturing diminished from 36 per cent to 34 per cent; a recent forecast estimates that public sector employment will rise to 21 per cent of the total by 1981, compared with a manufacturing sector of 31 per cent.[56] These trends might have created less interest if they had not been accompanied by persisting problems within Britain's economy, and some commentators have causally related the two phenomena. Bacon and Eltis, for example, argue that a massive transference of resources from 'productive' manufacturing to non-productive governmental bureaucracies has occurred. They claim that the major reasons for Britain's declining economic performance over recent decades are located in a shrinking industrial base unable to support an ever-expanding bureaucratic 'superstructure'.[57]

These ideas have political force as they are apparently shared by leaders of the major political parties; an all-party consensus exists as to the desirability of cash limits for public expenditure and the need to redivert resources into manufacture, while the parties strenuously compete in their efforts to support the claims of small businesses as part of the drive to 'get Britain's manufacturing industries moving again'. But Bacon and Eltis's assertions may be too sweeping; expansion in public service employment does not simply involve more 'non-productive' white-collar work but also 'productive' manual work, such as that provided, for example, by electricians and carpenters working for the Department of the Environment. Furthermore, in the mixed economy, it is not easy to distinguish public expenditure that is a drain on resources and that which is vital accoutrement to manufacturing enterprise, such as government loans and subsidies.

Nonetheless, the kind of assertions put forward by Bacon and Eltis have reinforced the tendency to regard middle-class occupations as no longer virtuous by definition. The questioning of what it is to be 'middle class', and the changes in occupational structure that lie behind it, is also symptomatic of what we may term the 'decomposition' of middle-class culture. King, for example, argues that 'if a middle-class identity ever existed the differentiation of the middle-class occupational world has ensured its passing'. Remarking on 'the internal divisiveness, fragmentation and, in some cases, brief existence' of middle-class organisations in Britain over many years, including recent groups such as the Middle Class Association, the National Federation for the Self-Employed, and the National Association of Ratepayers' Action Groups, he concludes that, 'there is little sign of a common class consciousness, an awareness of belonging to a class wth specific interests'.[58] King's conclusions are drawn from analysis of middle-class activists organising at a time of perceived, specific 'crises', but more general accounts of middle-class attitudes also suggest that middle-class culture is becoming fragmented. Bechhofer et al. believe that changes in education, particularly the decline of the grammar school, have disrupted 'cosy middle-class networks' and undermined the 'separateness' of middle- and working-class existence, with the result that the British middle class is now 'a less established, less unified middle class'.[59]

Clearly, it is no longer sufficient for sociologists simply to characterise middle-class attitudes as individualistic, achievement-orientated and displaying a graded, hierarchical (ladder) image of the class structure, in comparison with allegedly collectivist, 'live-for-today' working-class values; there is no *one* middle-class imagery. Roberts et al., for example, distinguish four types of middle-class imagery: 'compressed middle class', 'middle mass', 'ladder', and 'proletarian'. The small businessman typically expresses the belief that he is part of a 'compressed' middle class, squeezed between a large working class and big employers, although most of Roberts et al.'s white-collar respondents placed themselves within a large 'middle mass' category, with a view of the very rich and the very poor as placed at either end of the class system. The latter were not especially ambitious – many wished to climb to a comfortable occupational plateau – and displayed little hostility to the working class. A minority of white-collar respondents viewed the class structure in the dichotomous (us/them) terms employed by many manual workers, while a further small group of highly educated respondents, moderately left-wing in outlook, saw the social order as characterised by a series of fine gradations.[60]

These images reflect the absence of a single middle-class consciousness, and possibly indicate a slackening in non-manual career aspirations. Nor did Roberts et al. find a great divergence in orientations to social mobility between their working class and middle-class respondents once the respondent's own starting point was taken into account. Parents had similar educational hopes for their children, even if these were less likely to be realised by children from working class backgrounds.

'Social closure'

Problems encountered in the use of the division of labour, particularly the manual/non-manual distinction, for a general account of class societies, plus a preference for including elements of collective action and individual values within models of class rather than regarding individuals as merely the holders of economic positions, have led some theorists to analyse class structure in terms of 'social closure'. The notion of social closure rests on the well-established recognition that social mobility is a crucial element in the determination of class consciousness and that the boundaries on individuals' mobility chances provide the limits to who is recognised as belonging to the same class. Weber's concept 'social class', introduced to characterise social action by members of one class in relation to another, for example, arises on the basis of those class situations within which individual and generational mobility is easy and typical. Benson suggests that here the notion of blocked mobility is crucial, for it demonstrates that a social class has been able to attain something of a monopoly of access ('closure') to certain valued resources, such as private property or access to qualifications. Thus, the process of 'closure' is a vital part of the process of social class formation.[61]

A similar approach is adopted by Giddens. He identifies the distribution of mobility chances as the major variable in 'class structuration' – the process in which individuals sharing a similar market position become a social class, that is to say, they recognise collective interests. Restriction of intergenerational movement into valued occupations results in the reproduction of common life experiences over the generations, and this facilitates class consciousness. Thus, the connection between the existence of types of market capacities and the formation of identifiable social classes is primarily influenced by levels of mobility chances in a society; the more mobility is restricted intergenerationally, and the more an individual is restricted to a range of jobs with similar material rewards, the greater the likelihood of that 'homogenisation of experience' which facilitates class consciousness. Giddens argues that advanced capitalist societies are characterised by a threefold categorisation of classes – upper, middle and lower – based on three distinct sorts of market capacity: respectively, the ownership of property in the means of production, the possession of educational or technical qualifications, and the possession of manual labour power. To the extent that these forms of market capacity are joined to closed patterns of mobility, then the structuration of the basic three-class system is facilitated. However, 'closure' is always imperfect in capitalist societies in the absence of formal prohibitions on mobility, and Giddens argues that class structuration is also influenced by other, proximate, factors, such as the division of labour, workplace authority relations, and patterns of consumption.[62]

Parkin asserts that the notion of closure allows a conception of class relations as dynamic and conflictual, based on contrary principles of social action, which is largely denied by the division of labour model. Typically, dominant groups seek to maintain and enhance their privileges by a strategy of exclusion: the restriction of access to valued resources to a limited circle of eligibles marked out by certain social characteristics (e.g., race, education, religion). Exclusionary closure involves the subordination of 'outsiders', that is, it involves the exertion of power downward and the creation of a group of legally defined ineligibles. Ineligibles resist and challenge exclusion practices by a strategy of *usurpation*, by directing power upward and threatening the prevailing system of distribution. As Parkin remarks, 'Exclusion and usurpation may therefore be regarded as the two main types of social closure, the latter always being a consequence of, and collective response to, the former. . . . Modes of closure can be thought of as different means of mobilising power for the purpose of engaging in distributive struggle.'[63]

Consequently the distinction between bourgeoisie and proletariat, for example, is best regarded as referring to conflicting groups characterised by their predominant modes of closure – exclusion and usurpation – rather than position in the productive process. By definition the relationship between them is exploitative: 'Exploitation here defines the nexus between classes or collectivities that stand in a relationship of dominance and subordination, on *whatever* social basis.'

Parkin suggests that in modern capitalist societies the

bourgeoisie creates and maintains itself as a class by exclusionary devices based firstly on the institutions of productive property, and secondly on educational attainment. Both involve rules that effectively limit access to rewards and which profoundly affect the life chances of those excluded; the beneficiaries are those who own or control productive property and those groups possessing a state-backed monopoly control of access to professional occupations. These two sets of eligibles may be thought of as the core components of the dominant class under capitalism, and this is reinforced at the concrete level by similarity of social background and ideological and political predisposition. However, while the use of academic and technical qualifications as a way of restricting access to key positions in the division of labour tends to substantially benefit the offspring of those with professional status, Parkin notes that there are 'serious risks' attached to the transmission of status by way of 'cultural property' in comparison with the direct hereditary passing on of material property. The former demands at least minimal levels of ability and effort, and, as this can never be guaranteed, an element of hazard confronts those who wish their children to be as well-advantaged as themselves. We pointed earlier to the results of the Nuffield surveys on social mobility which indicate that only around one-half the sons of the highest professional groups attain their father's position; this, states Parkin, suggests 'a system designed to promote a class formation biased more in the direction of sponsorship and careful selection of successors than of hereditary transmission'.

Collectivities may adopt 'dual strategies' of closure in trying to maximise claims to resources, and this is commonly found among lower non-manual groups. Routine white-collar workers, for example, seek to employ strategies of exclusion based on formal qualifications, thus endeavouring to limit the supply of 'expert' labour on to the labour market and, as a result, keeping its 'price' high (i.e., exerting power 'downward' against manual workers). However, they are generally unable to attain full closure by gaining a legal monopoly to control entrants to their occupation. Consequently, they also adopt usurpationary strategies and demand improved pay and conditions by acting 'solidaristically' and forming or joining trade unions (i.e., exerting power 'upward' against employers). Professional closure and the use of exclusionary devices may remain as the preferred long-term goal, but intermediate groups 'strive to maximise their advantages by adjusting the balance between *both* types of closure activity according to changing circumstances'. Usurpationary challenges are often undertaken with reluctance; after all, exclusionary devices and full professional closure is more 'legitimate', better rewarded, and usually less costly in terms of time, energy and other resources.

Conclusion: Who comprise the middle class?

We have seen how Weberian approaches to class identification, including that of Giddens and Parkin, stress the importance of social mobility for class formation. The notion of closure or blocked mobility is regarded as crucial for class-consciousness. An analysis of the middle class must clearly address itself to the empirical importance of *recruitment*, and Goldthorpe, on the basis of the findings from the Nuffield study, suggests that the widening basis of recruitment to middle-class positions is a crucial factor in accounting for the middle class's declining normative coherence.[64]

Goldthorpe distinguishes for components of the middle class (see Table 10); 'established' and 'marginal' *salaried* groupings on the one hand (the 'new' middle class), and established and marginal *proprietors* on the other (the 'old middle class). These are characterised by different patterns of recruitment. Approximately one-half of the men in the 'old' middle class (large proprietors, independent professionals) are drawn from the established middle class, a third from the marginal middle class, and just under a fifth from the working class; but those who make up the 'new' component are recruited from these three sources in roughly equal proportions. Goldthorpe, however, points to the increasing 'establishment' of the new middle class of well-paid professionals and executives as they increasingly ensure that their offspring avoid downward social mobility. The more marginal sections of the new middle class, on the other hand, continue to experience much less recruitment from within its own ranks over the generations, and the contrast in structuration between the middle class groups helps to account for the 'fragmentary' character of the middle-class normative world.

TABLE 10 *Components of the middle class*

	'Old'	'New'
Established	Large proprietors, independent professionals	Salaried professionals, administrators and officials, managers, higher grade technicians
Marginal	Small proprietors, self-employed artisans and other own-account workers	Routine non-manual employees, lower-grade technicians, foremen.

Source: J. Goldthorpe, *B.J. Sociology*, December 1978.

Goldthorpe's scheme usefully outlines the major middle-class components, including the often disregarded propertied groups, and the four groups identified provide the subject matter of the chapters that follow. However, although any account of the middle class must necessarily include comparisons with the working class, a central goal in these chapters is the exploration of the tensions and conflicts, the changes and disparities in the market, work and status situations, within the middle class. When the middle class 'revolts', as citizens or producers, it is as likely to be symptomatic of an internal battle (middle-class ratepayers versus middle class bureaucrats, for example) as it is to be antagonism towards a trade union-led working class.

Firstly, however, we consider the historical development of the middle class.

2

THE DEVELOPMENT OF THE MIDDLE CLASS

The first known mention of the term 'middle class' is given by the *Oxford English Dictionary* as appearing in 1812. Before that time contemporary observers were more likely to see society as being composed of two different groups – the gentlemen and the non-gentlemen, with various ranks and orders within each of these two main groups. Before the Industrial Revolution society had its middle orders, of course, which lay between the nobility and the common people, but it was the rapidly changing society of the late eighteenth and early nineteenth centuries which demanded a new terminology to replace the old, as the new manufacturing interests developed their own sense of identity and distinctiveness during the political and social upheavals of the period. This identity of interest and attitude was shortlived, however, for the middle class was a group which was constantly in a state of flux, as it recruited members from below and exported others to the upper classes. But this first middle class left behind a legacy, in that its ideology became incorporated into the classical statements of bourgeois capitalist belief, in which labour was conceived as a commodity, economic struggle as a fundamental human drive, competitiveness as part of the human order, property as sacred and thrift the supreme virtue. Not for nothing did Engels complain of the English as being the 'most bourgeois of all nations'; it embourgeoised not only the aristocracy but the proletariat too.[1]

But the classical age of the bourgeoisie is over and its ideology is at an end, and, as Macrae comments, 'the culture of the new period of high consumption and reduced social distance is not yet defined'.[2] But if the ideology is dead the memory lingers on, and the old solid middle-class virtues are often seen as stabilising forces in a society of constant change and turmoil. Our images of the middle class appear very often to be frozen in the world of late Victorian and Edwardian England when the middle class – the backbone of the nation – reached its apotheosis, when taxation was low, servants easy to come by, status was assured and the sun always appeared to be shining; the bourgeoisie, which always seemed to have been rising had at last arrived. Since then some would have us believe the middle class has been in a process of decline (though from what point it has declined is never made clear) and the middle class today, though it may be the same genus, looks (as we remarked in the first chapter) to be a different species.

The middle class is continually proclaiming itself to be dying but never does die; rather it is in a continuous state of change both in composition and in function. Time was when the middle class appeared as an importer of the most talented individuals from the manual classes below, as well as an exporter of its élite to the upper class. Now, with the merging of the top end of the middle class with the industrial plutocracy of the upper class, no clear distinctions between upper and middle can be drawn, and similarly there is, as we have seen, a growing, though by no means complete, blurring of lines between the middle and working class.

The pre-industrial period

The term 'middle class' was coined, as we said earlier, in the early years of the Industrial Revolution. Of course, there were occupations in the pre-industrial period which we would now regard as being middle-class – those of merchants, lawyers, doctors and small businessmen – but these were not then a distinctive class within the rest of the local community. Artisans in the towns could become merchants and traders, but, equally, the sons of the local nobility could enter trade. It was, to a large extent, a one-class society, for there seems to have been common value systems, linking together the different status groups within the ruling stratum of society. As Laslett argues, 'rivalries and clashes between Englishmen in Stuart and even Tudor times, intellectual, political or military, can hardly have been of an inter-class character. They must have gone on within the same class'.[3] The struggle between King and Parliament in the Civil War is often regarded as a movement in which the bourgeoisie, allied to an impoverished gentry, 'rose up'. But this is certainly a simplification of a complex intragroup rivalry; the middle class were to be found not only supporting the King but also serving in the New Model Army.

The seventeenth century certainly saw a rapid expansion of middle-class occupations, though it is difficult to give figures with any degree of accuracy. But, if we accept Gregory King's figures as being approximately correct, there appear to have been in 1688, '110,000 merchants, 10,000 clergy, 10,000 greater or lesser officials, 16,000 persons in science and liberal arts, and 9,000 army and navy officers. To this figure for the commercial and professional groups needs to be added 16,000 gentlemen and 40,000 wealthy freeholders'.[4] The total income of the professional and commercial group was nearly as great as that of the landed proprietors.

During the seventeenth century, too, there was a rapid expansion in the numbers of clergy, following the decline in numbers at the Reformation; a 40 per cent increase in numbers called to the bar between 1603 and 1643; an expansion of secretarial and administrative posts following the English Revolution (three to four thousand had incomes over one hundred pounds). And if one adds to these figures the growth in the numbers of merchants and shopkeepers as a result of the expanded commercial activity during the period then the social importance of these middle groups in the pre-industrial period cannot be underestimated.

The rise in numbers was accompanied by a rise in the social status of many of these middle occupational groups. Rising incomes, through spiralling agricultural prices, affected all classes from the yeomanry upwards, but the increased rate of capital accumulation through expanding commercial activity made the merchant groups very acceptable neighbours to the landed gentry. In addition, members of the professions and of the commercial groups were becoming both better educated and of more genteel origins. There seems to have been an increased rate of intermarriage between the children of the gentry and those of the professional and commercial classes. Moreover, the younger sons of the gentry were often apprenticed to the prosperous merchants so that an observer of the time could write that the merchants 'often change estates with gentlemen as gentlemen do with them; by mutual conversion of one into the other'. It would seem that the linkage between the gentlemen and the merchant classes preoccupied some observers of the time as embourgeoisment concerns some people today. As Laslett writes: 'There can be no doubt that the sons of the Manor House married the daughters of the city merchants for as much money in the way of a dowry as they could possibly get, or that the son of a successful goldsmith, merchant, haberdasher or draper might marry the daughter of a country gentlemen'.[5] Furthermore, by the process of social mimesis the successful merchant retired at the first opportunity to the country and settled himself through the possession of estates as one of the gentry – a process which, though it might take a couple of generations to accomplish, could be achieved, and which is an example of the relatively flexible attitudes of the gentry of the time to the parvenu.

One should not exaggerate the rate of social mobility in the period. Apprenticeship of one's younger sons would only be to the prosperous merchants, and as many of these would be practically indistinguishable from some gentry one would not have to sink one's prejudices too far; trade, in the sense of what the small shopkeeper or blacksmith did, was certainly not attractive enough for sons of gentry to join.

What many sons of gentry did, however, and what their background and education fitted them to do was to become part of the middle class through joining government service at either a local or national level, or by entering the professions, particularly the ancient ones of divinity, physics and law. The seventeenth and eighteenth centuries saw an expansion of the professions. 'United by the bond of classical education . . . and deriving much of their status by their connections with the established order in the State',[6] the professions and public service together became important careers, both for younger sons of gentry and for those whose fathers worked in different middle-class occupations. The emergence of a professional class and the particular status acquired by that class were factors immediately associated with the slow growth of the civil service. By the mid-seventeenth century the equation linking the higher grades among the civil servants with those who practised medicine and law was already discernible. Already the bureaucracy was manifesting that capacity to survive through political changes which is the mark of an upper middle-class freed from military considerations and not dominated by the sovereign's court.

To the middle groups came also in the seventeenth century a dramatic increase in power. In foreign policy the mercantile classes could hold significant influence over governments simply by withholding credit from them. The role of both merchants and bankers cannot be overstressed; these middle-class groups had seized power for themselves. But this power did not exist in matters financial only, for middle-class principles of management came to be the dominant mode of organising public life. The state was coming to depend on the effectiveness of its administrative officers at both local and national levels and this gave the middle classes a growing influence in public affairs. As Stone writes, 'the landed gentry might continue to wield power and be arbiters of social status for another two hundred years, but they now had to temper the exercise of their authority with a careful regard for these newer elements in society'.[8]

The middle class and the Industrial Revolution

The challenge of the new middle class

It was the Industrial Revolution which gave the middle class a new self-consciousness and for the first time the sharing of common identity which seems to have lasted until the mid-nineteenth century. During that period the concept of class really applied to people in these middle occupations, for to their class-consciousness was often added a rejection of the values of the aristocracy and gentry as well as those of the manual classes whom they employed.

In the pre-industrial period the number of merchants, bankers and professional men was comparatively small, and intermarriage or investing their new found fortunes in landed estates was a manageable proposition, and this tradition continued during the early years of industrialism. Darby from iron, Mathew Boulton from engineering, Peel, Arkwright, Fidden and Strutt from cotton, Marshall from flax, Ridley, Cookson and Cuthbert from coal, and Samuel Whitbread from brewing are all examples of successful businessmen translating their fortunes into the purchase of large estates.[9] But many of the middle-class businessmen thrown up by industrialism were unacceptable to the gentry, while for their part they did not want to be assimilated to the traditional ruling groups. As Cole writes: 'These men emerged distinctively as a new middle class, conscious of their differences both from the gentry and from the main mass of the people below their economic level . . . the rising class of industrialists was differentiated at the outset almost exclusively by its economic position as the driving and directing force in the new forms of business enterprise'.[10]

These new men rose swiftly in the early years of industrialism. Still numerically very small (Colquhoun in 1814 calculated that there were only 25,000 manufacturers employing capital in all branches in 1801) they were, nevertheless, the aggressive and dynamic group whose energies and enterprise helped transform England. Of modest origins, owing little to birth, family, or education, they clawed and elbowed their way up, rejecting the values of the aristocracy and gentry while eliminating the petite bourgeoisie by pushing them into the ranks of the proletariat. Many seemed to be, as Hobsbawm says: 'Not merely a class, but a class army of combat.'[11] And this feeling of class-consciousness was strengthened by external factors which increased its self-awareness and helped direct it towards activism in politics.

Three factors seem to have encouraged this sense of class unity. The first was the imposition of income tax, by Pitt, which was thought to fall unfairly on the middle and industrious classes, who were being robbed of their savings by high taxation – a lament which has travelled well down the years – a grievance aggravated by the costs of the Napoleonic wars. The second was the view that, since the middle class was becoming the most important opinion making group in society, it should therefore be given parliamentary representation through the reform of Parliament, a conjunction for this purpose being made with the labouring poor against the aristocracy. The third was the campaign for the reform of the Corn Laws in the 1840s, 'a campaign which depended on class organisation for its efficiency and class vituperation for its energy',[12] and a movement against both proletariat and landlord through the middle-class body the Anti-Corn-Law League. By the 1840s the term middle class had become almost a term of self praise, and its values and ideology became those of the capitalist or bourgeois class that Marx wrote about.

It was the presence of the aggressive entrepreneurial spirit among the middle classes that came to confront the aristocracy with demands for the abolition of patronage; the reform of Parliament; the ending of protection and the institution of a system of free trade with no state intervention between employer and worker. This was the political platform. The philosophical justification was found in the writings of James Mill[13] and David Ricardo.[14] This class-consciousness gave them a strong sense of confidence as can be seen in these comments:

> The value of the middle classes in this country, their growing numbers and importance are acknowledged by all. These classes have long been spoken of, and not grudgingly, by their superiors themselves as the glory of England; as that by which alone has given us our eminence among nations; as that portion of our people to whom everything that is good among us may be traced.[15]

> By the people I mean the middle classes, the wealth and intelligence of the country, the glory of the British name.[16]

Accommodation of the middle class

This class-consciousness never emerged as a repudiation of aristocratic leadership. The bourgeoisie seems to have been perpetually rising throughout English history but never emerging as the ruling class, and at this time when a greater homogeneity of interest and attitude existed than ever before one would have expected a challenge to be made. Curiously the opposite happened. There are many reasons for this; one that is particularly significant is that there were changes taking place within the middle classes. The entrepreneurial spirit was the ideal of businessmen large and small, owning and managing their own firms and dismissive of the claims of idle landowners and irresponsible wage earners. But this view of the middle class is oversimplified because it leaves out two trends. The first of these is the recruitment of the larger and more successful businessmen into the hands of the new industrial plutocracy. The second is the growing numbers in the professional middle classes whose ranks trebled between 1841 and 1881.

This growth had the effect of dividing the middle classes and meant that the entrepreneurial ideal by no means carried the universal acceptance that was once believed. As Perkin puts it: 'Professional men . . . were freer than most to take sides in the socio-economic struggle . . . their increasing professionalism led many of them to differentiate themselves from the business class and to play a part in criticising the entrepreneurial policy of *laissez faire*.'[17] A challenge to the ruling classes was not made, but a defence against the lower orders was, and this led to the strengthening of the bonds of deference to the ruling class. For if industrialism threw up a new middle class it also produced a depressed proletariat, and the constant nagging fear of revolution by the lower orders made the new middle classes look to the established authorities to preserve their property at a time of unrest and challenge. If deference to the ruling orders was affected by the struggle over the Corn Laws, between 1846 and 1866 there still appears to have been a 'social stability and deference during which not even the scandals of military and administrative incompetence uncovered by the Crimean War disturbed a complacent acceptance of aristocratic leadership'.[18] It was an attitude of mind which, despite agitation for parliamentary reform, lasted until the 1880s when Joseph Chamberlain demanded that the rich pay ransom for their privileges. At a local level the repudiation of the gentry never occurred because the great country houses, after 1832, 'learned to pay proper attention to the interests, prejudices and opinion of the middle classes'.

The middle class did not merely look to the traditional ruling class for the maintenance of internal stability; they themselves recognised the influence they were having on government, even if they did not hold political office. They could see that the interest of land was not being favoured at the expense of commerce and industry. Between the Reform Acts of 1832 and 1867 domestic changes 'embodied in law and institutions the requirements of that industrial economy in which the major part was played by the middle class'. It was a Parliament of landowners who passed the Corn Laws in 1815 but it was also a Parliament of landowners who repealed them in 1846, under, of course, middle-class pressure. As Thompson argues: 'The landed interest continued to hold sway politically by the grace of the middle classes . . . the landed Member of Parliament of the 1860s and still more of the 1870s formed an upper crust resting on a middle-class electorate whose power to thrust them aside was already in existence even if it as yet lay dormant and unused.'[19]

A further reason for not presenting a direct challenge to the established ruling order was that until well on into the nineteenth century the middle class was still numerically small. Erickson has calculated, from the census of 1851 (the year of the Great Exhibition, the very testament to middle-class industry, enterprise and success) that the number of adult males in the middle class was less than one and a quarter million, or about 18 per cent of the occupied labour force. Half of these were engaged in commercial occupations of various kinds – merchants, bankers, shopkeepers and clerks – a quarter were farmers, and the other quarter belonged to the professional, administrative and employing classes in either industry or commerce.[20] As Deane writes: 'It was the last group from which most of the innovators and risk-takers were drawn. It numbered not many more than three hundred thousand people.'[21] It was only in the second half of the century that middle-class occupations began to grow, when the contribution of agriculture to the national product fell to be replaced by the mining and manufacturing industries. It was industrialism that called into existence a whole range of new professions and trades to minister to its needs – engineering, accountancy, surveying – as well as helping to expand the old professions of medicine, law and teaching.

At a micro level it was the middle-class manufacturing interests who took the economic decisions. It was they who expanded national wealth, improved standards of living, created demand, and invested their surplus wealth. At a national level, although the middle class was highly influential, the people who took the decisions were substantially the same group of people who were taking them before the Industrial Revolution. As Kitson Clark writes: 'The eighteenth century lingered at the top of society as obstinately and as self confidently as it did in the social pattern of Victorian England.'[22] And as Walter Bagehot noted in 1859: 'The series of Cabinet Ministers presents a nearly unbroken rank of persons who are themselves large landowners or are connected closely by birth or marriage with large landowners.'[22] It was not until the Reform Bill of 1867 that the middle class came into its political inheritance, and by then its challenge to the aristocracy was over. As we note in our final chapter, it was not until the last two decades of the century that Parliament came to be dominated by men of business and industry, when the balance of the economy swung from agriculture to industry.

It was, as Perkin has persuasively argued, the institutionalisation of the middle classes with its imposition of its ideas on others that led to the failure to create a middle class parliamentary party.[23] In truth their demands were absorbed into the framework of politics and especially that of the Liberal Party. It fell to Gladstone, as Chancellor of the Exchequer, to give the middle classes what they wanted: free trade, peace and economic progress, and it was through Gladstone that the middle classes came to be deeply associated with the fortunes of the Liberal Party. It is interesting to note that the present Conservative Government is not beyond claiming that it too is embarked on 'a crusade for Gladstone freedom'.[24]

By this time the successful middle classes and the landowning middle classes became interwoven to such an extent that the interests of the two were often the same. Joseph Chamberlain may once have wanted the rich to pay for their privileges, but he finished up a Tory minister. Landlord and industrial capitalist merged; together they prospered in the expansion of capitalism into the British Empire. The alliance of industrial capital and land secured the support of the second wave of the middle class in the towns. The old capitalist organisation was changing and here were the holders of jobs serving high finance capitalism. The work they did was no longer associated with the physical process of manufacture but with administration of factories, with decisions to produce, with marketing and with the growth of the service industries generally. It was yet another new middle class but this time without concern for how their capital was invested, and without independence, the ideal that the earlier middle class believed in so fervently. It was this middle class which could vote for the new Tory party, representing as it did land and manufacturing interests together, supporting it in its endeavours to exploit an imperial destiny.

Gentlemanly service

One consequence of middle-class reliance on older forms of authority was the continuation, in a rapidly changing social and economic order, of the notion of gentlemanly service, which has penetrated public life down into this century. If members of the middle class were too concerned with their own affairs to take the exercise of power into their own hands during the first seventy years of the nineteenth century, the traditional ruling class was only too keen to continue the traditions and ideals of gentlemanly service.

The qualities of gentlemanly service which the gentry brought to administration are difficult to capture, rooted as they are in a preindustrial order. Thompson suggests that 'honour, dignity, integrity, considerateness, courtesy and chivalry',[25] derived as they were from country life, were brought by the gentry to the administration of public life. Such qualities, to which can be added the general principle of disinterestedness, were honourable if not always appropriate. What they did, however, was to save the Victorians from the rule of the expert, for the gentlemanly mind held fast to the belief that a trained mind could cope with any kind of problem. 'The gentleman was not only individually cheap, collectively he was a safeguard against the ruthless and rootless expert, the Edwin Chadwick. He, or the method by which he was appointed, was a safeguard too against the sudden introduction of an administrative system based on abstract political principles and staffed exclusively by those who held such opinions.'[26]

The modern industrial state, depending as it does on a wide range of state involvement in economic activity, relies ultimately on the quality and number of trained people that governments can recruit. But lack of interest in the management of public life allowed the notion of gentlemanly service and amateurism not only to be continued but to be fostered. The state was expected to be the umpire rather that a player and experts were to be kept on tap but not on top.

This notion of the gentleman, with his distinctive qualities of mind, was fostered in the new public schools. Here was the place for the real interweaving of the gentry and the rising middle class, educated together on the reformed lines laid down by Arnold of Rugby. It was the new and rich middle class who supported the public schools, gaining social prestige through the schools' association with the upper class. The schools for their part taught the gentlemanly virtues and imparted the values of an established aristocracy to the prospective leaders of industry and business. The curriculum changed slowly, and although modern subjects were added the gentlemanly culture resting on the classics was retained. What was more important was the training of character through the virtues of discipline. Our politicians, civil servants, proconsuls and businessmen emerged with a set of qualities which produced the stereotype of the Englishman: self-reliant and correct, courageous and abstemious, inexplicit and taciturn, responsible but amateurish, always displaying loyalty and respect for tradition. It was the public schools which cemented firmly in the new middle class the notions of gentlemanly service. It was an achievement at which it is easy to sneer. Nevertheless, it was a valuable achievement.

Nowhere is this notion of gentlemanliness more evident than in the Civil Service which has always been pre-eminently a middle-class concern. The reform of the Civil Service in 1870 and the introduction of a competitive examination for entrance did not prevent this notion from persisting. 'La carrière ouverte aux talents' may be the maxim of the Civil Service but, even today, leading civil servants are drawn from the same class, if not the same families, as the Ministers they serve. The Member of Parliament who remarked that the British Empire was governed by Christian names was hardly exaggerating. The belief, too, that the trained mind could cope with any problem and that the recruitment of specialists was unnecessary survived into the reformed Civil Service and down, in fact, to our own times. And yet the system had strengths. As Smellie writes: 'The very slowness with which, in England, democratic government was substituted for aristocratic privilege made possible the success of our Civil Service. It was rescued from private patronage without becoming public spoils . . . the changes in the English political system and its administrative machinery were slow enough to secure the best of both worlds – the dying *noblesse oblige* and the disinterested scientific service struggle to be born.'[27]

End of the century

The last twenty years of the nineteenth century had considerable consequences for the country and for the middle classes. From the start of the Great Depression in the 1880s to its end in 1896, the world changed. Britain was no longer the workshop of the world and foreign competition with the United States and Germany was what the middle-class enterpreneur had to contend with. It was the existence of Empire which offered economic consolation to the middle-class manufacturer by providing a market for manufactured products and capital goods, through the employment opportunities it offered for the sons of the middle classes, and through the provision of cheap food, raw materials and gold to subsidise home industries.

Nevertheless, the writing was on the wall and in the period there arose a profound scepticism about the prevailing economic doctrines of the middle-class creed of individualism and a wider understanding of the economic writings of Henry George and Karl Marx. Attention shifted away from blaming economic failure and poverty on the individual to identifying faults that lay within the system, with the consequent need to look towards large-scale state intervention to correct the imbalances.

The Gladstone Parliament of 1880 was a 'no-mans-land' between the old individualism and the new socialism. The Social Democratic Foundation, the Socialist League and the Fabian Society provided the social critique, and the social legislation of the period and the numerous royal commissions were given philosophical justification by the neo-Hegelians led by T. H. Green. The age of collectivism was dawning.

Among the middle classes two responses are worth noting. The first was the view that middle-class vigour and drive were drying up – a view ascribed to what was thought to be the penal rates of income tax, rates and estate duties. *Punch* in 1881 could write: 'If you do not want your incomes exceptionally taxed, don't make money otherwise than by manual labour, and if you don't want your children or your brothers or your sisters to be fined for the public benefit on the amount you may leave, don't put any by.'[28] Such words could have been written yesterday.

The second response was the dissolution of the alliance between the middle and working classes. If the growing power of state intervention filled the middle classes with alarm, so too did the progress of the trade union movement. Gladstonian Liberalism became suspect to organised labour, with the lockout of the engineering employees in 1887 and the defeat of the South Wales miners in 1897. The coming to organised power of the unskilled labour unions who had no attachment to Liberalism led to moves to form the Independent Labour Party and the Labour Representation Committee. Sandwiched between growing state intervention from above and the rising power of organised labour below, the middle classes passed into the twentieth century with trepidation for what was to come.

Transitions in the twentieth century

Introduction

The momentous events of the twentieth century – war and civil strife, rising affluence and economic crises, social upheaval and shifts in political power, changes in belief and taste – have deeply affected class formation and class relationships in this country. Class, with its dimensions of political power and authority, income and wealth, life style and culture, has been affected both quantitatively and qualitatively by the events of this century.

The two world wars have, both directly and indirectly, had major effects on our social structure. More importantly, throughout the century there has been the steady decline of the British economy, the origins of which can be traced back to the last two decades of the nineteenth century. Periodic boom and affluence cannot disguise the fact that Britian has been in decline politically and economically for most of this period.

The consequences of this decline could have led to the different classes conducting a furious campaign for their existence. Paradoxically, this has not happened and throughout the 1930s, for example, when class divisions were at their sharpest, the language of conflict was rarely couched in class terms. Whether the same will remain true for the 1980s is anyone's guess. There is a deep continuity in our social life, and while history may not be a series of repeats, the responses to recurring historical events carry with them a high degree of predictability. The current response to our present economic crisis for many is for a return to the old talismanic virtues of duty, thrift, hard work, family and responsibility. Such responses are deeply enduring, and are found embedded in the middle-class frame of mind. This 'frame of mind' is not entirely solid, and within the ranks of the middle classes can be found a whole range of responses from complacency to conscience, self-righteousness to reforming zeal, philistinism to culture. Nevertheless, it is probably true to say that the broader values of society and those of the middle class are highly congruent in that they endorse the institutional order, celebrate the industrial ethic, lay stress on individualism, suspect collectivist tendencies, are apprehensive about the growing power of the state and celebrate, through its own socialisation processes, the internalisation of ambition, drive and success in its young[29] – points which are taken up in later chapters.

Within the broad continuity of the traditional industrial ethic there appears periodically to be a discontinuity between that ethic and the responses to it. In some respects, the 1960s witnessed a period of affluence when individuals, it seemed, no longer regarded thrift as the supreme virtue nor economic struggle as a condition of nature, and claims for liberty in the social and legal areas replaced individualism in the economic field. By the late 1970s that trend had been reversed, with cries for greater economic freedom, the return of the old virtues of hard work and thrift, while at the same time we have witnessed a demand for a tightening up on law and order, on industrial relations, and in areas in which greater personal freedom had been slowly negotiated: divorce, abortion and the independence of young people.

Throughout this century (and back into the last century on some issues) broadly similar kinds of responses can be discerned among the middle classes in the different periods. The heterogeneous groups that make up the middle classes have one common concern, and that is for the defence of economic and social inequality against levelling tendencies which carry threats to their income and to their property. The first response then is one of anxiety about any move that threatens their rights, privileges and wealth. The second is the manifestation of panic over the growing power of organised industrial labour, which they see as presenting a threat to their social and economic privileges.

In the rest of this chapter, the experience of the middle class is looked at period by period down to the 1950s, examining both the changes and the continuity of attitudes.

The Edwardian period

The ground plan of the class structure of this country, laid in the Victorian period, was developed in the years up to the beginning of the First World War in 1914. The Edwardian period has left a mythology of a settled and ordered society which continues to exercise a hold on the imagination, providing a reference point against which present day ills are judged.

It was a period best summed up by Keynes's comment:

> What an extraordinary episode in the economic progress of man that age was which came to an end in August 1914! The greater part of the population, it is true, worked hard and lived at a low standard of comfort yet were, to all appearances, reasonably contented with this lot. But escape was possible, for any man of capacity or character at all exceeding the average, into the middle and upper classes for whom life offered, at low cost and at the least trouble, conveniences, comforts and amenities, beyond the compass of the richest and most powerful monarch of other ages.[30]

The Edwardian golden afternoon was a myth, for it was a period in which social discord of one kind or another threatened the framework of society: the Boer War and its aftermath; the rise of feminism; constitutional crisis over the House of Lords; the revolt of organised labour leading to strikes and lockouts; the Ulster crisis. All this led many observers of the period to the conclusion that resolution would not come through parliamentary means but through civil strife.

The class structure of Edwardian England was perceived at the time to be a simple one. At the top, an 'upper class' consisting of the hereditary aristocracy and 'the gentleman'. At the bottom a working class of men and children – urban and rural poor – many living in conditions of primary poverty, whose lives were faithfully recorded in the Booth[31] and Rowntree [32] surveys. Between these two came the middle classes, with a number of different strata that were changing, growing and adapting in complex ways.[33]

The language used by commentators of the day to describe the class structure are revealing. Chiozza Money, a Liberal M.P., called his three groups 'the rich', 'the comfortable' and 'the poor'.[34] His contemporary Masterman, entitled them, 'the Conquerors', 'the Suburbans' and 'the Multitude'.[35]

The upper class To be a member of the ruling class in Victorian England was to belong to a small hereditary group – a few thousand who ran an Empire on Christian names – supplemented by the admission of the upper ranks of the Army, Navy, the Church and Law. By the Edwardian period the membership of the upper classes had been extended to include in its ranks that group of people called 'the gentleman'. To become a gentleman in Edwardian Britain was possible through business, banking, financial dealing of all kinds, and even through trade provided it was accompanied by a modified version of the life style lived by the traditional landed aristocracy. Such was the change in the composition of the upper class in this period that one observer could lament: 'Society itself, which throughout the whole of Disraeli's and the greater part of Gladstone's time had resembled a family party, was rapidly assimilating itself to a table d'hote whereat all who could pay the entrance fee can take their place.'[36]

The possibility of access to the ranks of the gentleman provided an important social function, making possible an accommodation between the old hereditary caste and the new thrusting middle classes aspiring to their ranks. As Middlemas puts it:

The gentleman was not necessarily an aristocrat. True he frequently became a peer, by creation for public or political services, or simply because he held influence in the shires... but the upper class was much wider than and different from the aristocracy with its exclusive habits and vast residual wealth in land and city property. On the one hand it behaved like a complex valve regulating the pressures between aristocracy and middle class caused by the explosion of industrial wealth, rising birthrate and political demands in the later nineteenth century and admitting a steady stream of suitable candidates for social betterment if not promotion to the peerage ... the gentry served as a buffer preventing the sharp cleavage between the aristocracy and the middle class which showed so clearly in early twentieth-century Europe, and prolonging the effective life of those above them, who they admired but sometimes envied and resented.[37]

Chiozza Money labelled this group as 'the rich', and that they certainly were. In 1913, Sir Arthur Bowley calculated that this group – about 2.5 per cent of the population – held over two-thirds of the country's wealth. A more recent calculation has put the top 1 per cent of the population in the years 1911–13 as owning 69 per cent of the nation's capital.[38]

The enduring tendency of the English ruling classes is that they never became purely urban or simply commercial. As has been noted earlier, each new wave of the successful and the rich married into the traditional ruling class and became indistinguishable from it in a generation or two. Orwell, in his classic essay, *The English People*, drew attention to this tendency and the sharp division among the middle classes between those who aimed at gentility and those who did not. That division he believed was cultural and not financial.

The manor house with its park and walled garden reappears in reduced form in the stockbroker's weekend cottage, in the suburban villa with its lawn and herbaceous border,... The widespread day-dream is undoubtedly snobbish, it has tended to stabilize class distinction... but it is mixed up with a kind of idealism, a feeling that style and tradition are more important than money.[39]

The 'solid' middle class Below the upper class came the ranks of the 'solid middle class'. Numerically quite small – perhaps less than 900,000 had incomes over £700 per annum in 1909 – it nevertheless allowed them the kind of life characterised by the suburban villa, servants and a carriage. It was the group with whom Arnold Bennett[40] conducted his famous love-hate relationship and they are best summed up in the words of Galsworthy's Jolyon Forsyte when he saw them as, 'half England and the better half, too; the three per cent half, the safe half. It is their wealth and security that makes everything possible . . . the middle men, the commercials, the pillars of society; everything that is admirable.' Echoes here of similar sentiments voiced by James Mill in the nineteenth century. Gretton, writing on the middle classes before the First World War, summed it up as 'wealth, money and possessions, and particularly their retention and use of them that are the distinguishing marks of the middle classes.'[41]

Middle-middle and lower-middle classes Below this solid middle class came the two status groups which we can label as middle-middle and lower middle-class. With their different occupations and somewhat different values, they were distinguishable one from another by fine degrees of social observation. The first of these was the group whose income lay somewhere between £150 and £700 per annum. They could afford a suburban villa, employ a domestic servant and with a smaller family and by careful housekeeping could spread their income further. With a rising standard of consumption, they could enjoy life though they had to keep an eye on their pence. Mrs Pooter, in the Grossmiths' *The Diary of a Nobody,* was able to indulge in that new middle-class habit of going shopping at Whiteleys, the first emporium, just as the Forsytes could indulge their fancies by shopping at Harrods.

And below this group there came the lower middle classes, the growing army of clerical workers, lower grade professionals, elementary school teachers and the emerging technician class. From these ranks came such literary figures as Leonard Bast in E. M. Forster's *Howards End*; Henry Straker, in Shaw's *Man and Superman* and, later, George Orwell's Mr Bowling of the England of the 1930s.

The expansion of occupations in the Edwardian period led to an opening up of the middle classes. If we group together all those classified as self-employed, higher grade professionals, employers and proprietors, administrators and clerical workers, then they account for about 20 per cent of the active population of the country, male and female. Marwick sums up the evidence on their size before the First World War as consisting of 400,000 salaried men earning above £160 per annum (the lowest point on which income tax was assessed); a professional group of 330,000; a proportion of 580,000 farmers; 620,000 employers and 60,000 men of independent means.

Where they lived One feature of the Edwardian middle classes that has to be taken into account is their geographical location. The mixture of country house and London season for the élite has attracted much attention with its rituals and conspicuous display of wealth. However, across the country in the rural areas and in small country and industrial towns there were local élites and complex status groups of which the local middle classes formed an important part. Edwardian England was not simply dominated by the landowning aristocracy but by the expanding new middle classes imitative of the gentry's life style and offering a clear hierarchy and patronage which kept both shopkeeper and working man both dependent and obsequious. As Thompson puts it:

> The diversity reflected local occupational structures, social superiors and inferiors. Edwardian Britain acknowledged their relative social standing in regular personal encounters: at work, in shops, at Church. Middle and Upper Middle Class families employed domestic servants; shop assistants were employed by local shopkeepers; craftsmen and labourers by local builders and manufacturers.[42]

Local status hierarchies were daily reinforced in social encounters and one quickly came to know one's place. But, at the same time, and more important in the long run, was the movement outwards to the suburbs and residential towns in which the middle classes sought out a more exclusive physical environment by which they could distinguish themselves from those in the classes below them. This process which started late in the nineteenth century has continued ever since. Only in the 1960s and 1970s have the middle classes attempted to recolonise areas of the inner city which they had previously deserted. And the word to describe that process is significant too: gentrification.

An indication of how towns expanded to accommodate the middle classes can be seen from the fact that the following twelve towns had a 75 per cent increase in the period: Blackpool, St Annes, Colwyn Bay, Morecambe, Ashford, Staines, Clacton, Bournemouth, Merstham, Reigate, Prestatyn and Southend. The increase was mainly due to the migration of the middle-aged and retiring businessmen. Middle-class areas which gained from importing of men and women in their thirties were Brighton, Southport, Blackpool, Hastings, Bath, Thanet, Scarborough, Harrogate and Llandudno.

The pattern was laid down in the Edwardian period, then, of migration of early middle-aged and middle-class groups to the suburbs and nearby residential towns, and, on retirement, a further migration by many to residential towns a long way from either place of work or birth. This phenomenon has led one observer to comment that 'pre-eminently the middle-class town of twentieth-century England is distinguished by the fact that a high proportion of its inhabitants were born elsewhere'.[43]

Uncertainty and anxiety The Edwardian frame of mind was one of deep uncertainty and anxiety, and many of our current concerns find their echoes in that period.

The first of these was the growing mood of self-doubt about the state of society. The various reports on poverty in the country;[44] the state of physical wellbeing of its manhood revealed in the Boer War;[45] doubts about its economic position in the world; anxiety about its power to defend itself; moral ambiguities over its Empire, all induced a mood of introspection and a concern for the future of the society. 'Beneath a prosperity so brilliant', wrote Sir Michael Sadler, 'there is a deeply felt unrest of heart and mind.'[46] In 1908 Arthur Balfour, the former Prime Minister, in a lecture in Cambridge chose as his theme that of *Decadence*,[47] in which he sought a parallel between old age in man and a period of decline of a nation in which there was a failure in national energy, a state he believed all nations passed through, but which he believed Britain had yet not reached.

One real and deep source of the uncertainty of the period stemmed from the conflict between the logic of the economic structure of capitalism on the one hand, and the moral claims for a society of free and equal citizens on the other. But Edwardian society was certainly not equal and the struggles to bring about such a society led to a deep fissure between the old liberal individualist solution and the trend towards greater collectivism.

The dilemma is neatly captured in Hilaire Belloc's *The Servile State*,[48] in which a line of criticism was developed which has led to a number of such books, including the compulsory reading for the modern Tory, F. A. Hayek's, *The Road to Serfdom* (1956). Belloc's argument was that capitalism was breaking down and a society in which a minority owned the means of production and the many were reduced to proletarian status was inherently unstable. The alternatives for Belloc were monopoly and restraint of trade, or state action for welfare. Such a state, with its implication for collectivism and redistribution, with its vision of state regulation hampering incentive and entrepreneurship, where work became a burden and not the means whereby a person could express himself in creative and productive ways, was anathema to many.

Accompanying the deep unease over the growing power of the state was the fear among the middle classes of the growing power of the working class. If the nineteenth century was apprehensive about the collapse of the Hyde Park railings, the years before the First World War were no less anxiety ridden. Just as today we see the power of the trade unions blamed as one of the root causes of current discontent. 'There was', wrote Masterman of the working classes, '. . . a note of menace in it . . . possibilities in its waywardness . . . one feels that the smile might turn into a fierce snarl of savagery.' And again he could write, 'the rich despise the working people; the Middle Classes fear them'.[49]

The fear of the working classes carried with it the tones of class war arising from the distribution of wealth and social inequalities of the period. The dilemma of the Liberal government of 1906, elected on a programme of reform, was that when those reforms were proposed and implemented, the government met increasing hostility and resentment from the middle classes towards the working classes. There was resentment at having to pay additional income tax, in paying insurance for their servants, at unemployment relief and at the 'gas and water' socialism of the local authorities. There was at this time a growing amount of comment on the antipathy of the middle classes towards the working class, and by their insistence on maintaining a proper social differentiation between them in insisting on particular habits of dress, manners and style of life. There was, too, a general opposition of those who paid income tax (above £160 per annum) to rises in taxation. The period saw the foundation of the Middle Class Defence Organisation, who wanted to 'abolish the absurd pampering of paupers at the expense of the struggling shopkeepers . . .', the Income Tax Reduction Society, and a series of articles in *The Tribune* (a Liberal newspaper) entitled 'The Bitter Cry of the Middle Classes' which was almost the swan song of the old nineteenth-century individualist creed.

It is hard to see, at this point of time, what the difficulties were all about, but the headlines following the 'People's Budget' of 1909 saw it characterised as a 'General Attack on Capital and Industry' by the *Morning Post* (the predecessor of the *Daily Telegraph*) and the slogan coined by the *Daily Mail* of 'plundering the middle classes'.

Bernard Shaw, lecturing on 'How the Middle Class is Fleeced', observed that the middle class had now fallen into an extraordinary state of neglect and contempt:

> It was not represented in Parliament. The aristocratic party had a chamber to itself and the Plutocratic class had the Commons very nearly to itself and the labouring class had the rest. The middle class was not represented at all; and had not the sufficient intelligence, apparently, to want to be. But it should be treated with respect; it was an important class, the class which ran the community. For the production of wealth, land and capital were required on the one hand, labour on the other, brains and business knowledge in the middle. Capitalist and labour would both starve but for the clever middle class, so clever in industry and so stupid in politics . . . beaten in political organisation by the working class.[50]

The fortunes of the Liberal government of 1906 were indeed sapped by this issue. As a government they were dependent on commercial middle-class support, but that class was resistant to growing government interference, to high taxation, and to support of the working classes. At the same time, the government was under pressure for further reform from the working classes and from radical reformers in its party and in the country. The Liberals procrastinated, and failed, allowing the Labour Party to become the party of progressivism in Britain.

The First World War

The long Edwardian afternoon ended in 1914 with the outbreak of the First World War. When it ended the world had changed and for the middle classes in England it marked a sharp transition in a number of ways.[51]

First, there were the casualties – the appalling slaughter of a generation and the loss of the brightest and the best from whatever class. Three-quarters of a million men were killed, which amounted to one in ten of Edwardian men, and, in addition, one in five were wounded. The shock and bereavement affected nearly all families in the country. Among the middle classes, from whose ranks the officer class was recruited, casualties were particularly high. It has been estimated that 20 per cent of the first generation of volunteer officers were killed. Of those officers from the public schools, 1100 Etonians out of the 5,600 were killed, one-third of those from Haileybury, 2,833 from Malvern and 687 from Charterhouse, and 2,608 out of 14,561 from Oxford University were killed. The consequences of such losses were incalculable; little wonder that an experience so vivid and searing on contemporaries has lasted down to the present, for many individuals only recently retired from public life had their whole outlook forged in such scenes of carnage.

But while a generation was being decimated a new formation was taking place. 'Temporary gentlemen' were recruited in the Services to fill the ranks of the depleted officer class and, more importantly, in civilian circles, through the expansion of wartime bureaucracy, and of businesses cashing in on the war boom. The greatest expansion was in clerical work, particularly for women, and in the supervisory and lower grade professional ranks. Altogether this meant an expansion of the salaried occupational groups by over one million and by 1921 they represented about 22 per cent of the working population.

Of profound significance, too, was the switch from domestic service by women who found employment in munitions, in transport and on the land. This switch helped to blur class distinction between the middle-middle and lower-middle classes, though here one has to see this in the context of local circumstances. The loss of domestic service was greater in the London region than it was in the rural areas where alternative work was not so readily available.

A most significant change which affected the middle classes was through the imposition of stiffer rates of income tax. McKenna's Budget of 1915 raised taxation by 40 per cent and this happened again in 1916. Additionally, the supertax threshold was lowered to £8,000. The imposition of an excess profits tax carried major financial consequences for the middle classes. A further consequence of the war was the effect it had on upper-class society. The high rates of casualties, of taxation and death duties, and the generally low economic return on land stripped much of the economic power from the gentry. But more than that, the localism on which the stability of the social order rested was lost with the conscription of the rank and file soldiers, and their posting outside their counties and their country. When they returned at the end of the war they were not as subservient or deferential as they had been. The hold the gentry had over rural society virtually ended with the war and local power and influence drifted away from the country house to the ranks of the working farmers.

Between the wars

The years between the two wars also had a considerable effect on the middle classes in this country, as might be expected. The events that took place in that period – the post-war boom, the collapse of the National Government, the first and second Labour Governments, the General Strike, the Slump, the impact of European Fascism and Communism – all impinged on the middle classes and helped shape their responses. The period is full of contradictions and paradoxes. It was a time of great change and yet there was a deep continuity. It was a time when status relationships between different groups was reconstituted and yet there was a growth of snobbery and exclusiveness. It was a period when there was both a repudiation and a reassertion of middle class taste and tradition. It was a period of extremes of wealth and poverty, with three million unemployed at the outbreak of the Second World War.

Continuity That there was a continuity between the pre-war world and the post-war world was, in part, directly attributable to the great losses that were sustained in the First World War.

This meant that the generation that would have succeeded to positions of power and influence in the 1920s were decimated and without leadership, and a gap arose between those who had known the good life before 1914, those who had known what the war was about from firsthand experience, and the subsequent generation who had been too young to go to war. Vera Brittain's *Testament of Youth* gives a very clear account of these differences.

This gap can be seen from the composition of Parliament during the inter-war years. In the 'Coupon Election' of 1918 only 100 M.P.s of the 'war generation' (that is, those under forty-one) were elected, and that figure never rose higher than 126 in all the inter-war parliaments. It was the old, the disillusioned and the stale who remained in power. Abrams has well pointed out that half the members of the 1939 Parliament were in their prime of life in 1914.[52]

The continuity of the pre- and post-war world could be seen in the symbolic leadership of George V. He and the dominating personalities in politics of the period – Baldwin, MacDonald and Chamberlain – looked back to the England before the Great War as did the Civil Service, the professions, business and finance:

> Nostalgia for the last period of British and Imperial greatness clouded and distorted for at least three decades the ideas held by the political élite about Britain's changing role and position in an unfriendly world. In Westminster, Whitehall, the City, the Stock Exchange, the Church, the Services, in short what came later to be called the Establishment – certain assumptions commanded general assent as if they had a talismanic virtue unaffected by passing time. Most if not all of them can be found stigmatised already in Masterman's Condition of England written in 1909.[53]

These men and their ideas found support from the middle classes. Whatever the twists and turns of policies may have been, and however insular and stupid many of the political actions were, it was what they represented in terms of continuity and reliance on older forms of authority that proved attractive to the traditional members of the middle classes. And in economics, in a world in which Britain's position was gravely critical, they held fast to the view that whatever ills the country faced could be dealt with without changing the basic structure of the capitalist economy.

Continuity was what the middle classes wanted in the main. In all the parliaments between 1918 and 1938 the middle classes were dominant. What is noticeable among Conservative M.P.s is the swing away from landowning M.P.s to a far greater representation of commercial and industrial background.[54] The Cabinets, too, became dominated by middle-class membership. In the Cabinets between 1919 and 1937, 81 out of 158 Cabinet Ministers were drawn from the ranks of the middle class.[55] As far as the Labour Party was concerned, after the debacle of the National Government of MacDonald in 1931, power passed increasingly into the hands of the middle classes. The middle-class centre of the party represented by Attlee (Haileybury and Oxford), Dalton (Eton and Oxford), and Cripps (Eton and University College, London) replaced the old trade union leadership of MacDonald, Thomas, Clynes and Snowden.

It is important, too, to note that it was more than a middle-class élite who were gaining ground in the Labour Party; it was now beginning to stretch down into the ranks of the lower middle classes epitomised by Herbert Morrison. As his biographers comment:

> Morrison was very much the spokesman of his own class. He represented the suburbs, the clerk, the minor civil servant, the municipal employee, the technician, the laboratory assistant, the elementary school teacher, the commercial traveller, the small trader and the shopkeeper and the office executive. Morrison realised their significance as a new force in politics, totally different from the middle class of the nineteenth century. In alliance with the working class they would overturn the established classes and create a well ordered, well-run society in which neither accident of birth nor occupation determined the status of the individual but only the efficiency of his contribution to the social whole.[56]

Continuity in the 1920s can be seen in many ways. 'Society' prospered and the pastimes of the privileged did not appear to be different from those enjoyed before the war – the country house weekend, hunting, Ascot and Goodwood, Deauville and Cannes for the more staid, and night clubs, parties, jazz for the 'café society' of the bright young things. In literature the dominant figures were still Shaw, Wells, Bennett, Galsworthy, Masefield and Forster – all pre-war writers. In art, traditionalism and the leadership of the Royal Academy were still pre-eminent, and in architecture, too, the dominance of Lutyens and the urge to build in a modified classical patrician style was prominent up to the 1930s.

Throughout the 1920s the middle classes exhibited again that note of despair about their plight and the deterioration of their economic position in comparison with those below them in the social pecking order. And always that concern is accompanied by the view that the country was on a downhill slope. Masterman described 'the general impression . . . of a whole body of decent citizens slipping down by inexorable God-made or Man-made or Devil-made laws into the Abyss, as if a table were suddenly tilted slanting and all the little dolls or marionettes were sent sliding to the floor'.[57]

Undoubtedly, the middle classes suffered in the post-war world. Domestic service declined and as prices rose after the war their economic position became more disadvantaged than it had been:

> Before the war it was living a little beyond its income . . . stretching forward to a more elaborate social life which is the motive power of its progress. . . . Now though its means are increased, in no case do these adequately compensate for the rise in the cost of living . . . the value of savings is but a half or third of the former total . . . in a vast number of cases, especially the old living on pensions, or small savings or cottage property, a more than doubled expense has to be met with no increase of income at all.[58]

Notwithstanding their seeing themselves as the 'new poor', it remains true that in this period the numbers paying supertax increased in this period as did the numbers of people with incomes in excess of £2,000. By 1929, Colin Clark estimates that 10 per cent of all income receivers took 42 per cent of the national income and 1.5 per cent took 23 per cent. Life for the middle classes was not easy in the inter-war years but it was not penury either, and the financial resources of a family could be spread further by reducing family size, which was a feature of the period.

Any account, then, of the inter-war years must consider the continuity of social life between the pre- and post-war world. It was a continuity that was deeply attractive to many members of the middle classes, promising the preservation of their position and a defence of their class and status positions. It can be argued, however, that it was an adherence to a set of values and beliefs in a structure of society that was ceasing to correspond with the social and economic realities.

Here then was the great betrayal . . . that for twenty years . . . one generation who had known the sweet life and lost it passed on its recollections to another slightly later generation which had been brought up to expect but never experience that life, and attempted to console its sense of deprivation. Things as diverse as cult of the old school tie, the old boy network and the inculcation of standard English by the BBC can be seen as fragments of a forgotton culture shored up against a ruin of a world without class landmarks. But many of our worst failures: the perpetuation of outmoded curricula in schools and universities, of outdated habits in industrial and business management, of an outworn culture can be traced back to this source.[59]

Movements for change in the 1930s If there was continuity there was also change and movements for change. Without that change, it is doubtful if the country could have survived the Second World War. There was a deep undercurrent of disillusion with the 'old gang' in politics, in business, in art and in letters, and in various movements struggling to change the existing order the middle classes were well represented. These different engagements were born of and promoted by a series of events at home and abroad: the General Strike; the Slump; the National Government of 1931; the rise of Fascism in Europe; admiration for the achievements of the Soviet Union; the Spanish Civil War.

Antagonism to the old order came from many sources: from the soldierly fascism of Mosley whose British Union of Fascists made recruits among the lower-middle-class white-collar workers. It came in the 1930s from the Communist Party, whose numbers rose to 56,000 at the outbreak of the Second World War, and from the young artists and writers – Auden, Spender, Cornford, Cauldwell – who took their writing beyond art and into the arena of politics. This latter group has often been severely criticised. Stephen Spender, writing in their defence says:

The writers of the thirties are often sneered at because they were middle-class youths with public school and posh university backgrounds, who sought to adopt a proletarian point of view. Up to a point the sneer is justified. They were ill-equipped to address a working-class audience, and were not serious in their efforts to do so. But that having been said it should be pointed out that up until the Spanish Civil War, when some hundreds of workers joined the International Brigade, the thirties writers represented a middle-class cris de conscience. And there is nothing despicable about this. The middle classes were the beneficiaries of the system which made them victims of the workers. Moreover, some of these writers were travelled and had an awareness of what was going on in Europe not just to the complacency of middle-class England and the apathy of most workers.[60]

An interesting question to be asked is why extremism in Britain between the wars did not flourish. The slump and the election of a National Government in 1931 suggested that all the ingredients were there: heavy unemployment, a leaderless working class, bankruptcy in ideas about reforming the economy, cuts in public expenditure and so on. There are many explanations for this and, clearly, one important factor was the massive rallying to the support of the National Government by the middle classes in the election of 1931. While the Labour vote held up, that election saw the virtual demise of the Liberal Party. It was a vote, therefore, for a certain kind of stability.

The second reason is that the middle-class groups never became militant and kept their distance from too close an association with the trade union movement. The economic position of many members of the middle classes in the 1930s led them logically towards some form of trade union organisation. However anxious they were to assert their distinctive middle-class status, their strategy was directed more towards being seen and treated like members of the higher professions. Thus, in 1933, the Bank Officers Guild and the Guild of Insurance Officials sought to arrange a conference of middle-class workers, only to find that their employers would not recognise their existence as organisations with whom they would negotiate.

The real reason why there was little extremism in the years between the wars is the perceptible improvement in the standards of living of many middle-class people. The slump and the subsequent Depression within the 1930s have been called the 'devil's decade', expressed in the phrases mass unemployment and appeasement. And yet, at the same time 'most English people were enjoying a richer life than any previously known in the history of the world: longer holidays, shorter hours, higher real wages. They had motor cars, cinemas, radio sets, electrical appliances'.[61] No wonder, as A. J. P. Taylor puts it, 'the two sides of life did not join up'.

As Stevenson and Cook have convincingly shown, the problem of the unemployed and the distressed areas in the old staple industries was not evenly spread but concentrated in the old industrial areas. In other parts of the country – in the South and the Midlands – a new industrial structure was being established. Economic growth for the decade averaged between 2.3 and 3.3 per cent, depending on the indices of production and the result was a rise in the national income per head of population. That fact alone, plus the fall in the cost of living meant for many of the salaried and middle classes (even if they had been in government service and had a cut in their salaries) a greater disposable income – a trend assisted again by careful family planning. It became possible in the 1930s for the average salaried member of the middle classes to buy his own house on a mortgage, run a cheap car and afford a range of consumer durables hitherto reserved for the more prosperous members of the middle classes. The period saw the expansion of personal saving through the building societies, growing job opportunities for women in office work, and an expansion of job opportunities for the managerial and professional salariat.

The period, too, produced a new picture of Britain, particularly in the South (where London had a population of 9 million and one-fifth of the population of Great Britain lived within a radius of fifteen miles of Charing Cross). It was here that the new arterial roads, the estates, the light industries and new factories sprang up. J. P. Priestley wrote:

> This is the England of arterial and by-pass roads, of filling stations and factories that look like exhibition buildings, of giant cinemas and dance halls and cafes; bungalows with tiny garages, cocktail bars, Woolworths, motor coaches, wireless, hiking . . . the smooth, wide road passes between miles of semi-detached bungalows, with their wireless sets, their periodicals about film stars, their swimming costumes and tennis rackets and dance shoes . . .[62]

The Depression had many faces: poverty, unemployment and hardship in some parts of the country were paralleled by increasing affluence and an improvement of living standards at the other. If the solid middle classes felt the pinch more, it was the new lower middle classes who came more into their own and where the distinctions between themselves and the working class grew sharper and more pronounced. Such was the growth of the service industries, of administration, of transport and distribution which expanded opportunities for this new lower middle class in ways hitherto unexpected.

Thirties into forties

The economic recovery in the 1930s had the effect of further separating the country into two nations. On the one hand a prosperous South and Midlands, economically prosperous from the new industries, and faithful in party loyalty to the Conservatives. On the other, blighted and industrially stagnant areas in the North, Scotland and Wales, where heavy industry was in decline but whose people remained loyal to the Labour Party.

The period of the 1930s saw two movements at work in the country whose effect was to be fully realised during the Second World War. The first of these was that part literary, part political movement in journalism which aimed to help the nation to understand itself and, in particular, to show the middle classes what working-class life was really like. The Grierson film documentaries; Allen Lane's Penguin Books; Mass Observation and *Picture Post*; the *Daily Mirror* – all provided a revolution in the communications industry. As one historian of the period puts it: 'This mission by the progressive middle classes to educate democracy and increase social understanding between the classes was to come into its own after the outbreak of war.'[63]

The second movement was that in politics itself which aimed for a reformed type of capitalism. The towering figure here was that of John Maynard Keynes with his ideas of economic management, which found support not only from within the Labour Party but also within a small section of the Tory Party, too. Harold Macmillan for one took an independent line on political and social questions throughout the 1930s and 'The Next Five Years Group' (Macmillan, Robert Boothby, Walter Elliot) was one consisting of 'men who felt that the Conservative Party must be given a more human face if it was to offer . . . a relevant policy for the country'.[64]

Certainly there was the view during the Second World War that change was expected even if the demands were modest, in a more class-conscious society.

As that lonely critic George Orwell wrote when considering how the war would make Socialism in Britain a realisable possibility:

We shall have to fight against bribery, ignorance and snobbery. The bankers and the large businessmen, the landowners and the dividend drawers, the officials with their prehensile bottoms will obstruct for all they are worth. Even the middle class will writhe when their accustomed way of life is threatened . . . But because patriotism is finally stronger than class hatred, the chances are that the will of the majority will prevail . . . If it can be made clear that defeating Hitler means wiping out class privilege, the great mass of middling people, the £6 a week and £2,000 a year class, will be on our side.[65]

The Second World War then accelerated the process of reform within capitalism. The Great War based its appeal for support on the theme of 'King and Country'; the Second World War on the grounds that it was a 'peoples war' and the outcome would be the improvement of the commonwealth. Certainly war itself did not have the effect of equalising and dissolving the status distinctions between class and class.

What it did not do was to herald a new social order but rather a reformed type of capitalism, with the existing social order remaining basically intact. As Paul Addison comments:

The nineteen-forties were the decade when the Conservatives were obliged to integrate some of Labour's most important demands into their own philosophy. They were able to do so without too much pain because Labour's demands had largely been cast in a mould of thought provoked by non-soçialist intelligentsia between the wars and during World War II. In his last years in politics under the premiership of Churchill, Attlee could argue that Labour had completed a peaceful revolution. When he revisited the Boys' Club in which he had worked in Stepney, he could observe how better nourished the boys were than they had been in Edwardian England. Such was Mr Attlee's consensus. The new dispensation which began after Dunkirk in 1940 and until recent years seemed the natural order of British politics. We were all – almost all Butskellites then.[66]

Postscript

Was the Butskellite corpse finally buried at the 1979 election? With the election of the Thatcher Government was the area of common ground between the two political parties finally abondoned? Suez, and the economic crises of the late 1950s provided the first shock to the system provoking a loss of national confidence. The 1960s witnessed a period of selfdoubt and self analysis about the institutions of society and the number of inquests into the 'state of the nation' were reminiscent of the years before the First World War. From the mid-1960s onwards both parties sought salvation through the seductive charms of technology and with an increased statism based on a tripartite relationship between government, industry and the trade unions. But economic decline still continues and the fact remains that the Social Democratic wing of the Labour Party and the Heathite wing of the Tory Party have failed to make a success of the mixed capitalist economy, opening up the possibility of power to the left of the Labour Party and real power to the radical right of the Tory Party under Mrs Thatcher. Uncertainty centres round whether the present government policies will provide the means of arresting our long-term economic decline, and/or, whether the consequence will be a sharpening of class conflict in a society that so far has somehow managed to avoid that condition.

3

WORK: THE ESTABLISHED MIDDLE CLASS

Introduction

In Chapter 1 we discussed how we might identify the middle class by examining a number of sociological approaches to class, and this also raised questions about the middle class's fate and values. Chapter 2 offered a detailed historical review of the middle class and in particular explored changes and continuities in middle-class attitudes. In this third chapter we begin to examine the contemporary condition of the middle class in several important sectors of social existence: work, family, education, leisure and politics.

Initially we examine the work situations of four groupings identified by Goldthorpe as comprising the middle class: an 'old' established sector of large proprietors and independent professionals: a 'newly' established middle class, including salaried professionals, administrators and managers; an 'old' but marginal stratum, exemplified by small businessmen; and a 'new' but marginal group of routine non-manual employees, such as clerical workers. Goldthorpe's classification is descriptive and residual, it contains virtually all groups that are not obviously working-class, and includes strata that some would wish to identify as other than 'middle class'. Giddens, for example, theorises an 'upper class' that is distinguished from the 'middle class' by a different form of market capacity, the ownership of property in the means of production. This is distinguished from the possession of educational or technical qualifications, the hallmark of the middle class, for it 'confers certain fundamental capacities of command' and is associated with a separate and restricted pattern of inter- and intra-generational mobility and thus a distinctive set of common life experiences. However, descriptively, Giddens's 'upper class' closely approximates Goldthorpe's 'old' established middle class.[1]

One could jib, too, at the inclusion of routine white-collar workers within the 'middle-class' category. We referred in Chapter 1 to the gradual blurring of the manual/non-manual distinction and the existence of some manual workers with a superior market capacity to that of many clerks, for example, which suggests that the latter may be middle-class only in terms of their own self-esteem, for their evaluation may be less than ever supported by material circumstances. This is a substantial objection; yet, as we have seen, white-collar work has long been associated with 'middle-class' office authority and other persisting, albeit narrowing, advantages in the work situation.

If the class location of routine non-manual workers is not unambiguously middle-class, neither is it obviously working-class, and this is sufficient for at least their initial inclusion within the scope of these chapters. On a different note, the inclusion of small proprietors within the middle-class category is objected to on the grounds that they lie outside the class system. Poulantzas suggests that small family firms do not engage in the extraction of surplus value from wage-labour but are simply involved in a minor way with the overall redistribution of value through the sale of goods.[2] Nonetheless, some 'small' businessmen are quite large employers, and even some of the smallest exercise an authority over subordinates and possess an autonomy not experienced by manual workers. We follow Bechhofer et al. in suggesting that small retailers may be viewed as precarious members of the middle class.[3]

The contemporary middle class is thus a diverse and complex group. Goldthorpe's 'catch all' classification, although lacking an explicit theoretical referent to the issues of class identification, is a useful starting point for an analysis of the likely sources of difference and antagonism within the middle class. Many of these conflicts stem from perhaps the major historical development in the social structures of modern industrial societies: the growth of large-scale, bureaucratic organisation, especially in the public sector, which has had important consequences for the nature and size of the middle class. Concentration and centralisation in manufacture, for example, has, for some observers, truncated the proprietorial powers of the old middle class and transferred industrial control to a new class of professional managers whose position is legitimated by claims to technical and organisational expertise rather than ownership. They are assisted by an enlarged clerical and routine administrative staff, essential for the efficient running of large corporations, but whose size and cost mostly rules out the close, special relationships with employers enjoyed by the nineteenth-century 'counting house' clerk.

These developments in the private sector have occurred alongside a steady expansion in the size and influence of the state. Many members of the middle class are public employees. The state employed 5.8 per cent of the total working population in 1911, but over 27 per cent in 1974 (see Table 11). Some are the 'new professionals' to be found in health, welfare and planning agencies that have expanded with the extension of social and other rights since the last war. As we noted in the previous chapter, a consequence of all these developments is that the older, marginal middle class – the small employer and the self-employed – has found itself diminished, threatened by the centralising, oligopolistic tendencies of large business and the fiscal and administrative burdens of an increasingly interventionist state, and fearful of collectivist challenges to its economic influence by a trade union organised working class.

TABLE 11 *Public sector employment, G.B., 1901–74.*

Percentages

1901	1950	1965	1974
5.8	24.3	23.5	27.4

Source: R. Brown, 'Work', in P. Abrams (ed), *Work, Urbanism and Inequality*, Weidenfeld & Nicolson, 1978, p. 71.

It is against these historical changes within the middle class, (see Table 12), that we analyse each of its major components. In this chapter we begin with a consideration of the 'established middle class'.

TABLE 12 *Major occupational groups as a percentage of total occupied population*

	1911	1931	1961	1971
Employers and proprietors	6.7	6.7	4.8	2.6
White collar workers	18.7	23.0	35.9	42.7
(a) managers and administrators	3.4	3.7	5.4	8.6
(b) higher professionals	1.0	1.1	3.0	3.8
(c) lower professionals and technicians	3.1	3.5	6.0	7.7
(d) foremen and inspectors	1.3	1.5	2.9	3.0
(e) clerks	4.5	6.7	12.7	14.0
(f) salesmen and shop assistants	5.4	6.5	5.9	5.6
Manual workers	74.6	70.3	59.3	54.7

Source: R. Brown, op. cit. (Table 11), p. 75 (adapted).

The old-established middle class

The modern middle class in Britain presents a complicated image to observers for it is composed of the legacies of a number of historical developments, described in Chapter 2, which have gradually transformed the class into one characterised less by private ownership of the means of production than by salaried employment. Several more or less plausible stereotypes of the middle-class individual are now readily found in popular literature: the public school educated, well-connected and urbane merchant banker; the grammar school educated, hard-driving managerial executive; the comfortable, rather leisurely professional in private practice; the secure, if less independent, professional in education or the health service; the conformist, unambitious clerk; the tax-avoiding, grousing small businessman; and, occasionally, the dynamic, arriviste parvenu with his working-class accent, such as Sir Billy Butlin or Sir Freddy Laker. These several caricatures indicate that the middle class is no longer stamped by one recognisably 'authentic' group in the way that, as we have seen, independent trading and manufacturing entrepreneurs became the exemplars of middle-class life in the last century. Kumar also notes, like us, that the bourgeois ascendancy of the nineteenth century marked 'the heroic age . . . a honeymoon period of praise and support for the energy of the bourgeoisie,'[4] – but that it did not last long. The alleged gaucheness, social insensitivity and narrow economic-minded-ness of the entrepreneur has now become a long-standing source of derision for other claimants to middle-class moral leadership, such as intellectuals and the salaried intellegentsia.

These last groups include most social scientists, and this may provide one explanation for the remarkable sociological distinterest in the established proprietor. Despite increasing 'official' approval of entrepreneurship in recent years, as both Labour and Conservative administrations strain for the industrial regeneration of the British economy, we know almost nothing about the businessman's work, how he operates, what he does. Instead, sociologists have largely confined themselves to answering one broad question: do private owners of the means of production still possess real industrial power or has this passed into the hands of working executives? This raises the issue of the so-called 'managerial revolution'.

'Managerial revolution'

A familiar theme in analyses of British manufacture suggests that it is misleading to view the commanding heights of the economy as remaining in the control of private owners, and that, at this level at least, the picture of family-owned businesses run by, and in the interests of, a small group of closely related individuals is outdated. In its place we have instead large joint stock corporations with ownership dispersed among many shareholders, and this leaves 'real' powers in the hands of full-time professional managers whose interests may diverge markedly from that of owners. Even if ownership remains in the hands of a few individuals, perhaps one family, then, the argument runs, the administrative and technical complexity of modern industry still ensures that owners have little option but to leave control in the hands of working directors and managers who intervene only if profits fall below a 'reasonable' level.

This thesis of 'proprietorial spectatorship,' which clearly informs some of the influential sociological theories of class structure explored in the first chapter, particularly those of Carchedi and Dahrendorf, has several variants. The seminal work on the separation of ownership and control, *The Modern Corporation and Private Property*, by Berle and Means, suggested that the emergence of the joint stock company as a legal entity which owned its own assets meant that those who provided capital for a firm need not necessarily be the same as those determining the uses of that capital. The question raised is whether those managers in operational charge of a corporation also exercise strategic corporate control. Berle and Means argued that the diffusion of shareholding in public companies leads, *pari passu*, to a weakening of self-interested, profit-maximising control by owners and its replacement by that of a more 'socially responsible' managerial class. Although also committed to the goal of profitability, the new class balances this with a concern for the interests of employees and consumers.[5] However, as Child[6] observes, Berle and Means hardly consider the possibility that the dispersal of share ownership may increase the power of those with sizeable holdings. Other writers also have been less sanguine with Berle and Means's additional claim that the managerial class, being disinterested in political, as opposed to industrial, power, merely formed one of several competing élites in the political system. Burnham, for example, envisaged a new ruling class of managers drawn from both industry and government whose influence sprang from their technical indispensability to the modern industrial order. However, Burnham accepted Berle and Means's argument that the new 'controllers' of the modern corporation are managers who depend upon competency and expertise, not ownership, for their position and legitimacy.[7] Dahrendorf also argues that these managers act differently from the old-style entrepreneur: they are not consumed by profit maximisation but, albeit by economic and political necessity, required to behave with one eye on good 'human relations' with their workforce and the other on the ethical prescriptions of more enlightened and interventionist governments. Thus, as we have seen, the key to class conflict within industry is participation in, or exclusion from, authority rather than the distinction between the propertied and the propertyless.[8]

Recent Marxist writers, too, have suggested that a transformation has occurred in the composition of capital. Carchedi, for example, maintains that under monopoly capitalism a hierarchical and bureaucratic structure – a complex of managerial roles which he terms the 'global capitalist' – replaces the individual capitalist in exercising surveillance and control over the work-force. Legal individual ownership is less important than the 'real' collective ownership of top managers in performing the function of capital, which continues to be the expropriation of surplus value from the 'collective worker'.[9] However, although we noted in Chapter 1 that Carchedi's analysis bears a striking resemblance to Dahrendorf's in its insistence that power and control rather than private ownership are the hallmarks of the new controllers, there is one crucial difference. Dahrendorf emphasises the importance of individuals, their actions and the decisions they take in his examination of changes in class structure. This hardly matters for Carchedi; classes are identified in functional terms. It is the 'function' of capital in the system of production to further the process of capital accumulation and whilst the agents, or 'bearers', of this system may change, there can be no question of a new managerial class, or a new stratum, with objectives contrary to this longstanding capitalist function. As Crompton and Ubbay, who follow Carchedi's analysis, put it, 'Capital in the modern firm should not be conceived of as a set of people, top managers or major shareholders, but a complex structure of roles defined in functional terms.'[10]

It is easy to be sympathetic to attempts to 'depersonalise' or 'functionalise' the capitalist industrial process, to refer to 'agents of capital' rather than managing directors, because the picture of ownership in the means of production in the contemporary British economy is, as elsewhere, complex. The growth of the multinational corporation, matched to the increasing internationalisation of ownership (a quarter of British firms are foreign controlled), and the developing importance of unit trusts, pension funds and other forms of investment accounts in the ownership of British manufacture and commerce, make it less easy to associate ownership with identifiable individuals or families than with institutions. Patterns of consumption hardly help us, either, for the 'conspicuous display' of the established middle class as outlined by Veblen is more fiction than fact.[11] 'Ownership' appears a less tangible, less visible feature of economic power than the direct, day-to-day authoritative involvement of managers. Yet the evidence for the proposition that such ownership is irrelevant for corporate power is open to several objections.

Firstly, company shareholdings are concentrated in even fewer hands than other assets, such as bank deposits or insurance policies, and are not as widely dispersed as the 'managerialists' imply. Ownership is sufficiently monopolised to provide at least a potential source of effective power. In 1961 the top 5 per cent of wealth-holders owned 96 per cent of all personally owned shares, whilst the top 1 per cent of income earners in 1970 received 7 per cent of all income, but 17 per cent of investment income.[12] This, as we observed in the first chapter, reflects the crucial importance of inheritance in the acquisition of personal wealth. Harbury and McMahon relate how this role has hardly changed this century: about three-quarters of those leaving estates of £100,000 or more in 1954 had inherited at least £10,000 from their fathers and about half had inherited £50,000 or more.[13] This demonstrates how difficult it is to build up substantial share control in a company from modest beginnings, or to resist takeovers by larger concerns once an enterprise begins to expand.

Secondly, family-owned companies have not been eliminated from the ranks of the economic giants; some quite large companies are still family- rather than publicly-controlled. Family links are particularly important in brewing, merchant banking, farming, and retailing. In Stanworth and Giddens's analysis of leading company chairmen, 47 per cent of merchant bankers began their careers in firms which were either controlled by members of the same family or in which they were strongly represented among shareholders.[14] Strong family influence is even more noticeable in the top positions of the leading brewing companies: 64 per cent of these chairmen had direct family links with the firm of which they became chairman, and 'this proportion varies little over time'. Although Stanworth and Giddens note some decline in family influence in recent years, they still calculate that nearly 'one quarter of those who became chairmen of major industrial and financial corporations in Britain after the Second World War had a family link with the firm over which they presided'. Furthermore, even in the largest joint stock companies, where share ownership is quite scattered, it may require only a small tranche of shares with voting rights (leaving the non-voting stock dispersed) to gain direction of a company's fortunes, whilst the setting up of 'holding companies' and other such devices may enable such control to reverberate beyond the specific firm concerned. Interlocking directorships may have the same effect. Stanworth and Giddens found 'many chairmen at the centre of a radiating circle of business connections', holding an average of ten directorships during the course of a career. In such ways private and family ownership may exercise more influence than is immediately apparent from analyses of particular companies. Some family boards, particularly those of recently arrived 'newcomers to the big league', may remain, at least temporarily, relatively isolated from the City and the traditional large manufacturing élite. Whitley points out, nonetheless, that many soon 'stabilise' into companies with major institutional investors and merchant bankers on the board.[15]

Thirdly, there are grounds for believing that sociologists have generally tended to underestimate the strategic corporate power of private ownership. Pahl and Winkler stress that ownership involves the important 'right of transfer' to other buyers, or to descendants, which does not shift to management in joint stock companies. Some shareholders are extremely aggressive and exercise, or threaten to exercise, their capacity to withdraw capital. Pahl and Winkler note that, in recent years, 'asset strippers' engaged in quick-fire mergers have reorganised shareholders and given them greater influence in matters concerning takeovers. Major institutional shareholders – the pension funds, for example – have long exercised their 'market prerogative' to invest in the most profitable areas of industry, but have shown increasing willingness to seek more direct involvement in the running of firms where they have investments (although, strictly speaking, this is less control by 'owners' than by the owner's representatives, i.e., pension fund managers).

Finally, we should distinguish between what Pahl and Winkler describe as allocative control and operational control in considering the economic influences of the 'old' established middle class. They suggest that control over the allocation of resources is analytically and often empirically distinct from control over the day-to-day use of resources already allocated. Owners are much more directly involved in strategic planning and financial decisions ('allocative control'), especially when negotiations and the financing of mergers and takeovers are on the agenda, than in more routine matters.[16] Furthermore, Whitley notes that the increasing sophistication of financial control techniques and the importance of financial decisions, the preserve of Boards of Directors, 'make it more rather than less likely that owners could exercise control'.[17]

Thus the evidence for the demise, if not the 'invisibility', of the established entrepreneurial middle class is slight. Yet if there has been no 'managerial revolution', it is indisputable that at least a 'managerial evolution' has occurred. To understand changes within the established middle class more fully we need to turn to its 'newer' elements – the managers and administrators – and the claim that they have become 'less the servants than the wardens of their capitalist employers'.

The 'newly' established middle class

The managers

Although we may be sceptical about a radical decline in the power of ownership in the large modern enterprise, there is little doubt that one of the most significant industrial developments since the late nineteenth century has been the growth of a new 'auxiliary' class of top managers and salaried professionals. The everyday operations of most large firms today are in the hands of full-time experts – accountants, lawyers, economists, technologists – and form what Kumar has described as 'a "salariat" without capital of their own but highly placed in the market by virtue of their scarce professional and technical skills'.[18] These skills have appeared increasingly essential for companies in large complex and competitive modern economies in their efforts to guarantee internal efficiency and achieve some control over their external environment. Table 12 (above) indicated that between 1911 and 1971 the number of managers, administrators and higher professionals (not all in the private sector) trebled, from 4.4 per cent of the total occupied population to 12.4 per cent.

These higher-level managers are clearly distinguished from routine white-collar employees, whose numbers have also rapidly swelled in the last fifty years, in terms of authority,

TABLE 13 *Changes in relative earnings of non-manual occupational groups 1913/14–1960*

Occupation (men only)	**Indices of earnings – occupational group average expressed as a percentage of average for all men in same period**				
	1913/14	**1922/24**	**1935/36**	**1955/56**	**1960**
Higher professions	357	326	341	244	253
Managers and administrators	217	269	237	234	230
Lower professions	169	179	165	97	105
Clerks	108	102	103	82	85
All non-manual workers	142	158	152	144	145

Source: Westergaard and Resler, op. cit., Ch. 1, n36, p. 74 (adapted).

income and prestige. Table 13 indicates that in the period 1913/14 to 1960, in terms of earnings, a large gap persisted between the established professionals and managers at the top and other non-manual workers further down the scale. Table 14 shows that in the 1970s senior executive salaries remained substantial, especially in the private sector. As Nichols remarks, there has been 'a progressive division of labour within capitalist society' as top managers have increased their power and status 'along with that of the corporation'.[19] It is even arguable that 'managerial' norms have superseded 'entrepreneurial' norms for certain public bodies. Following an analysis of reports from the National Board for Prices and Incomes in the period 1965–70, Crouch suggests that the Board worked with the notion that pay structures should be 'rational' and reflect differences in skill level and responsibility, rather than demand and supply forces in the labour market. The Board's preference was for a system 'whose features are overt and clear, calculable in precise terms according to a body of internally consistent and logical principles'.[20] The criteria were those of the manager rather than the risk-taking entrepreneur, and the Board was extremely sceptical of attempts at responding to market fluctuations.

As noted above, the expansion in top management has led some writers to claim a revolution in the behaviour of capitalist institutions based on the obsolescence of property and its replacement by possessions of skills and qualifications. The

TABLE 14 *Average salaries (including bonus, commission and profit-sharing) of top management: September 1973*

Sector of industry and size of undertaking	Chairman £	Deputy Chairman £	Board members £	Sales executives £
Nationalised industries				
Capital employed:				
£1,250m and over	23,400	18,400	14,600	10,900
£250m but under £1,250m	20,600	17,000	13,700	9,600
£50m but under £250m	14,800	11,000	11,000	8,600
£10m but under £50m	17,200	12,200	10,000	7,400
Private sector				
Capital employed:				
£1,250m and over	59,800	53,200	35,900	18,300
£250m but under £1,250m	42,000	28,800	18,400	10,900
£50m but under £250m	29,500	24,100	17,000	10,500
£10m but under £50m	21,600	17,100	11,300	7,100
Financial	32,000	23,200	18,200	14,200

Source: NBPI Report No. 107, *Top Salaries in the Private Sector and Nationalised Industries*, Cmnd. 3970, HMSO, 1973, p. 53.

major elements of the 'managerialist' argument in terms of its implications for the role of management, the implications for the role of private ownership having already been analysed, may be summarised as follows:

1. Power. The central aspect of the managerial thesis suggests that in large, joint stock companies effective control has passed into the hands of working managers, and this stems from their functional indispensability in such firms. Burnham,[21] Drucker,[22] and Galbraith[23] are among those who have proposed that the demands of the modern corporation for technical and scientific skills necessarily gives power to competent, achievement-oriented managers who 'earn it', rather than to the merely wealthy. In a more extreme version, Galbraith suggests that power resides even further down the corporation than top management, in the 'technostructure' which consists of all those who contribute specialised knowledge in company decision-making or possess professional skills.

2. Behaviour. The rise of the managers leads to schisms within the economic élite based on differences in outlook. 'Organisational' or 'bureaucratic' man is allegedly less adventuresome, less inclined to 'maximise' profits than preferring a 'reasonable' level of profitability, and becomes more concerned with achieving stability in the organisation and building up his own separate empire. Schumpeter[24] and Geiger[25] go further in suggesting that professional managers are more sympathetic to the public interest – that they are more 'soulful' or 'socially responsible' – than owners.

3. *Mobility.* It is claimed that the arrival 'at the top' of the salaried manager reflects changes in roles and avenues of mobility. Bureaucratic structures in large industrial and commercial organisations offer substantial career opportunities for the less wealthy; education provides a more open method of recruitment to high-ranking economic positions than property ownership and family connections. Furthermore, the executive with a grammar school or comprehensive school education is more in tune with changing consumer demands than the old-style property owner, and is thus more successful.

However, support for these propositions is, at best, patchy. To begin with, the claim that effective power obtains with 'indispensibility' is logically flawed. The oft-quoted observation by Max Weber that if this proposition were correct then slaves would hold power in slave economies is pertinent here. And, as we have seen, there is evidence that considerable power remains with property owners. Secondly, the argument that the separation of ownership and control 'produces two sets of roles the incumbents of which increasingly move apart in their outlook on society in general and toward the enterprise in particular' is exaggerated.[26] For example, directors of large corporations are not remunerated solely in terms of salary but are at least part owners of their firms, often possessing sizeable shareholdings. In December 1967 *The Times Business News* published the results of an inquiry into the capital assets of major directors which showed, among other examples, that the average director's holding in ICI was worth £22,000, in Shell it was worth £11,000, and in Unilever 'only £9,000'.[27] Nor were these the largest average holdings. And while they represent an insignificant proportion of a company's shareholding, they still form a substantial personal investment. Scott notes, too, that directors in British companies own shares in companies other than their own and comprise the largest single group of private shareholders, suggesting that 'managers' and 'shareholders' are not distinct social categories.[28]

However, it would be misleading to claim that managerial property holding provided sufficient evidence of a property orientation among senior executives, for directors still generally gain more from salaries than share dividends. Nonetheless, managerial behaviour displays little signs of a lack of commitment to company profitability for they have to operate in a system where national and international competition ensures that particular firms have constantly to strive to maintain their profits in order to survive. If some top managers do seek to achieve a 'satisfactory' level of profit rather than to 'maximise' profits, preferring organisational growth and enhanced individual status, then these objectives still depend on securing an adequate level of company income. This is not to suggest that maximising profit is the only managerial motivation. Barratt-Brown points out that 'monopoly profit may not always be pushed as far as it might be for fear of encouraging new competition, e.g., from men like John Bloom. But it does imply that profitability must be an overriding goal'.[29]

Furthermore, we must be careful not to accept uncritically the image of the profit-mad, rapacious nineteenth-century Victorian entrepreneur against which one contrasts modern, self-effacing, security-seeking 'organisation man'. Profit maximisation under perfect competition was more a valuable premise in classical economics than an accurate description of old-time business behaviour. Owners of property have always pursued a variety of 'non-profit' oriented objectives such as organisational size, 'satisfaction' and personal status. In this sense, both types of businessmen – managers and owners – share a similar frame of reference; indeed, Barratt-Brown suggests that it is managerial-dominated companies that are more likely than family concerns to pursue profit rather than growth. They may feel they have more to lose, or to gain, than the comfortable, well-established owner-proprietor.

Two further points may be made that cast doubt on the proposition that modern corporations are less profit-oriented than their predecessors. First, the range of new costing and financial techniques makes it more rather than less likely that the modern businessman – manager and owner – will be sensitive to profitability and take it as the best guide to managerial performance. Second, the increase in scientifically trained managers – the 'technostructure' – has not been accompanied by a significant increase in their presence in the highest managerial echelons. Barratt-Brown notes that the role of the technical expert is essentially advisory, and rarely are more than one or two found on the board of top companies. As he remarks, 'technological choice is determined not so much by consideration of technical efficiency or cost saving as of marketing and price management'. Nor does it appear that attitudes to profit are attenuated further down the management line. Benyon and Nichols, in their work on a leading chemical company, 'ChemCo', highlight the tendency for departmental and other managers to act as 'little owners' and to see their own sub-units almost as independent companies with a consequent need to compete efficiently and aggressively for profits.[30] This is encouraged by the greater ability of the company to monitor departmental and individual performance through the use of computer and statistical techniques, and to use this in continuous assessment of a manager's potential.

Top managers may be no less profit-oriented than owners, but what of the claim that they are more 'socially responsible'? To begin with, it is worth remembering that managerial claims to social responsibility have a long history, its modulation depending on the degree of public criticism levelled at managers.[31] Furthermore, traditional owner-managers, especially those imbued with certain religious convictions, most notably Quakerism, have long expressed a rather paternalistic concern for their workforce and the nation. Today many smaller, older family concerns still retain this air of moral guardianship, and unlike thrusting, manager-controlled new companies, are prepared to countenance 'inefficiency' for the sake of a quiet life.

However, there is little evidence that the 'ethic of social responsibility' is generally taken seriously as a prescription for everyday business behaviour by either owners or managers, for its articulation is simply regarded as good 'public relations'. Nichols's study of northern businessmen, for example, indicates that when a 'social responsibility' ideology is espoused it marks less a sense of disinterested moral conviction than a pragmatic awareness that to act and to been seen as acting 'responsibly' is in the company's long-term interests and consequently does not conflict with the major aim of increasing profitability. More particularly, most managers equated social responsibility with profitability; they reasoned that, after all, high profits benefited the country by providing valuable employment. But few managers felt that they had the moral or political clout to act as the 'soul' of the community.[32] As Scott observes, 'corporate careers depend upon contribution to the success of the company, and managers tend to acquire the personality which meets the needs of the system'.[33]

Winkler's study of directors in nineteen British companies also demonstrates the necessity for regarding 'moral' managerial ideologies with a leery eye. Despite recent management and academic emphasis on the 'human relations' approach to employees by the modern executive the most notable feature of Winkler's investigations was the discovery of an almost total 'lack of psychological concern for workers' interests, goals, opinions, problems or personal situations'.[34] This was not simple 'passive unconcern' but 'active disinclination' and workers were regarded 'almost exclusively as a cost'. Although Winkler's sample did contain a small group of 'progressives', their 'liberality' was confined to the rejection of overt manifestations of status differentials and compliance with social legislation; furthermore, these individuals 'then had heightened expectations of orderliness and co-operation from workers'. This process of directorial isolation and exclusion, and the adoption of an 'us/them' model normally associated with manual workers, is viewed by Winkler as a coping device for avoiding difficult situations and argumentative workers. Isolation is believed to have a strategic value for managers. It preserves 'managerial prerogative' and retains a sense of mysteriousness and mystique necessary to safeguard the authoritativeness of managerial commands.

Finally, the view that the new breed of manager has less

exclusive social origins than the older owner-manager lacks substantial support. Certainly at the highest level directors and managers tend to be drawn from the same social stratum as shareholders. Clark's[35] study of industrial managers in the 1960s revealed that six or more out of every ten senior managers had fathers in social classes I or II, a finding that replicates Clement's[36] research in the 1950s which indicated that while some 30 per cent of managers were from manual backgrounds very few reached top management status. The higher the level of management the more restricted is recruitment likely to be and this is even more noticeable for larger firms. Around two-thirds of their directors still have public school and/or Oxbridge backgrounds. Stanworth and Giddens's study of company chairmen showed that 'the vast majority, 66 per cent of the total, were upper class in origin', while the proportion was even higher for bankers.[37] The Nuffield surveys on social mobility suggest that this picture is unlikely to change substantially in the near future: while the 'service class' (the higher echelons of professional, administrative and managerial employment) has generally recruited a large proportion of the upwardly mobile as these positions have expanded, subsequent immobility and the probability that top managerial jobs will expand at a much slower rate in the next decades indicates that the top stratum of the new middle class is becoming a more established, self-recruiting category.[38] But this need not imply changes in managerial orientation; the upwardly mobile may be presumed to have displayed the 'right character' in their climb to important executive positions and, if anything, conform even more assiduously to norms of 'good business practice' and accept the pre-eminent goal of company profitability.

We are not proposing that owners and managers experience no conflicts of interest, but that their business outlooks are fundamentally similar. Of course, despite 'an overall homogeneity of value and belief, and a high degree of social solidarity, as manifest in interpersonal contacts, friendship and marriage ties', there are differences between managers and shareholders, but, as Giddens remarks, 'these do not appear to be any more common than those between shareholding blocs and, if anything, they are probably less so'.[39] Winkler maintains that two principles lay behind directors' relationships with investors in his study: 'to pay the minimum dividend that would keep them quiet, and to keep all promises of future corporate performance sufficiently ambiguous or hedged about with qualifications to cover any actual results.'[40] He goes on to remark that 'if it is correct that managers have the same interest in profitability as owners, it is equally true that there is a genuine conflict of interest when it comes to distributing that profit'. Pahl and Winkler, too, suggest that managerial interests may be furthered by the information control they possess in dealings with the Board. Major decision-making frequently takes place outside the Board, often within staff coteries and 'adjuncts' built up by groups of managers, and the Board simply confirms prearranged outcomes. They also point to 'the well-articulated norm' that non-executive directors resign or withdraw from a situation of conflict within a Board rather than take up the cudgels with executives. However, it is doubtful that managers relish such offers (threats) of resignation as they could prove extremely damaging to their company's reputation. Pahl and Winkler thus conclude that managerial stratagems do not diverge 'from the traditional corporate goals of profit, return on investment, asset growth, earnings per share etc, nor the substitution of individual self-interest'.[41] It may be that the characteristic mode of control in modern large corporations is what Scott terms 'control through a constellation of interests'. Major shareholders are 'in a position of effective possession but do not constitute a coalition of associates. . . . No coalition can achieve minority control, but the board cannot disregard the interests of those in effective possession.'[42] Thus the major shareholders may agree on the composition of a board and its way of doing things but the board does not become their instrument nor does it achieve autonomy from the shareholders.

Increasingly the crucial share interests are those of financial capital which have become much more closely linked to industrial corporations in the last twenty years. The Royal Commission on the Distribution of Income and Wealth estimated that by the early 1970s insurance companies comprised nearly 40 per cent of the large shareholders in British companies. A complex system of interlocking directorships, in which financial representatives sit on a variety of corporation boards, forms the basis of an 'informational network' which enables banks to influence corporate policy even where they do not intervene directly (although direct financial intervention is on the increase). However, as Scott puts it, 'intercorporate configuration is a system which is based upon the power relations among its constituent elements, but in which the overall structure is so complex that it is unrealistic to depict a particular group as having the ability to form an 'empire' subordinate to its wishes'.[43]

Middle and lower management

Entry into the 'established' managerial class has come to depend increasingly on the possession of formal, often graduate, qualifications. This can lead to a clearer differentiation between higher and lower level management in terms of authority and prestige and firmly root the latter in the 'marginal' middle class. Resentment by lower, poorly educated and older management at apparently 'blocked' careers is reinforced in those industries where management structures are slimmed in the pursuit of greater efficiency. Nichols and Benyon, in their account of a new productivity scheme at ChemCo, show how the management hierarchy became 'flattened out'. As a number of middle-level management jobs disappeared many of the older managerial superintendents found that their careers had 'come to a halt in the middle'. Most had been with the company for a considerable number of years and had become classified as 'ChemCo men', which meant that their experience, which might have counterbalanced lack of formal qualifications, was likely to be too 'ChemCo-specific' to allow promotion with other employers.[44]

This is one aspect of the pressure exerted on some middle managers as boards, aided by new microprocessors and other computational control devices, seek to reduce administrative overhead costs in an effort to maintain a competitive edge in the costing of their products. Consequently, some less well-qualified managers are likely increasingly to experience not only reduced promotion opportunities but the stronger possibility of unemployment. Reactions to these developments may vary. Nichols and Benyon, for example, see a clear division emerging between their foremen at ChemCo: the great majority of 'traditional foremen' felt largely overwhelmed by the 'new' methods of management which, allied to minimal technical knowledge, induced a sense of inferiority and a resort to strategems based on 'tricks and bluffs' for coping with both their seniors and their workers. A small number of foremen, however, were 'management men'; they identified with senior executives, enthusiastically pursuing the goal of greater efficiency in their own plants, and were generally younger and better qualified than their traditional counterparts.

It is probably unwise to generalise at great length on the basis of Benyon and Nichols's findings at ChemCo, but changes in the structure of management of the kind they describe may be an increasing feature of continuous process industries. Gallie's[45] investigations of two British and two French petrochemical refineries also support Benyon and Nichols's findings. All four plants had recently experienced reductions in the ratio of lower managers to workers in the search for greater productivity. Furthermore, recruitment from the shop floor into the lower ranks of management had declined and, combined with policies of more direct graduate entry into management positions, had led to the feeling that managers generally were becoming 'distant' from the shop floor. This did not apply only for manual workers, for routine lower-level managers also felt that other managers were socially aloof and operationally isolated from them.

The problems of middle or lower managers have also been well documented by B. Roberts et al.[46] in their study of technicians. The technicians' category contains a mixture of occupations, including draughtsmen and quality controllers, perched somewhat precariously between higher-level, technologically trained managers and skilled manual workers. As in studies of the refinery industry, Roberts et al. note that technological posts are increasingly filled by young graduates and this severely reduces mobility prospects for most technicians. To make matters worse, technicians also experience encroachment 'at the other end' from skilled craftsmen who have been expanding into technicians' jobs by having their job definitions widened, often in productivity schemes. If this was not sufficiently galling for technicians, who feel that such schemes enhance both the status and income of the skilled worker, Roberts et al. discovered that technical managers are expected to exercise increased responsibilities over manual workers as the result of these productivity agreements. To add insult to injury, even when senior management is sympathetic to the technicians the use of 'job evaluation' procedures as a way to secure extra money for them tends to reveal that technicians are not substantially 'worth more' than skilled workers.

Clearly, the technician's work situation is decidedly ambiguous. He is expected to exercise authority over shop-floor workers and yet to fulfil a technical work function as well. Companies are apparently more 'aware' of the latter role, for technicians are often treated as being on a similar level to manual workers in the provision of status facilities, such as canteens, and, more importantly perhaps, on matters such as redundancy.

Technicians display all the signs of Carchedi's typical 'middle class, outlined in Chapter 1, by carrying out both the function of capital – control and surveillance of the workforce – and the function of the worker in the labour process. Furthermore, the balance between these two functions in the technicians' work situation appears to be changing in the way described by Carchedi; increasingly they are losing their capitalist, authoritative function while their 'worker' function increases, and this is reflected in declining income differentials and loss of status. This echoes Braverman's[47] thesis that the never-ending search for the rationalisation of production under conditions of monopoly capitalism involves increasing managerial control over the labour process, but that this control is confined to smaller groups of executives assisted by computerised and mechanised labour-saving devices. Lower-level managers come to be viewed mainly as 'costs' to be pruned and cheapened, and to be increasingly regarded as little different from manual workers. Crompton, too, has specifically adapted much of Carchedi's analysis to Roberts et al.'s technicians. She argues that with the development of monopoly capitalism an increasing share of surplus value is used initially to employ lower level supervisors-cum-workers, such as technicians, to exercise surveillance over the workforce. However, the escalating costs of this 'wage labour employed within the capitalist function' leads to efforts to use it more efficiently, by reducing its size and by enhancing its accumulative rather than its control function. The effect is 'to split the technicians' occupational role between graduate manager and manual workers, while downgrading the remaining elements of the technicians' work role'.[48] Technicians come to participate more explicitly in the labour, rather than capital, function – that is, to act as collective workers – and the consequence is a loss of authority, earnings and status.

However, closer scrutiny of Roberts et al.'s study reveals a number of difficulties with Crompton's analysis. First, it is not clear that technician's incomes have narrowed significantly in comparison with manual workers. Certainly, technicians themselves thought they had, but this is a common (and often unfounded) feeling in many occupations, especially non-manual, and Roberts et al.'s findings on the matter are at best inconclusive. Conversely, while they discovered that technicians' advantages in fringe benefits had more obviously declined, which could be viewed as threatening their 'special status', the technicians appeared to regard this as a less serious development than an alleged deterioration in their income advantage.[49] Second, Crompton suggests that the willingness of technicians to join trade unions is indicative of them having become 'truly proletarianised'. However, Roberts et al.'s research indicates that the turn to unionism is part of the attempt to maintain those class and status advantages still possessed by technicians, and this sense of 'being different' is a barrier, ill-founded though it may be, to a convergence in their class position with that of manual workers.

Managers and industrial relations

One common explanation for Britain's poor economic performance in recent years, found in newspaper editorials and the speeches of political leaders, centres on the alleged inability of British managers to exercise their traditional authority over workforces. The result, it is claimed, is low profitability, inefficiency and a general disinclination by both managers and workers to pursue and adopt new methods and products along the lines of our foreign competitors. Reasons for this apparent managerial reluctance to manage vary. For some the major factors are to be located on the management side. 'Punitive' rates of direct taxation, for example, are alleged to penalise those prepared to take on responsibility and exercise initiative, thus impelling the most able to go abroad and encouraging those that remain to accept comfortable, established career plateaux. Alternatively, lack of managerial authority may be viewed as part of an inbred spinelessness encouraged by Britain's 'old boy' network, formed in the public schools and Oxbridge, and which devalues manufacturing entrepreneurial zeal in favour of easy pickings on the financial markets.

There are those, however, who regard Britain's economic ills as at least partly explained in terms of economic and social changes in the workforce. Goldthorpe, Hirsch and others[50] have suggested that the social causes of inflation may lie in worker aspirations which have risen in recent years as the state has encouraged individuals to lay claim to certain minimal provisions of economic, social and political life as 'entitlements' or 'rights' rather than to regard them gratefully as the product of 'good fortune'. A more deferential, subservient age thus passes with the extension of citizenship and the 'maturing' of the working class. This is reflected in the determination of working-class institutions, notably the trade unions and their officials, to challenge managerial prerogatives. The flexible deployment of labour, for example, is allegedly hampered by the obstructionism of a powerful trade union movement that is sustained by capitulations on industrial relations legislation by Labour and Conservative governments. Lower-level management, it is suggested, may be even more demoralised than their bosses, for when the really big decisions need to be taken trade unions go straight to top management (and vice-versa). Less senior managers thus feel impotent in the face of these 'unholy alliances' above their heads.[51]

This is undoubtedly an exaggerated portrayal of the factors surrounding British management, but it does point to certain characteristics of British managerial 'style'. Duncan Gallie's study of industrial life in British and French oil refineries is particularly valuable here because of its comparative reference. It suggests that British managers tend to operate in a less assertive style than their French counterparts. Gallie describes British management's strategy as 'semi-constitutional' and that of the French as 'paternalistic'. Whereas French executives seek to maintain the maximum degree of managerial discretion over employees, the goal of their British counterparts is to secure the loyalty of the workforce 'by making sure that the terms of employment and the rules of work organisation had secured the explicit consent of the workers' representatives'.[52] The latter are unwilling to stress managerial power; unlike the French system, for example, there is no system of individual bonuses that depend on 'good behaviour', and while the French emphasise managerial prerogative, British managers recognise the central role of the union's as representing the collective interests of the workers. A prime managerial objective is stability, and this is firmly associated with the British view that it could only be obtained by securing employee 'consent' on major matters. Managers held a pluralistic conception of industrial relations in which different group interests were recognised and accepted, together with the attendant requirement for bargaining and negotiation. Furthermore, important salary negotiations in the British refineries take place at plant level, which means management negotiators are encountered by the workforce in other, less contestful roles outside the wages round, unlike the situation in France where national negotiations ensure that a much more impersonal and often bitter atmosphere prevails. The recruitment to the British management team of individuals from the shop floor who display negotiating skill also reinforces the mediating approach in British industrial relations.

However, British consent has its price, for Gallie notes that, 'in accepting the principle of productivity bargaining, for example, the management committed itself not only to laying out its plans to the unions for a period of several years, but it also de facto surrendered its formal prerogative to unilaterally control substantial areas of work organisation, and this correspondingly led to an important increase in the formal extent of union control'.[53] In part this reflects the organisational strength of the British craft unions and the long-standing work freedom of skilled employees. This results in a strong commitment to preserve work autonomy and a loose and informal system of supervision which increases the pressures from the shop floor on first-line management. Union strength and management's desire to negotiate must be viewed as mutually reinforcing, for the price of non-agreement can be high. The French unions, however, lack the membership and unity to stage long-running plant disruptions, a factor that is both reflected in and partly the consequence of the more autocratic French manner of management. French authoritarianism and interventionism certainly appears more efficient than the British style. British managers concede issues that would horrify the French, and operational speeds are generally slower than in the French plants.

However, the case for 'weak' British management must be kept in perspective. There is no indication of a desire for greater control by workers or union officials in the sense that they want a right of veto over managerial decisions, as there is in the French refineries. Although workers criticise their bosses for 'inefficiency', it does at least indicate that they 'were essentially looking at the organisation from the same point of view as management itself'. Even those employees who want increased control are after more consultation than a share of managerial authority. They accept that long-term or strategic decisions are the prerogative of the Board, and that 'it was management's job to manage'.

Managerial 'careers'

Sociologists have often emphasised opposing orientations to ambition and mobility possessed respectively by the 'individualistic' middle class and the 'collectivist' working class. However, K. Roberts et al.'s survey of class images, for example, found that 'a positive evaluation of upward mobility was neither confined to nor even concentrated within the middle classes'.[54] Not only did they detect widespread work aspirations among manual workers, but their survey suggested that white-collar employees were not 'uniformly anxious to climb further up career ladders'. Instead, many prefer to climb only to those positions that ensure a comfortable, reasonably well-paid occupational existence. These findings may partly confirm recent articles suggesting that the middle class has become disenchanted with the psychological ravages of the competitive world of work, and that it is even becoming 'work-shy'.[55] The archetypal 'organisation man' of the immediate post-war period is now 'laid back' man, apparently more concerned with developing his 'true self', and seeking satisfaction in the family, the garden or the local night school.

However, intimations of a declining commitment to the work ethic have to be taken with a pinch of salt. The 'rat-trapped' manager is in the habit of whimsically proclaiming that if only he could leave it all behind for a more leisurely life as an academic or a postman then he would; but he rarely does. The newly established middle class expects and mostly receives opportunities for continuous, predictable and increasing rewards from work, that is, a 'career'. Nonetheless, there is certainly evidence of role strain in managerial orientations to work. The Pahls, for example, in their study of career and family relationships in the middle class, found that many managers were cross-pressured throughout their careers by two equally strong cultural forces, one emphasising success in occupation, the other stressing involvement in the family.[56] The consequence was an apparent ambivalance in attitudes to the notion of a 'career'; few managers were found to be 'advancing along a clear and structured career line', and for some moves up the occupational ladder were described by the Pahls as more the result of 'a series of almost fortuitous circumstances' (explained in terms of 'luck'), a form of passive progression, which suggested to the authors that the notion 'career' was basically a 'retrospective concept', a means of 'structuring one's biography and making sense of the past'. Most 'career' moves for the Pahls' managers had not really changed their social position, and perhaps, as a result, many displayed a marked indifference to actively planning to achieve new jobs. Their lifetime 'project' involved securing the best educational and thus occupational opportunities for their children and achieving a satisfying domestic life. These educational hopes for their children included the desire that they attain sufficient qualifications to enable them to escape the competitive pressures of industrial organisations and to lead more autonomous, 'professional' lives, although there was little evidence that the parents appreciated how competitive and 'organisational' is contemporary professional existence. The Pahls conclude that 'the emerging style of the new middle class in Britain is not the self-conscious, status seeking typical of the American literature, but rather a contented domesticity, centred around shopping trips on Saturday and annual camping holidays with the children'.[57]

Yet the Pahls' conclusion requires certain reservations. One further British cultural value is worth mentioning: that the ambitious take careful steps to ensure that their ambition is not seen to be 'naked' or 'vaunting' but is discreetly covered – though not entirely – by a disclaiming modesty. Furthermore, publicly eschewing career hopes provides a useful escape route if these expectations are not fulfilled – the ready-made 'excuse' of 'I did not want promotion, anyway'. It is noticeable that, despite their protestations, many of the Pahls' managers did move frequently, did regularly obtain better jobs, and often stayed late or went to the office on a Saturday morning. The 'typical manager', while emphasising the importance of his family to his life, also admitted 'that work supplied him with a sense of security and advancement'. The responses in the Pahls' sample should perhaps be construed as the reactions of individuals in situations over which they have little control. The constraints of their everyday work existence are experienced as oppressive – hence romantic yearnings for alternative life styles – but it still has a compulsive, inescapable attraction that produces the sense of ambivalence in their attitudes to work. Besides, organisational structures are not composed of a number of never-ending escalators; they 'taper' at the higher levels and progressively narrow promotion opportunities. Most managers, especially in their middle years, have to accommodate to fewer opportunities, and one way of protecting their sense of adequacy and esteem is to renounce ambition for domestic contentment. As the Pahls' remark, too, 'what would happen if everybody did share the same striving attitudes – there would be widespread disorder'.[58]

It is probably best to regard managers' orientations to their 'career' as variable and dependent on a range of structural as well as individual factors, for example, the level of opportunity available in a particular organisation, including its 'age structure', and levels of growth and expansion in an industry. A study by Sofer of middle-level executives and technical specialists in the chemical and car industries discovered apparently more promotion-conscious managers than the Pahls. Work played an important part in nearly all their lives, whilst most had an 'overwhelming wish for promotion' and 'feared that they might not get it'. This was reflected in a marked sensitivity to age-grade status, for individuals were able to make fine calculations relating relative ages to position and progress in the company's 'pecking order'. However, Sofer, like the Pahls, found some ambivalence in their statements on the question of promotion, for most recognised possible psychic and familial losses with advancement. When interviewed a number contradicted themselves, disclaiming ambition at certain points but then at other stages clearly discussing their particular promotion chances with relish and high expectation. For the most part their fantasies differed from those found in the Pahls' study: Sofer's managers generally favouring self-employment or small business activity to the 'professional occupations' desired by those in the Pahls' sample.[59]

Professions and professionalisation

No analysis of the established middle class would be complete without a consideration of 'the professions', for, as was noted in Chapter 2, the notion of 'being in a profession' has been central to conceptions of the archetypal middle class. Lewis and Maude, for example, when bewailing the decline of middle-class influence and values in *The English Middle Classes*, published in 1949,[60] made clear that their image of the middle-class individual was the independent professional or small businessman, such as the propertied practitioner of medicine or law. These had style, autonomy and substance. It is an image with a persisting enchantment, for, as we have seen, the managers in the Pahls' sample wistfully regarded green 'professional' pastures as the ideal alternative to the world of competitive business. Yet, as Raynor has remarked, 'the concept of a profession is not very precise . . . [and] has a curiously old-fashioned air about it'.[61] Modern 'professions' have little in common with Lewis and Maude's idealised portrayal of them; the restriction of the term 'profession' to the traditional, independent practitioner – virtually a businessman selling medical or legal skills to clients for a fee – is no longer appropriate following the steady growth we outlined in earlier chapters of 'professions' in which the individual is more likely to be found secure in a bureaucratic position (see Table 15). Scientists, engineers, planners, teachers and the 'welfare professionals' are predominantly salaried employees, servants of the state rather than businessmen.

Perhaps these developments lie behind the two dramatically opposed meanings conveyed by the word 'professional'. In one sense it implies a relaxed and disinterested exercise of learned knowledge; in another sense it suggests a cynical, win-at-all-costs attitude ('professional foul'). This divergence of meaning is to be found repeatedly in organisations: the managers in the Pahls' study obviously had the first interpretation in mind as they yearned for an alternative 'professional' existence, but Pahl and Winkler in another study found their executives took the word 'professional' to mean 'the ability to produce a competent performance in any circumstances', which was taken to be the production of good profits and growth.[62] Similarly, in one of the oldest 'professions', agriculture, Newby notes that '"professionalism"...is interpreted as an unremitting economic rationality'.[63]

The term 'profession', however, still retains vestiges of high status noted earlier as being associated with the 'older professions', such as the Church, medicine and law, and this connotation is found also within the influential sociological perspective associated with Emile Durkheim. This regards 'professional' occupations as moral communities, their members imbued with the spirit of altruism and service, and offering havens from both the oppression of an ever-powerful state and the cut-throat, exploitative, self-interested ethic of capitalist corporations.[64] Carr-Saunders and Wilson provide one of the earliest major British contributions to this tradition, although they maintained that 'professionalism' was also becoming an increasing characteristic of business with its growing employment of specialised, university-educated management.[65]

This rather lofty view of professional life accords closely with the older professions' views of their exalted status, which has been traced by Elliott to their links with the status professions of pre-industrial society. Particularly, 'the ideology of liberal educa-

TABLE 15 *Number and percentage distribution of persons in 'professional occupations', 1891 and 1971.*

Profession	Male	Female	Total	
1891				
Religious	41,919	8,872	50,791	(11.0)
Legal	19,978	—	19,791	(4.5)
Medical	26,755	448	27,203	(6.1)
Nursing	601	53,057	53,658	(12.0)
Medical auxiliary	24,077	2,227	26,304	(5.9)
Teaching	54,220	146,375	200,595	(44.9)
Engineering	35,399	488	35,887	(8.0)
Scientific	1,920	42	1,962	(0.4)
Accounting	7,930	50	7,980	(1.8)
Literary	7,485	787	8,272	(1.8)
Librarian				
Officials of associations	1,530	465	1,995	(0.4)
Social welfare				
Artistic	9,250	3,032	12,282	(2.7)
Others				
1971				
Religious	35,730	5,410	41,140	(1.5)
Legal	36,050	2,470	38,520	(1.4)
Medical	64,980	15,040	80,020	(2.9)
Nursing	37,950	401,030	438,980	(16.1)
Medical auxiliary	40,570	41,350	81,920	(3.0)
Teaching	307,690	380,530	688,220	(25.3)
Engineering	744,670	59,630	804,300	(29.5)
Scientific	146,690	54,590	201,280	(7.4)
Accounting	73,960	2,650	76,610	(2.8)
Literacy	38,790	12,680	51,470	(1.9)
Librarian				
Officials of associations	7,240	700	7,940	(0.3)
Social welfare	21,550	39,690	61,240	(2.2)
Artistic	27,040	16,070	43,110	(1.6)
Others	69,120	38,100	107,220	(3.9)

NB. Figures in brackets show distribution of each group of 'professional' occupations as a percentage of all occupations classified as 'professional'.

Source: R. Brown, op. cit. (Table 11), 72–3 (adapted).

tion, public service and gentlemanly professionalism' which was elaborated in superior contrast to the raw materialistic creed of early industrialism, although never as radical opposition ('it called on business to recognise its limitations'), owed much to older notions of gentlemanly leisure.[66] As we observed in Chapter 2 the public school system of the nineteenth century consolidated those virtues associated with the gentry and the landed classes although emphasising occupation rather than ostentatious non-work or leisure as the key to status and the service ideal. These ideas gradually provided a uniform moral cement for British élites during the nineteenth century as the sons of businessmen and industrialists were inculcated into the world of 'honour' and 'civility', and undoubtedly facilitated the persisting status of the landed aristocracy and the 'professional ideal' long after that class had lost much of its economic power. We may find, too, the source of the lingering distaste for commercial manufacturing, and the lack of an explicit 'business ethic' (in contrast to the United States, for example), in the idealisation of the 'professional man' by the British middle class.

A similar, historically based explanation for the status associated with 'professional occupations' is forwarded by Jackson. Distinguishing their prime legitimating authority as based on the manipulation of knowledge, rather than craft experience, Jackson suggests that the professions depend on the notion of the university as the institution of the intellectual. This reinforces the conception of professional competency as located around problems of social concern (life, death) and thus requiring a special, 'sacred' or mysterious knowledge beyond the powers of most individuals. However, the level of professional prestige, according to Jackson, rests on more than the priestly, esoteric character of the knowledge possessed, and also derives from the status of its recipients. The lowest professional status is experienced by primary school teachers – 'to whom everyone goes to learn what everyone knows'. School teaching thus lacks the exclusive knowledge and the exclusive clientele characteristic of older professions such as medicine and law; the rise of mass education compromises ('secularises') its mystique.[67]

A third, but similar, explanation for the high prestige of the professions is a functionalist one. The claim is that the abstract and theoretical knowledge possessed by professionals and expressed in performance is functionally relevant to both society in general and the client in particular. Professionals comprehend the major existential issues for individuals (illness, anxiety) and this involves treating problems and emotions once confined to the inner sanctums of the family. Thus, it is argued, professional codes of conduct are essential to protect the confidentiality of practitioner–client relations on these crucial and sensitive matters. The professional association is important here: as well as controlling the formal education of its members, it socialises new entrants into the norms and values of professional practice. Thus the functional relevance of professional knowledge and the autonomy and integrity apparently required for it to be properly executed lead to success being conferred in terms of status, rather than money.[68]

However, these arguments have been less easy to sustain with the growth of salaried professional employment by the state and other large organisations, for these involve tasks that have never been performed in the family, such as those undertaken by specialised scientific and technical groups. Yet rather than indicating an attenuation of the professional ideal, 'post-industrial society' theorists, such as Bell[69] and Halmos,[70] regard the expansion of service industries and the development of technical and administrative occupations based upon the application of abstract knowledge rather than machinery as extending the 'service' ethic. Such employment is characterised by interaction between individuals rather than between individuals and machines, and this necessarily involves the dissemination of norms of sociability and civility. The objection here, however, is that the growth in the professions has been largely confined to the more routine, less 'sacred' occupations such as welfare work and teaching. As Table 16 shows, their income is sharply differentiated from established professionals, such as medical practitioners, solicitors and architects. These lower-level professions have a high proportion of females, and as women's earnings are generally much lower than men's, this is reflected in their low level of relative earnings. Furthermore, commitment here to older notions of professional prestige appears tenuous, as members increasingly incline towards trade unionism rather than independent professional associations. Indeed it could be argued that the term 'profession' has become simply a status symbol, one of the strategies employed by all manner of occupations in their search for increased remuneration and autonomy, rather than a characteristic of a clearly identifiable group of high-prestige positions. Johnson suggests, too, that most so-called professionals employed by the state no longer enjoy either autonomy or participate in the exercise of control and surveillance of subordinates. The spread of technical rationality virtually extinguishes the free professional association, while most professional work becomes so routinised that a remuneration divide clearly exists between top 'authoritative' positions and those subject to the commands of private or public employers.[71] Yet this argument is perhaps exaggerated. Parry has remarked that, in Britain at least, although autonomous professionalism is constantly besieged, in many areas – medicine, for example – it has resisted full incorporation into the state machinery.[72]

TABLE 16 *Gross weekly earnings of adult full-time male employees in selected occupations, 1971*

Occupational groups (male, f.t.)	**Median gross weekly earnings (£)**
Managers – general and administrative	69.6
Medical and dental practitioners	58.5
Architects and planners	47.2
Solicitors	46.2
Accountants	43.4
School teachers	37.1
Welfare workers	30.3

Source: Westergaard and Resler, op. cit., Ch. 1, n36, p. 78 (adapted).

TABLE 17 *Median earnings of full-time employed women compared with men in selected occupations, 1971*

Occupations	**Median gross weekly earnings**	
	Women (£)	**Men (£)**
Nursing matrons, sisters	30.3	—
School teachers	28.4	37.1
Welfare workers	25.8	30.3
Medical auxiliaries	22.8	—
Nurses – all (including matrons, etc.)	20.0	23.5
Laboratory technicians	1.4	30.0

Source: Westergaard and Resler, op. cit., Ch. 1, n36, p. 103.

It is increasingly difficult, nonetheless, to maintain that 'the professions' are identifiable by certain characteristic occupational traits. Millerson, after trawling the sociological literature on the professions, found twenty-three 'elements' that have been used by authors in defining the ideal typical profession, the most popular being (1) skill based on theoretical knowledge, (2) the provision of training and education, (3) testing the competence of members, (4) organisation, (5) adherence to a professional code of conduct, and (6) altruistic service.[73] Similarly, Goode's list of the characteristics of a professional community emphasises shared values, a common language, and the socialisation and control of community members.[74] Turner and Hodge, however, believe that such categorisations are too rigid and do not allow for recent changes in the notion of 'professionalism'. They prefer to develop a framework for the analysis of occupations, rather than of professional occupations alone, which would allow questions to be raised about any occupation without worrying overmuch whether it was a 'true' profession or not. Variables could include the degree of substantive theory and technique required for particular occupational positions, the level of monopoly exercised by occupational associations, and the extent of external recognition or occupational claims to control, and the degree of internal organisation.[75]

More damaging criticisms of the 'trait' approach have been levelled by Johnson. Firstly, he argues that the notion of a 'true' profession draws too heavily on the older, established 'professions', and accepts the claims of the 'professionals' themselves too uncritically. Secondly, the relationships between the 'elements' or 'traits' are rarely articulated theoretically, but simply compose a descriptive list. Thirdly, while altruism may be a valued component of occupational role, it may not form the motivation of individual practitioners. Finally, and most fundamentally, the 'trait' approach does not recognise that 'professionalism' is best viewed as referring to a specific institutionalised form of occupational control. Johnson argues that the social division of labour, the increasing specialisation of occupational skills and production of inaccessible knowledge, leads to a form of 'social distance' or 'indeterminancy' between practitioners and clients. Their relationship inevitably involves a conflict of interests; for example, client accessibility to professional competency, although reducing uncertainty in their relationship, also reduces professional authority and autonomy. In cases where alternative consumer judgement is mainly ineffective, such as in medicine, 'social distance' is increased in favour of the practitioner.[76]

Johnson suggests that 'professionalism' as an historically specific form of occupational control is most effective when the occupation is relatively unified and when there is strong demand for its expertise from a large, relatively homogeneous set of customers. Professional associations play an important role here in ensuring collective practitioner identity and interests through control of recruitment and enforcement of ethical practices. Professional associations, too, are most concerned that the occupation does not become less unified by internal competition for business among its members: thus the British Medical Association bans advertising and has traditionally aimed to prescribe or incorporate new or alternative medical skills.

A claim to exclusivity is a central component of 'professionalism' and may be viewed as a process by which certain occupational groups achieve higher social positions. The relationship between professionalism and class formation has been well explored by the Parrys who point out that 'professionalism' operates as a form of 'collective social mobility'.[77] They define professionalism 'as a strategy for controlling an occupation in which colleagues set up a system of self-government and restrict recruitment through the control of education, training and the process of qualification'.[78] This strategy can then be used by the members of an occupation to achieve entrance into higher status groups while erecting their own obstacles to entry by those lower down the scale. Claims to 'professionalism' and higher social status are not guaranteed to succeed, however, and the Parrys provide instances of both non-successful and successful 'professionalisation'. The doctors provide the successful example.

During the nineteenth century a unified medical profession was formed from three distinct and relatively closed occupations, each of whose functions were legally prescribed and circumscribed. They had their own corporate bodies – the Royal College of Physicians, the Royal College of Surgeons, and the Worshipful Company of Apothecaries – which controlled recruitment and training. The Royal College of Physicians had the highest status, and, until the middle of the century, new members were required to relinquish membership of the other bodies immediately. However, the Parrys note that 'the old system of "orders" was breaking down as part of the general decay of guild control over occupations'. In medicine a more prosperous and better-educated middle class stimulated the rise in the general practitioner whose operations cut across the system of distinct boundaries. Furthermore, the decline in guild and church control heralded a struggle between groups trying to maintain or improve their standing; in particular, surgeons, general practitioners and apothecaries challenged the physicians dominance of the more lucrative and higher-status opportunities within the medical field.

The result was a long process of political manoeuvring and compromise between the 1820s and the 1850s, characterised by calls for a unified, self-governing medical profession which would include the general practitioners, the surgeon apothecaries and the prestigious physicians, but exclude the low-status chemist and general apothecaries. This was achieved with the passing of the Medical Registration Act (1858), which created a General Medical Council charged with maintaining a register of qualified practioners and was invested with powers of removal. From then on 'the doctors, through the Council, sought to consolidate their position by a process of fostering cultural and educational homogeneity', particularly by recruiting those with high-status, mostly public-school backgrounds. Over the last hundred years, the General Medical Council has thus served as the 'classic' professional association, maintaining a self-governing and free medical profession. Increasing intervention by the state in the field of medical care, notably the National Insurance Act (1911) and the introduction of the National Health Service in 1948, has hardly affected doctors' autonomy or control of medical institutions. The doctors remain as self-employed contractors to the National Health Service, rather than as salaried employees, and still have considerable opportunity for private practice. If anything, the extension of social and medical rights by the state to its citizens has sustained the medical profession by providing a guaranteed 'clientele', although the relative replacement of the independent 'special' fee-paying client by state-supported 'consumers' of social services may have led to the attenuation of the professional service ethic. This is not to suggest that the power of the medical profession is so established or entrenched that it will remain immutable. Doctors are having to resist challenges to their autonomy and control by trade unions and Labour governments over such issues as pay beds in national health hospitals and the conditions and terms of contract for hospital doctors, and this may lead to a long-run weakening in their professional influence and autonomy.

Teachers have been less successful than the doctors in establishing an autonomous, self-governing profession. One important historical factor was probably the lack of firm roots in an older estate or guild system: by the nineteenth century the teachers, unlike the doctors, had no well-established corporate institutions that might have provided a framework for a unified profession. This was doubly unfortunate, for the state was far less disposed to the professionalisation of teaching than it was to medicine. By the mid-nineteenth century teachers faced an uphill struggle for occupational autonomy, as there was already extensive state control over elementary education, particularly the supply and training of teachers, together with a developing inspectorial bureaucracy, and these developments were gradually spreading to the other educational sectors. As a result, governments were reluctant to dispose of their powers to a new body along the lines of the General Medical Council, and teachers became firmly established as salaried employees. In the period following 1860, during which pay and training facilities were considerably truncated, and the inspectorial net tightened, teachers were clearly relegated to a lowly status in the eyes of the state, with a position below that of school managers. The Parrys suggest that with the defeat of professionalism, unionism became 'the prime strategy' for coping with the new situation. It is 'no coincidence' they remark, that the formation of the National Union of Elementary Teachers occurred in the same year (1870) as an Education Act firmly establishing a system of school boards. 'It soon became clear that unionism was to be the way of the future although the struggle to gain any real purchase on the administrative structures, which were laid down to control education, was to be a long one.'[79]

The Parrys notion of 'collective social mobility' as characterising 'professionalisation' is similar to Parkin's conceptualisation of 'professional closure'. Parkin suggests that professionalisation may be regarded as a strategy seeking 'to limit and control the supply of entrants to an occupation in order to safeguard or enhance its market value'.[80] With the increasing significance of 'credentialism', the use of educational qualifications in restricting access to important occupational positions, professional strategies generally involved raising entry requirements in the face of increasingly large numbers of potential candidates. Although such moves are justified on the grounds that work tasks are more complex and require greater amounts of skill, they also ensure (if successful) that the supply of labour is sufficiently scarce in relation to demand for its 'price' to be fixed at a 'reasonable' level. Such claims are framed in such a way, however, that they rarely allow observers to distinguish between that specialised knowledge which is vital for work tasks and those 'ritual embellishments that prolong the period of training, thereby protecting market capacity'.[81]

Professionalism and bureaucracy

As we have seen, sociologists have generally used the term 'professional' in the first of the two senses outlined above, to imply a disinterested, essentially non-utilitarian urbanity, rather than cold-eyed, rigorous calculation. This is one reason why a substantial sociological literature is devoted to the alleged conflict between 'professional values' and managerial goals in the new private and public bureaucracies. Scientists employed by the modern corporation, for example, apparently struggle between the commercial imperatives of large organisations, whose conception of 'value' centres on profitability, and the commitment to autonomy and the advancement of 'pure' knowledge enjoyed by their peers in a wider professional community. Reluctantly they are forced to undertake less interesting practical or applied research, within strict accounting and financial procedures, the results of which are subject to the ultimate test of commercial viability.

It is worth noting that in some cases at least, this dilemma may be more apparent than real. Sofer's investigations are interesting here.[82] At one of his firms, Novoplast, substantial top managerial efforts were made to ameliorate possible cross-pressures from competing professional and administrative value systems, most notably by providing a scientific career ladder separate from administrative career opportunities. Novoplast contained a significantly higher proportion of scientists than the other major firm sampled, Autoline, and many were shown to be especially involved with the intrinsic content of their work and were anxious to ensure that the company did not dominate their lives. But despite this the Novoplast men still expressed more interest in the career advancement dimension of their moves than with the possibilities of increased task satisfaction or greater autonomy. Additionally, Sofer provides evidence of 'organisational socialisation', for management orientations increased with length of service and promotion. Understandably, for the major work tasks of heads of departments or divisions are mostly well removed from scientific research: the central work 'problem' for such people is 'organisational' – the maintenance of a smooth, relatively stable system of administration.

Sofer's scientists certainly exhibited more organisational loyalty than the 'professional-bureaucratic dilemma' may have led us to expect although 'academicism' may be greater where firms encourage some of their research departments virtually to resemble university departments, with an emphasis on autonomy and 'scientific' research. However, Novoplast is a highly scientifically based chemical company, and organisational rather than professional identification may be even higher elsewhere.

4

WORK: THE MARGINAL MIDDLE CLASS

Small businessmen

In Chapter 3 we examined the work experience of the relatively well-established middle class, paying particular attention to such issues as 'the managerial revolution' and professionalisation. We now turn to the marginal middle class and, as in Chapter 3, consider both proprietors and employees. We begin with the small entrepreneur, a category that has received such vociferous encouragement in recent years from all shades of 'establishment' thinking.

Small businessmen have long regarded themselves as on the verge of extinction and prey to large collective predators in the jungles of modern monopoly capitalism: big business, organised labour and a powerful, interventionist state. Marxists believe these fears to be soundly based for they suggest an historical tendency for the petite bourgeoisie to polarise between the two major classes associated with the capitalist mode of production, the owners of productive property and the sellers of labour power, capitalists and proletariat. The search for profitability in harsh, competitive and international world markets results, it is argued, in larger, more concentrated and centralised business enterprises and small entrepreneurs are inevitably displaced by this process. Small capital has regularly appeared at least to half-believe gloomy forecasts of its demise, and even the relatively politically quiescent British small business sector which, unlike many of its European counterparts, has generally channelled its political energies into conventional party politics, has reacted vehemently to various legislative 'attacks' on its position, for example, the ending of resale price maintenance (1963), the introduction of VAT (1973), and the introduction of additional national insurance charges on the self-employed (1975).

There is little doubt that the small entrepreneur in Britain has had much to worry about. The Bolton Committee on Small Firms, which reported in 1971, pointed out that 'the declining share of small enterprises in economic activity is a universal process but . . . has gone further here than elsewhere'.[1] In manufacturing, the share of small firms in employment has fallen substantially since the 1920s (see Table 18). Between 1958 and 1963, while total manufacturing output rose by 25 per cent, the total real output of small firms hardly changed.[2] The Bolton Committee suggested a number of reasons for this decline, but two stand out as having special importance: the increased role of the state and the emergence of the giant company. By 1969 the public sector, if public corporations and nationalised industries are included with central government and local authorities, accounted for 25 per cent of the employed population and 27 per cent of GNP.[3] This adversely affects the size of the small firm sector in at least five ways:

1 the nationalisation of industries effectively prevents entry and growth of new small firms into that industry;
2 the purchasing activities of the state as a major or dominant buyer of a range of goods are based on large orders, often by inviting selective tenders, and this favours the large, well-established contractor;
3 the state has sought to 'rationalise' a number of industries and improve economic efficiency by encouraging concentration, e.g., shipbuilding, textiles;
4 the range of regulatory controls enforced by the state, e.g., pensions, health, and planning, places a bigger administrative burden on small, more labour-intensive firms than on large companies, and may increase the costs of the labour employed;
5 taxation on profits may have reduced the ability of small firms to finance their expansion through reinvested earnings and threatened the continuation of family businesses.

Perhaps more dramatic than the decline of the small firm is the growth in very large companies. The share of manufacturing

TABLE 18 *Employment in U.K. manufacturing, 1924–1968*

	All establishments thousands	Small establishments thousands	Small as percentage of total %
1924	5,115	2,257	44
1930	5,179	2,238	43
1935	5,409	2,375	44
1948	6,871	2,538	37
1951	7,382	2,576	35
1954	7,537	2,500	33
1958	7,781	2,498	32
1963	7,960	2,436	31
1968	7,870	2,280	29

Source: Bolton Committee Report, op. cit., Ch. 4, n1, p. 38.

companies with more than 5,000 employees as a percentage of total manufacturing employment rose from about 25 per cent in 1951 to 43 per cent in 1963.[4] As firms grow larger, like the state their bulk-buying activities stimulate further concentration while the dominant position of large companies in certain markets may result in obstacles to the entry of small firms, for example, by discriminatory price competition. Thus, together with changes in the occupational structure, the appearance given is 'that the petit bourgeois is marking time while all around him work situations and job relationships are altering rapidly'.[5]

By 1971, therefore, less than 8 per cent of the occupied population either ran their own business and employed others, or were simply self-employed. Brown indicates that commercially they were important only in agriculture, forestry and fishing (about 63 per cent of all occupied), construction (26 per cent), distributive traders (18 per cent) and 'miscellaneous services' (19 per cent). Nonetheless, small business firms remain numerically important. In 1971 there were over 1.25 million small firms in the UK, giving employment to 6 million, and contributing nearly 20 per cent of the gross national product.[6] Furthermore, some burgeoning new areas, notably electronics, which tends to involve batch rather than mass production, have recently spawned a fresh generation of small businesses. The growth in service industries may also provide further opportunities for the small entrepreneur, while the much lamented decline in traditional small business sectors (e.g., landlordism) has been less dramatic than is often portrayed, as both Eversley,[7] and McCrone and Elliott[8] have noted. There are substantial reasons for expecting the small business sector to survive in reasonably good shape, despite tendencies to larger concentrations of economic power, that stem from its functionality for capitalism generally.

Poulantzas details a number of economic reasons which explain the usefulness for monopoly capital of preserving smaller concerns. First, by operating in and maintaining areas of limited profitability in given periods, small businesses keep open opportunities for the larger concerns into which they may expand when the economic climate is good. Secondly, they provide a source of innovation of new products, enabling large firms to intervene when the risks have been minimised, as, for example, in the computer industry. Technological advances, too, sometimes derive from the small sector, which lacks the ability to develop them, and are forced to hand them to the giant firms at relatively low cost. Thirdly, the relatively labour-intensive small firm provides a valuable training ground and source of employment for the young, the least well-qualified and the downwardly mobile, who may then move on to larger concerns. Fourthly, small capital provides for secondary lines of production not suitable for largescale units, such as car accessories. Finally, because smaller firms lack the economies of scale of the larger concerns, monopoly capital may fix its prices by reference to those of the smaller sector and reap large profits.[9]

Poulantzas provides little empirical support for his propositions, and there is insufficient British evidence available either. But there is little denying that 'establishment' thinking is currently sympathetic to the role that small enterprises may play in modern economies. A general 'small is beautiful' philosophy dominates official circles, and has replaced the 1960s view that 'big is efficient'. All the major parties now laud the small businessman, and while many in the Labour party distrust the small employers' Conservative, anti-trade-union tendencies, Labour leaders at least have echoed the other parties in affirming the small entrepreneur as a source of employment in an age of increasing unemployment, especially for the inner city areas, and as a social and moral counterbalance to the larger industrial battalions.

Notions of what constitutes a 'small business' vary, however, and it is possible that while the Conservative image of a 'small businessman' is a rather large employer, such as the embattled George Ward of Grunwick, with up to four hundred employees, it is the self-employed craftsman that finds most favour within the guild socialist tradition of the Labour Party. And clearly, as the Bolton Report remarks, 'a manufacturing business employing up to 200 people has very little in common with a small shop owned and run by a married couple'.[10] Perhaps, therefore, it is not surprising to discover that academic and official definitions of a small business display startling variations. At the lower end, Goldthorpe et al.[11] define 'a small-scale employer' as one with less than ten employees, although this is upped by Caplow[12] to around thirty, a parameter within which he argues it is possible for members to form a 'primary group' where all possible pair relationships are attainable. Ingham,[13] and Stacey,[14] go higher – to 100 employees – although Ingham suggests that the greatest structural changes, particularly the level of bureaucratisation, are likely to occur when an organisation reaches between thirty and sixty members. The most influential official definition, found in the Bolton Report, fixes the upper limit in manufacturing at 200 employees, although Bolton adds three further characteristics: a small firm has a small share of the market, it is managed by its owner(s) in a personalised fashion and not via a formalised structure, and it does not form part of a larger enterprise, leaving the owner/managers free from outside control in decision-making.[15] A final example we offer, from Boswell, complicates the issue further by defining small businesses as those employing up to 500 workers, suggesting that at this level the financial, personnel and administrative problems faced by employers are generally similar and contrast with those experienced by bigger employers.[16]

Attempts to arrive at a precise definition based on number of employees are probably futile: circumstances and working conditions vary considerably from sector to sector. Ingham's inclusion of structural contrasts between small and large firms, particularly as it affects types of managerial control, and Bolton's stipulation of autonomy in decision-making, usefully provide more qualitative criteria, although Bolton's characteristics would leave out of calculation the small but highly specialised firm dominating a given market by technological knowhow or ethnic appeal. More satisfactorily, Bechhofer and Elliott suggest that the 'motley collection of occupations to which reference is made when people speak of the "small businessman"' have three essential characteristics in common: the employment of capital, the dominance of a relatively low technology, and an uncomplicated managerial overhead, that is, 'the social organisation of work is simple, the span of authority small',[17] although this perhaps underestimates the increasing number of small businesses employing quite sophisticated technology, in such areas as electronics, for example.

In many small industrial organisations functional specialisation in the system of administration does not extend beyond a small degree of delegated authority; 'the general manager, often the owner, will act as buyer, sales manager and public relations officer. His immediate subordinate – works manager/foreman – is likely also to act as personnel officer, inspector of products, and research and development officer'.[18] Thus small firms lack the impersonal bureaucratic control mechanisms of larger enterprises, and activities are less rigidly circumscribed by procedural rules. Small employers require job rotation and the diffusion of skills in a flexible workforce, and this it is often claimed increases the level of shopfloor interaction, intrinsic task enjoyment and identification with 'visible' owners. While these small-scale particularistic work environments may be increasingly overshadowed by the growth of large companies, in some sectors the reverse may be happening. Newby, who found that workers on large, bureaucratised farms were more calculative in their attitudes to their employer than those employed on smaller farms, notes that 'the decreasing size of the labour force has enabled the traditional authority typical of agricultural employers to become more securely rooted'.[19]

One has to guard against the too misty-eyed view of industrial relations in the small firm found in a number of studies. Some small employers are demanding task masters, and, in the absence of trade unions, provide poor working conditions. Paternal, religious, community-orientated small employers who take a benevolent interest in employees outside the company may be thinner on the ground than in a previous period. Newby et al. outline how the modern farm manager and owner rarely adopt the squirearchy role of their predecessors in the local community, while competitive pressures from the agro-business sector is inducing a more economically rational approach to agriculture from even the smallest farmers.[20] Curran and Stanworth also question the image of warm, close relations between workers and management in small companies, pointing out that 'the Arbitration, Conciliation and Advisory Service spends a disproportionate amount of its time in small firms'. Furthermore, around one-half of registered unfair dismissal claims involve companies with less than 100 employees. Nor did Curran and Stanworth in their researches find simple correlations between workers' orientations and size of firms: 'the major influences were far more likely to be differences in workers' market situations and employers' selection practices – that is, factors beyond the workers' control.' These selection practices were often idiosyncratic, with small employers quite willing to disregard formal qualifications and relevant experience. The employers displayed a temperamental individualism which made them shy away from large organisations – 'their entry into entrepreneurship is often a protest against such a society' – and antipathetic to trade unionism.[21]

Autonomy and independence are highly cherished commodities in the petit-bourgeois world. The work by Bechhofer and his colleagues at Edinburgh University on shopkeepers indicates the strength of commitment by small retailers to 'economic individualism', a general feeling that individuals should stand on their own two feet and make the best of their skills in the open market, but be free to enjoy the rewards of this effort. Bechhofer and Elliott note two 'corollaries' of this competitive individualism in their Edinburgh sample:[22] a strong anti-collectivism, which manifests in vigorous opposition to state intervention in the economy, but which also instils a coolness towards their own protective associations; and a belief in individual mobility – a feeling that hard work will bring material success and high status, especially for their children. Yet these retailers are no swashbuckling, entrepreneurial cavaliers, but cautious, stolid and financially rather timid. They display a reluctance to change their working operations, or to use outside finance as a means of expanding the business, preferring instead to settle for a reasonable income, security and the feeling of independence that comes from being your own boss. One result of this unwillingness to 'go for broke' is a persisting economic marginality which means that many do not achieve the security of comfort they value. Around 20 per cent of Edinburgh's shops 'failed' (i.e closed or changed hands at least once every six to twelve months) while a considerable number of shopkeepers (18 per cent) also supplemented their income tax by working in another occupation. The smallness and 'marginality' of retailing units is underlined by the finding that 84 per cent of the Edinburgh sample had less than two full-time employees, confirming the impression that the small shop is 'essentially a family business'. The shopkeeper may value his autonomy, but his scope of authority is very restricted. Furthermore, hours are long and premises frequently drab.

It would be misleading to infer that the shopkeeper's lot is an unhappy one; although the shopkeepers in the Edinburgh study were often little better off than many manual workers in terms of income, their market situation was generally much more advantageous. Unlike manual workers, shopkeepers are able to accumulate small amounts of capital within the business, and these could be used to purchase consumer goods. The individualism and traditionalism of these small property-holders is well revealed in the propensity to own these consumer durables outright without recourse to credit, while the level of house ownership without a mortgage, for example, was very high, 'even for professional groups'.

The small independent business stratum is clearly characterised by its economic 'marginality': they 'sit uncomfortably between the mass of manual workers and the lower echelons of the middle class'. Although they do not possess the economic security of the established middle class, their market and work situations, their ownership of property and relative autonomy at work, distinguish them from the working class. The economic marginality of shopkeepers is reflected in the heterogeneity of their social origins, for they are drawn in roughly equal proportion from the working and middle classes.

Finally, it is worth noting that many of the characteristics of the urban small businessman are replicated in an agricultural setting. Farming is a sizeable component of small entrepreneurial activity in Britain, although the urban manufacturing connotations of the term 'business' may have served to disguise the fact (in a recent occupational breakdown of their support, the National Federation of the Self-Employed listed 'farmers' as comprising the largest category[23]). Despite the recent emergence of large-scale 'company farming', agriculture is still characterised by small-scale, family-owned businesses, and these are subject to the same economic pressures as their industrial counterparts. Newby et al. indicate, for example, that in East Anglia at least, as farms become larger and more capital intensive, encouraged by the interventionist policies of successive governments, the marginal producer is being squeezed out and the number of farmers has fallen, slowly but consistently, since the war.[24] Yet, as with Bechhofer et al.'s retailers, hostile economic currents, although reinforcing suspicions of size and big business, have done little to stimulate acceptance of combination and farmers' organisations.

The multiplicity of roles performed by the independent 'town' businessman is a well-established feature of the small farmer's working day: he is entrepreneur, manager and labourer combined. The smaller the farm, the more likely is the farmer to spend his time labouring, and the more probable that the farm provides an extension of family identity with its 'employees' all closely related. It is understandable, therefore, that 'the personal' or the idiosyncratic remains a feature of farmers' attitudes to their workforce. If anything, they are even more thorough than other small employers in investigating the private lives of potential workers, and are profoundly distrustful of formal qualifications and trade unionists. The paternalism of farm relationships has, of course, long been reinforced by the tied-cottage system, for this not only gives farmers a powerful sanction over their employees – losing your job means losing your home – but exposes the labour force more continuously to the farmer's definitions of the situation. Close proximity to, and frequency of interaction with employers, however, is no guarantee of harmonious relationships, either on the farm or in other small enterprises, for, as Newby et al. observe, 'intimate personal contacts can be every bit as intolerable as the impersonality of the market place'.

Routine white-collar workers

The contemporary British middle class, as we have noted, no longer approximates to the select, well-rewarded and cultured 'haute bourgeoisie' of the late nineteenth century. Although some 'professional' roles may still exhibit characteristics found in idealised accounts of middle-class existence, the expansion of non-manual occupations in the last seventy years largely reflects the growth of routine white-collar employment. While the non-manual section of the labour force increased from 30 per cent to 45 per cent in the period 1931–71, the proportion of white-collar employees rose from 18 per cent to over 30 per cent, a numerical leap from 3.75 million to over 7 million.[25] The Arkwrights employed only three clerks to look after 1,063 workers in 1804, but most modern businessmen employ nearly as many clerks as manual operatives and some industries, such as banking and insurance, are composed primarily of clerical employees. As noted in Chapter 2, however, the expansion of the white-collar sector has been accompanied by a decline in the economic and social standing of the clerical worker: a range of indices – income, working conditions, promotion opportunities – indicate a severe narrowing of differentials with manual workers, emphasised perhaps by the fact that many white-collar workers are from manual backgrounds and include an increasing proportion of women. For example, the percentage of all non-manual women in routine grades rose from 51 to 72 in the period 1921–66, but that of men in similar positions from 38 to 40.[26] As a result, claims to the special middle-class status of the kind employed by the clerk in the nineteenth-century counting house now appear as either a serious form of self-delusion or sheer snobbishness. However, data from K. Roberts et al.'s investigations in Liverpool indicate that those in typically low or routine white-collar jobs are not especially inclined to claim this status, but rather take the working class as their reference group.[27]

It is no surprise, therefore, to find that a prominent theme in sociological analyses of class is concerned with the possibility that white-collar workers are becoming 'proletarianised' and that this is evidenced by recent rapid developments in white-collar trade unionism. As we previously noted, the case for regarding the routine clerical worker as a member of the working class is not new; Marxists have long made such a claim, while in the late nineteenth century the Labour movement employed the term 'white-collar proletariat' to describe what was regarded as the 'pathetic self-deception of the blackcoated worker who was seen as indulging in middle class pretensions on a working class level of living'.[28] Between the wars, referring to the essential 'propertylessness' of the clerk, Klingender argued that clerical stubbornness in refusing to recognise the elemental fact that like the manual worker he also was a seller of labour was best regarded as 'false consciousness'. But he believed it would pass with the inevitable polarisation of the classes.[29]

An interesting contemporary variant of the 'clerical proletarianisation' thesis has been advanced by Braverman, although it is mainly based on American material. Braverman locates the expansion of clerical and other forms of non-manual employment in the need for capitalist owners/managers to control the labour process more fully if they are to secure greater efficiency and profitability in their enterprises. Employers tend to seize traditional, informal work knowledge and skills from operatives and translate them into abstract rules and procedures that become legitimated as managerial directives and act as a form of control. The result is a more disciplined and 'deskilled' workforce whose jobs become 'cheaper' as they become more specialised and routinised. A consequence of capital's enforcement of its conceptions rather than those of the workers on the organisation of tasks is for 'brain' or 'mental' labour to be socially and physically separated from 'manual' and 'physical' labour. The separation of conceptualisation from execution in the work process creates large clerical and technical office staffs to assist the aim of managerial control. And as capitalism becomes more complicated it requires more efficient administrative and accounting systems which also increases the number of white-collar workers. However, the main point of Braverman's argument is that the expansion in clerical labour changes it from a marginal to a substantial 'cost' to management. Like manual jobs white-collar work becomes subject to routinisation and 'deskilling' as management seeks to make cheaper the cost of the administrative overhead by, for example, introducing mechanisation and computerisation into the office. Consequently clerical labour has become more tightly and impersonally controlled and disciplined. As the clerk loses his special marketable skills with the spread of literacy, and experiences declining relative income and prestige, 'mental knowledge' passes to an ever smaller stratum of top managers.[30]

Braverman's thesis is very persuasive and offers numerous insights into the origins and changing nature of contemporary white-collar work. Yet there are a number of difficulties with his analysis which suggest that he exaggerates the convergence of manual and non-manual work. First, his notion of 'deskilling' is elusive. As B. Roberts et al. indicate in their work on technicians, 'skill' involves different degrees of knowledge, responsibility, physical capability and experience, and the relative amounts of each factor contained within a job specification will be influenced over time by a changing sociotechnical environment. However, 'these elements are not always capable of quantative measurement and therefore it is difficult to validate claims that levels of skill are either falling or increasing'.[31] Secondly, mechanisation may not have the same effect for clerical workers as for factory operatives. Lockwood observes that calculators and typewriters are useful supports for clerical functions: machines are ancillary to human labour in the office, whereas the reverse is the tendency in the factory, where technology dominates the worker.[32] However, computerisation may come to have similar unemployment consequences for white collar employees as some forms of advanced mechanisation have had for manual workers. Thirdly, the 'cheapness' of at least certain kinds of clerical labour, the narrow income differential with manual employment, is less of a contemporary feature than Braverman suggests, at least in Britain. It is easy to assume too stark a contrast between the well paid and well regarded nineteenth century clerk in a cosy small establishment and the lower-status modern clerical worker in large, impersonal office blocks earning virtually the same as manual employees.

Lockwood's *The Blackcoated Worker*, although published in 1958, still stands as virtually the sole, empirically-based account of the British clerk, and it remains a valuable source of material for the analysis of white-collar occupations and helps to shed light on the historical continuities and discontinuities in the economic and social standing of routine non-manual employees. Lockwood portrays the nineteenth-century office as small, with the division of labour slight, and where office records were more 'a rule of thumb guide to business decisions than a statistical basis for rational costing and sales'.[33] The clerk's knowledge was learnt on the job and gave him particular skills that were not easily transferred to other employers, although the personal relations he enjoyed with his own employer, plus reflected authority and status, induced little sense of thwarted ambition. There was sufficient sense of distance from the proletarian which was reinforced by clerical aspirations to be thought a 'gentleman'.

Yet Lockwood's evidence casts some doubt on the typicality of this kind of 'blackcoated worker', at least by the turn of the century. Then, as today, the clerical situation covered many possibilities: 'there was an immense range in the remuneration of functions that were termed clerical'.[34] Some were simply pen-pushers, whereas others had the authority of top management, differences that were expressed in 'the bewildering lack of uniformity in clerical salaries'. However, the great proportion of clerks at the end of the last century earned little more than the artisan; it was only in banking, the civil service, insurance and the top clerical echelons of the commercial sector that clerks 'were able to maintain a fairly respectable middle-class way of life without strain', and many of these were the sons and nephews of employers, temporarily gaining 'experience' before moving to higher positions. Nor were large clerical offices unknown, especially in the Civil Service, insurance and on the railways – after all, the Dickensian image of the nineteenth-century office, as found in old movies at least, is of long rows of clerks scratching away under the beady eye of the senior clerk, and it was these industries that saw the first stirrings of white-collar trade unionism. Conversely, the extent of clerical employment in modern, large office blocks may be exaggerated, for many clerks are to be found in small establishments. Although Lockwood's analysis of the clerk in the post-war period is based on large concerns, he is careful to warn that only 'in a relatively few instances do office sizes approximate the workforce concentration that is typical of factory production'.[35] Despite the increase in the number of clerical workers in a unit of administration, the size of the clerical work group has not substantially expanded. Clerks tend to be dispersed among a variety of specialised departments, within which they are still distinguished by considerable degrees of skill and responsibility. And while 'pools' of secretarial or sales employees are to be found engaged on mind-numbing, repetitive assignments, office routine is generally more unpredictable, less obviously rhythmic, than that in factories. Managers and clerks cooperate in day-to-day routines, cocooned in relative isolation from the manual worker, and resistant to attempts by top management to impose uniform or factory routines in the office.

It is undeniable, of course, that the nature and circumstances of clerical work has undergone substantial change, even if Braverman overestimates its scope and pace. Lockwood's account is based on the premise that the fact of 'propertylessness', which the clerk shares with the manual worker, is an insufficient index of class position, and by submerging 'objective' class differences between the two groups provides little understanding of clerical reluctance to identify with the working class. The key, instead, is to regard 'class position' as composed of three separate dimensions: market, work and status situations.

Market situation

The market position of the higher-status, better-paid clerk has undoubtedly declined in recent years. Although clerical fortunes until the mid-1930s fluctuated – periods of narrowing income differentials were soon followed by a restoration of relative earnings – the post-war years mark a more permanent loss of comparative advantage with manual incomes, as well as a compression of rates within clerical ranks itself. Manual workers enjoyed higher earnings, if not higher wage rates, in the period of labour shortage which characterised the twenty years following the ending of the Second World War. A further, longer-term factor behind the relative weakening of the clerk's market capacity has been the steady expansion of compulsory education which has ensured that literacy is no longer a scarce resource and may be purchased at cheaper rates from traditionally 'less expensive' labour pools, such as that comprised by married women. Male clerks may have benefited in the more general expansion of the established managerial strata since the war by seizing better opportunities for promotion, but the increasing adoption of graduate trainee recruitment schemes has probably restricted upward clerical mobility. Certainly, although young male clerks may still reasonably hope to eventually achieve managerial positions, the great majority of female clerks have no such expectations.

Work situation

We have already commented on a number of changes in the clerk's working conditions, such as the expanding size of the administrative unit and the implementation of office machinery, and it was suggested that the consequences of these changes were less dramatic than indicated by Braverman. Nonetheless, one important modification in the white-collar employee's work situation does indicate a convergence with the manual operative. This is the decline of 'administrative particularism', the special personal relationship enjoyed with the employer, and its replacement by a more impersonal mode of conduct. The emergence of large-scale organisations in such industries as banking and the civil service has been accompanied by 'the introduction of uniform scales of remuneration, the rigid classification of jobs, explicit criteria of merit, and the articulation of the individual career with prescribed exams'.[35] While clerical tasks are still less precisely defined than manual work, and their variability ensures that clerical competence is less homogeneously classified than factory skill, individual white-collar employees are increasingly related to each other by formal, bureaucratic standards. In the public sector especially one is more and more likely to find a mass of clerical subordinates 'whose functions less and less justify their classification as brain workers'[36] and who are sharply separated from the small group of executives who undertake important strategic and conceptual work.

Status situation

Writing in the late 1950s, Lockwood suggests that a crucial distinction in the class positions of the manual and non-manual employee lay in the latter's 'status consciousness'. Even the most junior clerks saw themselves as possessing greater social prestige than any manual worker, and such feelings served 'to dampen any incipient feeling of identification clerks may have had with the working class'.[37] Clerks claimed, and generally received, a 'status differential' compared with the operative. However, the clerk's status links with the established middle class have always been tenuous, for they have lacked the latter's necessary material resources, with the result that they have tended to compensate by becoming 'snobbish', 'priggish' and 'petty'. The erosion in their economic circumstances in recent years has left an even more rickety material foundation for their status claims. To add insult to injury, as we noted in the opening chapters, even previously 'friendly', i.e., Conservative, governments, now regard much white-collar work as a burden on the country's productive sectors and a damper on the country's entrepreneurial spirit, rather than as a source of civility and stability. Undoubtedly the militancy of certain white-collar trade unions, especially in the public sector, has also weakened official and public sympathy for the special status claims of the non-manual worker. Besides, the working class has long asserted its own competing claims to social worth based on virtues allegedly foreign to clerical behaviour and has seen its members as the 'real' producers of wealth in contrast to the effete, timid, and conformist office worker.

Perhaps the most significant sign of the crumbling of clerical status is to be found in the feminisation of clerical positions. The relatively low prestige of predominantly 'female occupations' such as junior school-teaching and clerical work is ample testimony to the claim that 'the effect of a high proportion of women in an occupation on the social status of that occupation is a function of the general status of women in society'.[38] As

Wainwright observes, noting the 'feminisation' of a range of routine white-collar positions:

The mass increase of women in paid labour has not involved the majority of women in forms of labour that clash with the cultural definitions of women's domestic identity. Women as a social group have not become separated sufficiently from domestic labour to break down the cultural image of masculinity and femininity which reflects and justifies the sexual division of labour . . . the small areas where women do have some degree of control are those in which, as domestic labour they control the organisation of children and other women.[39]

Women are thus concentrated in those 'jobs – secretarial and clerical – where servicing others, primarily men, will in effect be the main task'. Table 19 also indicates the extent to which the established middle class has generally been protected from feminisation by the expense and length of training necessary for entry.

TABLE 19 *Economically active females by socio-economic groups, Great Britain*

	Thousands (1) Females	(2) Total	(3) (1) as % of (2)
Professional	87.5	886.9	9.9
Employers and managers	431.5	2382.0	18.1
Intermediate and junior non-manual	4418.9	7201.0	61.4

Source: 1971 Census, Economic Activity Tables, Part IV, Tables 29.

There are still degrees of differences between manual and non-manual workers on all three dimensions of class position, but perhaps the crucial difference is found in the work situation, especially in the commercial sector. The distinction between office and factory work continues to reflect 'the structure of industrial organisation and especially the relations of authority in the enterprise . . . the clerk is the man (or woman) on the other side of the desk who is somehow associated with authority'.[40] To the extent that clerks maintain their position at the fingertips on the extended arm of managerial authority, despite the relative decline in their social prestige and the similarity of their income levels with manual workers, they will remain marginally and tenuously members of the middle class.

This marginality in the clerk's class position is exemplified by the ambiguity that they display in their attitudes to their organisations. The quite high status clerical superintendents in the insurance companies investigated by Davis displayed what he terms a 'collusive consciousness' in their orientation to work. They did not closely identify with their company but there was a recognition of mutual life ties, a sense of managers and employees inhabiting the same life space. While the supervisors recognised the unitary nature of the social system, they were also aware of conflicts of interest: a major problem for these employees was reconciling the often incompatible demands of the job, interpreted as keeping a 'happy department' with a low turnover of labour that produced accurate and efficient work while complying with the wish of management to apply efficient business methods. The solution 'was to collude in the management's rationalisation schemes as being in the company's interests',[41] but to try and minimise their effects on themselves and the other clerks. It is 'this ability to see and argue from the management's point of view, though without necessarily identifying with management or approving of what they do', that Davis describes as 'collusive'. It means that the legitimacy of the system is rarely doubted, even when individual interests are threatened, and this is accompanied by a tendency 'to identify upwards rather than downwards'.

Davis's clerical employees were not interested in joining trade unions. But many of the arguments over the alleged 'proletarianisation' or otherwise of the routine white-collar worker rest on conflicting interpretations of the increasing tendency of such employees to become unionised. Does it indicate a recognition of the similarity of their class position with manual workers, an identification with the working class and its organisations, or does it signal a recognition of separate interests and the need for these to be defended?

Middle-class trade unions and associations

We argued in Chapter 2 that until recently it used to be considered, if not exceptional, then slightly odd for members of the middle class to join trade unions. However, we must note that white-collar unions have existed since the nineteenth century and, as Jenkins and Sherman remark, 'the NUT, the various Civil Service unions, the police organisations and the national and local government officers have all been in the field for most of this century with substantial memberships',[42] although it is only recently that some of these unions (e.g., NALGO) have affiliated to the TUC. Nonetheless, in comparison with their manual counterparts most non-manual employees have been disinterested in union membership. In 1966 a review of unionisation among white-collar workers by G. S. Bain, Director of the SSRC Industrial Relations Research Unit at Warwick University, revealed that while the number of white-collar trade unionists increased in absolute terms between 1948 and 1964 (from 1,964,000 to 2,684,000) this simply matched the growth in non-manual employment.[43] In fact the density of white-collar unionism – the percentage of potential union membership actually organised – marginally declined in this period, from 30.2 to 29.6 per cent, while manual union density increased slightly from 50.7 to 52.9 per cent (see Table 20).

TABLE 20 *The growth of white collar and manual unionism in the U.K., 1948–1974.*

	1948	1964	1974
Union Membership (000's)			
White collar	1,964	2,684	4,263
Manual	7,398	7,534	7,491
Union Density (percentage)			
White collar	30.2	29.6	39.4
Manual	50.7	52.9	57.9

Source: R. Price and G. Bain, 'Union growth revisited', *B.J. Industrial Relations*, Vol. 15, 1977, p. 347.

By the end of the 1960s a number of explanations for the apparent reluctance of non-manual employees to join trade unions had become established. One, associated particularly with David Lockwood, emphasised persisting differences in the class position of white-collar workers in comparison with manual employees, especially in their work and status situations. They generally possessed greater authority and status, experienced more personal and relaxed relations with their employers, and enjoyed better fringe and other benefits. This encouraged non-manual workers to identify with management and to emphasise their separateness from manual workers; trade unions were regarded as 'workers' organisations' and given a wide berth. However, as we have seen, Lockwood thought that the more the work situation of the non-manual employee was bureaucratised and relations with bosses were impersonal, the more likely were groups of workers to join trade unions. Bain also observes that bureaucratisation and trade unionism 'proceed from the basic assumption that generally applicable rules are necessary to govern the relations between men in the plant'.[44] In large organisations particularly, it becomes harder for individuals to come to their own salary agreement with supervisors, as the rules apply to a person as a member of a group rather than as an individual. He comes to acknowledge that 'the most effective way of modifying them in his favour is by collective rather than by individual bargaining'.

A second explanation, drawing on surveys from the 1950s and 1960s asserted that the middle class has 'individualistic' values while the working class is disposed to 'collectivism'. As collective associations, trade unions are not perceived as appropriate vehicles for advancement by non-manual employees. These contrasting value systems are expressed in different images of society; manual workers view society in conflictual, 'us/them' terms, with the best hope for improved pay and rewards in group action on behalf of all its members. The middle class, however, perceives society as hierarchically but harmoniously arranged in strata based on status, and prefers to climb the ladder of success by individual effort. These different class orientations are also institutionalised in two types of organisation, the professional association and the trade union. Prandy has argued that 'trade unions are class bodies – they bargain with employers; professional associations are status bodies – they bestow a qualification and seek to maintain or enhance its prestige'.[45] Thus trade unions give expression to class conflict, an interpretation with which others, such as Lockwood and Blackburn,[46] appear to concur, when they suggest that unionisation for white collar workers is one indicator of class consciousness.

This leads to a third, but slightly different account of white-collar unionisation. Lockwood and Blackburn also suggest that even when non-manual employees do join their own trade unions, their organisations tend to maintain their distance from manual unions by, for example, being more reluctant to call strikes, join the TUC or affiliate to the Labour Party. In other words, the 'character' of middle-class unionism differs from manual unionism: it is less militant and more instrumental.

The argument that the middle class does not join trade unions because they have a different outlook on life in comparison with the working class is no longer as persuasive as it may have been ten years ago, if only because white-collar workers are now proportionately more organised. Since the mid-1960s non-manual trade unionism has accelerated much more than the expansion in non-manual positions. In the period 1964–74 white-collar union density increased from 29.6 per cent to 39.4 per cent, an increase in absolute terms from 2,684,000 to 4,263,000. A graphic illustration of the take-off in middle-class trade unionism since the late 1960s is provided by one of the major white-collar unions, the Association of Scientific, Technical and Managerial Staffs (ASTMS), which increased its membership by 700 per cent between 1964 and 1977.[47] Yet the development of white-collar unionism has been remarkably patchy: union membership and density in the white-collar section of manufacturing still falls considerably short of that for manual workers, while the percentage organised in the private sector industries which employ a large number of non-manual employees, is much lower still (see Table 21). Though the proposition that the middle class is especially averse to trade unionism may be weakened by this data, considerable class differences in union membership still remain, particularly when 'managers' and other members of the established middle class are brought into calculations. To what extent do the three explanations for this contrast, outlined above, still hold?

The first problem with these explanations relates to definitions. As May observes, 'the notion that there is something unusual about the middle class joining trade unions does not make much sense if we are prepared to regard as trade unions various bodies that many members of the middle class have

TABLE 21 *Union membership and density by sector in the U.K., 1974.*

Sector	Labour force (000's)	Union membership (000's)	Density (%)
Public sector	6,112.6	5,079.4	83.1
Manufacturing	7,778.9	4,836.4	62.2
Manual	5,678.6	4,164.2	73.3
White-collar	2,100.3	672.2	32.0
Agriculture, forestry and fishing	427.7	99.7	23.3
Private sector services	6,689.3	810.0	12.1

Source: R. Price and G. Bain, op. cit., (Table 20), p. 342.

always accepted that it is right and proper for them to join'.[48] Thus, if professional associations or staff associations are regarded as 'trade unions' the reluctance of the middle class to organise in collective defence of occupational interests is less apparent. However, most writers do not see these bodies as essentially trade unions on the grounds that professional associations are less concerned, if at all, with negotiations over wages and working conditions, the central task of trade unions. Instead, as Bain notes, 'the major functions of professional associations are education and certification'.[49] Similarly staff associations, while lacking the autonomy of the professional association, may not be sufficiently independent of employers to warrant the description 'trade union'; indeed, as May indicates, many are set up by employers to *avoid* trade unionism, although firm evidence is hard to find.

The claim that the goals of professional associations and trade unions are radically different has a long sociological pedigree. Carr-Saunders and Wilson distinguished between the 'single purpose' of trade unions to protect the economic interests of their members, and the multi-purpose professional association which protected the public but, more specifically, sought to advance the knowledge, techniques and status of particular disciplines.[50] More recently, Millerson had identified four types of professional bodies: (1) prestige associations, such as the British Academy, whose members have a special prestige; (2) study associations, such as the British Sociological Association, which promotes a specific subject; (3) qualifying associations, such as the Law Society, which control recruitment to an occupation through an examination system; and (4) occupational associations, which include groups such as the British Medical Association that seek 'to improve the working conditions and remuneration of the individual professional'.[51]

Occupational associations come close to performing many of the functions of a trade union than allowed for by some sociologists; they are concerned with job regulation, controlling the supply of professional labour, and increasing the incomes of their members. The line between professional associations and trade unions becomes even hazier if one accepts Bain et al.'s point that the concern of qualifying associations 'with study, qualifications, and public service has always been closely linked with their concern to control the supply of professional labour and to increase the incomes of their members'.[52] In support of their claim that although qualifying associations do not usually negotiate directly on salaries and conditions they may considerably influence such issues, Bain et al. quote Blackburn, who observes that,

> Control over the numbers gaining a desired qualification means control of the market, which is of prime importance in determining pay and conditions... Other protective devices which may be adopted include: (a) remuneration surveys among members; (b) advice to individual members on terms of contracts and suitability of salaries; (c) advice and information on contracts and salaries (to employers); (d) use of an appointments register or journal to inform members of vacancies; (e) support in the formation of a new body to conduct negotiations.[53]

Bain et al., referring to qualifying and occupational associations, remark that, like a trade union, their major tasks are to help make the rules and regulations governing their members' working conditions and to protect their 'economic' interests. Both employ restrictive practices and closed shop tactics to this end, although these are more likely to be referred to as 'professional control and autonomy' when it involves professional associations. Bain et al. conclude that 'rather than being distinct from trade unions, professional associations can more accurately be portrayed as the craft unions of a different social group'.[54]

A second difficulty with the proposition that a significant connection exists between class position and trade union membership concerns the nature of the 'decision' to join. This is increasingly not a completely voluntary act as membership of a union steadily becomes the norm, even for some white-collar employees. The spread of the closed shop reinforces the 'institutionalisation' of the unions and in some cases its membership may be encouraged by employers, especially the larger ones.[55] Bain et al. argue that it is therefore unlikely that trade union membership is strongly related to various dimensions of stratification, while the thesis that routinised working conditions and lack of authority leads to organisation is challenged by the observation that those with the most skill and control, such as draughtsmen, tend to be the most unionised. In the public sector, too, position in the authority structure appears to have no dramatic correlation with union membership.

Recent findings also seriously question the distinction made between the allegedly individualist values of the middle class and the collectivist orientations of the working class. A number of white-collar workers do not see themselves as middle-class but identify with manual workers, and for them joining trade unions appears not to be regarded as at all abnormal. As we noted in our discussion of 'social closure' in Chapter 1 'collectivist' and 'individualist' strategies may coexist with their appropriateness depending on the issue. White-collar workers may turn to trade unionism once 'individual' or other tactics fail, and few are faced with a straight choice between union and employer but adopt twin loyalties. Similarly many professional employees see no contradiction in belonging to both a professional association and a trade union. K. Roberts et al.'s evidence also sustains Bain et al.'s conclusions that 'the aims of both white and blue-collar trade unionists appear to embrace a similar mixture of individualism and collectivism'.[56] Their research reveals that, if anything, more blue-collar non-members than white-collar non-members objected to trade unions 'on principle', and among white-collar non-members 'there was relatively widespread indifference to the entire subject – the issue of joining has simply never arisen'.[57] As they remark, 'this hardly suggests that white-collar workers are especially opposed on ideological grounds to the type of representation that trade unions offer'. We have already noted, too, the Parrys' argument that professional associations are formed to attain collective social mobility. Thus, this typical organisation of the established middle class is not distinguished from trade unions by a different value structure – individualism as opposed to collectivism – but by the former's efforts in seeking a higher position in the social hierarchy for all its members.

In the light of these objections to the claim that differences in levels of unionisation stem from stratification factors, George Bain, in *The Growth of White Collar Unionism*, emphasises three major variables especially crucial in the development of middle-class unionism: employment concentration, employer recognition and governmental action. Bain's data, like Lockwood's, indicate a fairly strong association between concentration and unionisation, which he suggests follows from the adoption of standardised, impersonal rules and regulations. This reduces manager – employee interaction, and with an individual's wages and working conditions little affected by special 'personal' circumstances, sensitises white-collar employees to their collective interests. Secondly, we have seen that non-manual union density is highest in the public sector and this emphasises the importance of employer recognition for levels of unionisation, for employees have generally been encouraged by the public authorities to join trade unions. Employer recognition of unions removes a number of fairly obvious barriers to membership for many non-manual employees. Most importantly, there is less chance of offending one's employer and jeopardising career prospects by joining. However, Bain's point that employer recognition will advance levels of unionism because non-manual workers identify with management is, as May observes, not fully supported by K. Roberts et al.'s investigations, which indicate that routine white-collar workers at least tend not to identify with management. Moreover, employer recognition is often less than enthusiastically conceded, and in some cases 'partial' recognition may be a strategy for reducing possible union influence by, for example, refusing to extend full negotiating rights. Employers may insist, too, that unions make structural modifications to their organisations before they will be considered 'appropriate' representatives for white-collar employees. This may help recruitment in cases where general or manual unions have been reluctant to seek white-collar recruitment aggressively, and where such employees may have doubts that their 'special' interest would be adequately safeguarded.

The third factor emphasised by Bain – governmental steps to advance unionism – has been of increasing importance in the last fifteen to twenty years. This period has been characterised by various pieces of legislation, such as the Trade Union and Industrial Relations Act 1974 and the Employment Protection Act 1975, that considerably extend and protect trade union rights. Also, bodies such as the Commission on Industrial Relations (1970) and the Advisory, Conciliation and Arbitration Service (1975) have seen their roles as 'to encourage, promote and uphold collective bargaining'. The extension of the principle of the closed shop, however, may not have had as much effect on levels of non-manual as on manual unionism. In K. Roberts et al.'s survey far fewer non-manual employees gave the existence of the closed shop as their main reason for joining a union than manual workers (one-fifth compared with nearly a half), and May notes that while 'the civil service unions have been offered a form of closed shop, it is hedged around with so many escape clauses that the unions concerned consider that they have been offered very little'.[58]

A number of writers have suggested that trade unionism is a reflection of class consciousness: Blackburn, for example, implies that recognition by employees of their common interests is a feature of class solidarity, while Lockwood goes further in suggesting that, in the case of clerical workers, at least, it involves the additional recognition that their common interests are not fundamentally dissimilar in type from those underlying the concerted actions of manual workers. But it is not clear why middle-class unionism should indicate identification with the working class; if unionism does indicate class consciousness (and, as Bain et al. observe, neither Blackburn nor Lockwood explicitly indicate the set of beliefs constituting 'class consciousness') why should it not indicate a form of middle-class consciousness? The technicians in B. Roberts et al.'s study certainly appeared to be joining trade unions with the aim of preserving their separate status and material interests, and the actions of white-collar unions more generally seek to defend or improve differentials with manual workers.[59]

This brings us to the question of 'union character' and the proposition that non-manual unions pursue different objectives to manual organisations and 'behave' less militantly and more 'economistically'. If such a distinction exists, it hardly runs deep. Reviewing the evidence in 1973, Bain et al. conclude that both non-manual and manual unions differ little in the extent to which they are prepared to take up issues removed from their members' specific interests, while participation in strikes and other forms of militant action, as well as affiliation to other employee organisations and political parties, is not the sole prerogative of manual unions. In examining the period of high union militancy during the Conservative administration of 1970–4, May notes that whereas a number of middle-class unions did not welcome industrial action against the Industrial Relations Bill, two (ASTMS, NUBE), came close to opposing the TUC policy of non-registration, and the white-collar Technical, Administrative and Supervisory Section (TASS) of the Amalgamated Union of Engineering Workers (AUEW) strongly supported industrial action against the measures. In 1973 the Civil and Public Services Association emerged as one of the most strident opponents of the government's statutory incomes policy and was openly contemptuous of the more conciliatory TUC position.

In conclusion, it would appear that non-manual and manual trade unions adopt remarkably similar tactics in the pursuit of their claims; certainly 'professional' employees such as teacher and civil servants have few qualms about possible loss of 'status' incurred by strikes or other forms of industrial action. Such attitudes are likely to be reinforced if, as seems likely, the government begins to treat them as though they were no different to manual employees and exacts a fuller penalty for militancy. In January 1979, for example, in the face of a strike threat from the nine civil service unions, the government threatened civil servants that they would have their pay cut, their sick leave entitlement reduced, and requests for holidays refused. Furthermore, it warned that 'unauthorised absence' does not reckon or qualify for superannuation, or count for increments, annual leave, probation or seniority'.[60] Yet it would be misleading to suppose that because white-collar methods are similar to those of manual unions this implies a convergence of identity. As May notes, the tactics may be similar, but their purpose 'is precisely to assert their differences'.[61] Non-manual militancy is less an indication of emerging 'worker' consciousness than recognition of separate class interests.

5

FAMILY AND EDUCATION

In previous chapters, especially in Chapter 2, we raised the question of differing value orientations between working-class and middle-class adults and pointed to the growing, if not completed, blurring of these traditional distinctions. We noted, too, that whereas the classical late Victorian and Edwardian age of bourgeois culture is over, its imprint remains in popular conceptions of the middle class, particularly in claims that the old middle-class virtues remain as a source of stabilisation in an increasingly turbulent age. The importance of culture in the rapprochment between aspiring manufacturing and commercial élites on the one hand, and an older feudal and landed class on the other was also highlighted, especially its fusion around notions of 'gentlemanliness' and civility and its possible effect in damping entrepreneurial zeal. This reliance by the middle class on traditional forms of authority in securing the stability, order and predictability which are necessary prerequisites for capital accumulation resulted in the new parvenus postponing claims for political power in exchange for the right to make money. Despite the apparent decomposition of traditional authority, in part at least the result of the success of capitalist consumerism and its demand for individual gratification, its persistence over the ages requires explanation. In this chapter we examine in more detail the crucial socialisation agencies of family and education and the part they have played in the maintenance and change of middle-class values.

One of the main points at issue will be whether it is now possible to characterise a distinctive middle-class family life, for much writing on the modern family regards it as characterised by a sense of crisis and change which is clearly connected to diversity in middle-class values. We have discussed both the occupational diversity and normative heterogeneity of the middle-class, and this is reflected in differences in family practices. Usually it is the highly educated members of the middle class who are involved in experiments which challenge the family as a traditional institution. It is these who are involved in 'alternative life styles',[1] 'dual-career families'[2] and other departures from what has come to be considered normal family life. However, sections of what we have referred to as the 'old' middle class, such as shopkeepers, tradesmen and members of the older professions, such as the clergy, are the most vehement defenders of the traditional family.[3]

In their efforts to understand the nature of the modern family, sociologists have taken a renewed interest in its history. The conventional sociological wisdom used to be that the pre-industrial family had an extended structure which maintained strong relationships between kin outside the conjugal family. The view that this type of family gave way under the impact of industrialisation to the predominance of the nuclear family type, consisting of mother, father and children, is now felt to be inadequate. Not only did Young and Willmott find that relationships outside the nuclear family have continuing contemporary importance,[4] but the presence of extensive networks in pre-industrial England has also been shown to be highly questionable.[5]

Recent historical work on the family has suggested that the modern family is unprecedented in its child-centredness and by its characteristically privatised, self-enclosed nature. The family is now pre-eminently the sphere of personal satisfaction where modern man escapes an impersonal world. Furthermore, the emergence of these distinctive features has been linked to the rise of the middle class itself. Aries's work has been seminal in this field. He maintains that the whole idea of 'childhood' as it is now commonly understood in western societies evolved with the modern family. In medieval society the child was regarded as a little adult, who, after a brief period of 'coddling', was expected to join 'the movement of collective life' that 'carried along in a single current all ages and all classes'. The family had its place, 'it fulfilled a function, it ensured the transmission of life, property and name, but it did not penetrate into human sensibilities'.[6]

With the rise of the middle classes a new pattern emerged and work and home life became more and more separate. This process started among merchants and the early professions, and spread with industrialisation. The home became the distinctive place of leisure and personal life. By subtle shifts through the sixteenth and seventeenth centuries the family became more self-enclosed until it was 'cut off from the world and opposed to society the isolated group of parents and children'.[7] 'Childhood' now became an extended period of social learning and the idea was born that the 'child is father to the man' and that childhood experience determines adult personality and behaviour. As we shall see the needs of middle-class parents at this time gave an enormous impetus to the development of specialist educational institutions.

Other historians and sociologists have followed the broad drift of Aries's thesis. As Harris notes, the modern family can now be seen as one feature of that emerging social form of which industrialisation and the middle class were key elements.[8] Shorter observes that the modern family has three crucial characteristics which distinguish it from its predecessors. First, the conjugal bond is based on a 'romantic' conception of the relationship between husband and wife; this stresses emotional attachment and self fulfilment over economic and pragmatic considerations. Second, children assume prime importance; the family becomes child-centred. Third, the family becomes relatively isolated from the wider society.[9] Shorter, however, tends to neglect underlying social and economic factors, for the emergence of the modern family form is linked to the developing individualism and economic activity of the middle class. Poster, for instance, argues that 'the modern family arose among the bourgeoisie in Europe around 1750, later in some places, earlier in others'.[10]

Young and Willmott writing specifically of the English family, also draw a historical connection between the modern family and the middle class. They maintain that the modern 'symmetrical family', so called because of the emphasis on an equal relationship between husband and wife, began in the Victorian middle class and percolated down through the rest of society as living standards, housing and education improved. The movement for women's rights, the first use of modern contraceptive techniques and the notion of marriage as a partnership are all associated with this period and have served to delineate the contours of modern family life. They also note a tendency for the family to become a self-enclosed enclave for purely personal satisfaction. 'As the disadvantages of the new industrial and impersonal society have become more pronounced, so has the family become more prized for its power to counteract them.'[11]

These various formulations all suggest an intimate historical link between the form of the contemporary family and the middle class, for it took shape when the property-owning and professional middle classes were the driving force behind industrial growth. These groups have been joined by new elements, referred to in earlier chapters, notably the salaried, managerial and 'service' classes, and as we proceed to examine some of the recent research into middle-class kinship and family life, the complex relation between 'traditional' and 'new' elements in middle-class families will become clearer.

The middle-class family in contemporary Britain

One important feature of research into middle-class families has been the attempt to establish the relationship between middle-class occupations and careers on the one hand and family and social networks on the other. Geographical mobility in particular has been recognised as an important factor in many middle-class occupations for, as we noted in Chapter 3, a successful career in many national and international organisations may well necessitate frequent movement. Many members of the middle class have benefited from the expansion of managerial and administrative posts and have been upwardly mobile socially, and as the Nuffield Surveys referred to in Chapter 1 indicate, social and geographical mobility can obviously have a profound effect on family life.

An early attempt to conceptualise these problems was made by Watson.[12] He distinguishes between 'burghers' and 'spiralists' as distinct elements in the middle class. 'Burghers' are locally based and property-owning individuals who commonly have extensive networks in their neighbourhood. 'Spiralists' are drawn from the salaried, geographically mobile middle class and tend to be relatively cut off both from ties of kinship and from the local community. The term derives from the image of the organisational middle-class career involving spatial mobility and movement upwards in status; hence metaphorically describing a spiral. If a 'spiralist' becomes blocked in his career, then local ties may reassert themselves. Watson is more interested in the relationship between the middle class and the community than in the effect on the family and, unfortunately, he does not distinguish between 'spiralists' from different class backgrounds. Furthermore, a second study of Banbury suggests that geographically mobile individuals who work for organisations which require local knowledge, such as bank managers, local civil servants and clergymen, have wide social networks in spite of being immigrants to the area. Stacey et al. argue that 'the place of origin, personal orientation and interest all interact to determine the extent to which businessmen are involved in local affairs. It is no simple matter of natives and immigrants nor of burgesses and spiralists.'[13]

The Banbury re-study found that kinship ties outside the nuclear family continued in all classes, both personal relationships and the flow of economic aid and services, from parents to children during the former's child-rearing phase and from children to parents during the latter's old age. The flow of aid was, however, greater in middle-class families, and operated over longer distances. Rosser and Harris also note that middle-class families sustain their kinship ties over longer distances, although they claim that the basic pattern of kinship is similar across all classes.[14] As we shall see, this claim is challenged by other studies of middle-class kinship, particularly those investigating individuals from working class backgrounds.

Middle-class families and their networks

Kinship networks are extremely important for middle-class families. They provide flows of economic aid, emotional support and a host of minor services. This is most likely to be the case where family-held property is substantial. Newby et al. found that among Norfolk farmers family inheritance of land led to very strong family ties. Most of the farmers in their sample were themselves the sons of farmers and their social networks were overwhelmingly rural and middle class.[15] Middle-class occupations, however, are these days more typically managerial and professional, and here amounts of family property are insignificant and family ties altogether looser. Firth and his colleagues report, in contrast to Newby et al.'s findings, that in their study of professional families in North London substantial aid, such as large sums of money, although by no means absent, was relatively infrequent. 'Petty services, letters, visiting, runs out in the car were,' they observe, 'that which loomed large in the mental ledger of services which nearly every person seems to keep as a measure of specific kin relationships.'[16] They suggest that British middle-class kinship is characterised by a lack of formal rules and firm structures. Although children are not directly taught about their kinship system many people had indirectly acquired a great deal of knowledge and were surprised to see the extensive genealogies which the researchers had been able to compile from their recollections. Kinship responsibilities, though acknowledged, were also the object of ambivalent feelings. In the words of one respondent, 'relatives are the only people you can dislike and still be on good terms with'. Personal judgements are crucial in determining the extent of these obligations and a close relationship might exist, for example, with one cousin but not with others. Even relationships between brothers and sisters are highly variable and decided by personal considerations.

Kinship ties are seen as different from friendship ties but they do take some of their characteristics from them. The families recognised geographical mobility as an occupational necessity and proximity was not seen as crucial for the relationship to be 'close'. Letters, visits and, most importantly, telephone calls enabled relationships to be maintained over long distances and over substantial periods of time. Connections with the family are associated with the life cycle, being typically important for young children, diminishing through adolescence and early adulthood, but becoming progressively more important after marriage and the birth of grandchildren. Relationships between parents and children, although close, are also highly realistic, for 'there is apt to be a very cool, rationalistic appreciation of the parents' virtues and faults and an almost clinical attitude at times towards responsibilities for parents'.[17] A strong expectation exists that the marriage bond takes precedence over the relationship with parents and Firth et al. found no sign of the mum-complex which anchored the daughter to her family of origin revealed in some studies of working class kinship.[18] By retirement middle-class families are more likely to be independent than those of the working class, and retired middle-class couples live greater distances from their children and are more likely to move to a special retirement area, normally at the seaside. There is, however, a tendency to move back nearer children in late old age when infirmity occurs.[19]

Firth's study does not distinguish between families from middle class origins and those who had been socially mobile. In his study of 120 families on two middle-class housing estates in South Wales, Bell was able to investigate more fully the relationship between social and geographical mobility. He distinguishes socially mobile families who, without exception, had also been geographically mobile; geographically mobile families from middle-class families of origin; and local middle-class families who had not been either geographically or socially mobile. The latter tended to work in smaller firms with fewer branches, possessing fewer formal qualifications than their geographically mobile counterparts and likely to be working with relatives in a family firm or else to have owed their job in some other way to kin connections. The social networks of these locals were very different from those of the non-locals; 80 per cent of locals had their 'best friend' living within twenty-five miles, whilst 50 per cent of non-locals reported theirs to be over a hundred miles away. The non-locals were therefore much more dependent on neighbours for those everyday services like baby-sitting and mutual practical help that the locals received from relatives. Local and non-local families constituted distinct 'gossip cells' and had different visiting patterns. Mutual visiting on the estates was much more frequent between non-local families. In fact local families tended to be highly suspicious of neighbours who tried to be too friendly, whereas almost any approach was welcomed by non-locals anxious to make contacts.[20]

Bell found that neighbourhood services like baby-sitting and mutual help in laying lawns and drives were commonly exchanged, particularly between non-locals. No substantial goods and services were involved, however, and neighbours had in no way replaced family relationships. Whereas family networks in the local community were related to geographical mobility, social mobility was the key factor in kin relationships, although regardless of geographical mobility, kinship ties were more important for the families of middle-class origin than they were for the socially mobile one. As in Firth's study, personal contact might be infrequent but close relationships were maintained by letter, telephone and periodic visits. There were substantial flows of aid from parental family to the children's family. This tended to be financial aid in matters like house purchase and help with the needs of grandchildren for items like clothes and bicycles. The crucial relationship in these transactions was that between father/father-in-law and son/son-in-law. Such aid was never demanded outright, for blatant requests clash with deep-seated middle-class notions of independence and standing on one's own feet. Wants and difficulties are made known, offers are then made and can be accepted. The rules are subtle. Children must not ask outright or see the help as an obligation of their parents, and parents must not ask too much in return. One man described how he had outlined his prospects to his father-in-law, mentioning that if he could raise £10,000 he could buy himself a partnership. He was well aware that he could not ask for the money but he was equally well aware that his father-in-law would consider the matter. In the end the money was offered and accepted. Bell suggests elsewhere that this kind of aid can make a significant difference to the standards of living of socially mobile and non-mobile families where the husband is at the same point in his career. He adds that this may account for the slight tendency to greater family size amongst those sections of the middle class in receipt of such aid.[21]

The socially mobile families in Bell's study tended to have fewer contacts with relatives than the locals. If any aid flowed at all it tended to be back to parents. Many families reported that contacts with relatives were difficult to maintain. Bell illustrates these differences by contrasting involvements in family rituals; whilst one local middle class family entertained seventy-two guests, mainly relatives, at their christening, a geographically and socially mobile family, who held a christening in the same month, entertained seven guests, none of whom were related.

Kinship networks, then, still seem to play a significant role in the lives of middle-class families. They provide flows of aid and support despite geographical mobility. Indeed, a certain degree of geographical mobility is expected and accepted as an integral part of many middle-class careers. If 'getting on' also means 'getting away', then the means of maintaining close relationships are readily available. This is less true of those who have also been socially mobile. In the next sections we examine how these factors influence internal family relationships, in particular the relationship between husband and wife.

Personal life and the conjugal bond

As we have seen, the notion of a pragmatic economic relationship between husband and wife, and its replacement by a more romantic personal conception stressing self-fulfilment, is one of the hallmarks of writings on the development of the modern family. Indeed, the greater cultural emphasis on 'self-expression' and 'self-actualisation' is seen by many as a crucial feature of contemporary industrial society and the alienating, impersonal world of work is usually distinguished from the personal, expressive worlds of leisure and the family. Daniel Bell, for example, has gone so far as to suggest that the 'bourgeois world view', or 'protestant ethic', stressing duty and responsibility, has declined to the extent that 'self-actualisation' is now the 'axial principle' of modern Western culture. This stands in contradiction to the hierarchical and bureaucratic 'techno-economic structure' governed by the 'axial principle' of rationality.[22]

These views overestimate the universality of these changes and underestimate their class basis, for these values are still largely confined to certain sections of the middle class. Research into the membership of personal growth groups, for example, shows that they predominantly attract those in the caring professions and education.[23] This seems to indicate an extension of the concerns of work rather than an opposition to it. The evidence available on the membership of communes also tends to support this conclusion, for their memberships are usually comprised of the young middle class.[24] Abrams and McCulloch observe that, 'communes are made by teachers, psychologists and students, by unattached mothers, potters, silversmiths and architects; by, as one commune member put it, the 'sons and daughters of the middle class'.[25] While personal and expressive values are probably becoming increasingly widespread it would be mistaken to see them as dominant across all sections of society or, indeed, even across the middle class as a whole. Furthermore, the values embodied in communes are only anti-family in a very restricted sense, for they may be regarded as representing the logical extension of the values of self-expression that the family has come to serve for many people, although in most families it is the husband and wife relationship that is valued as the emotional core of a fulfilling family life.

The pioneering work in British sociology on the husband and wife relationship is Bott's *Family and Social Network*. She distinguishes between couples who have 'joint conjugal roles' (i.e., live highly interdependent lives, share household tasks, take joint decisions and have a common social life), with those who have 'segregated conjugal roles' (i.e., are highly independent of each other, operate in distinct social networks and have a strict division of labour within the home). She argues that the key factor in the nature of conjugal role relationships is the connectedness of the family's social network. Where this is tight and overlapping the relationship tends to be segregated; in effect, there is a woman's world and a man's world in the local community. Loose-knit networks increase the likelihood that couples will develop joint conjugal roles, for 'the degree of segregation in the role relationship of husband and wife varies directly with the connectedness of the family's network'.[26]

Bott's work emphasises the nature of the social network but leaves social class and occupational factors relatively unexplored. We have already noted the extent to which middle-class families accept geographical mobility as normal and the influence of this variable in determining joint conjugal roles may be considerable. Young and Willmott have extended Bott's analysis, and

Table 22 shows their data on the distribution of tasks within the home in the different social classes. While noting the importance of social networks, they include the effects of the feminist movement, the availability of contraception, miniaturised domestic technology, and educational and occupational opportunities for women among other contributing factors in the emergence of 'symmetrical' role relationships. The availability of these resources is itself largely determined by social stratification and they are far more likely to be available to middle-class women. In any case Young and Willmott undoubtedly overestimate the symmetry of contemporary conjugal relationships even for the middle-class. The shifts which they report are little more than trends that have certainly not become fully established.

TABLE 22 *Occupational class and husband's help in the home*

Reported help to wife at least once a week	**Professional and managerial**	**Clerical**	**Skilled**	**Semi-skilled and unskilled**	**All**
None	14%	13%	14%	24%	15%
Washing up only	16%	7%	13%	12%	13%
Other tasks (cleaning, cooking, child care etc), with or without washing up	70%	80%	73%	64%	72%
Total	100%	100%	100%	100%	100%
Number	171	70	236	107	585

Source: M.Young and P. Willmott, *The Symmetrical Family*, p. 95 (adapted).

Particular attention was paid in Young and Willmott's study to a sample of managing directors, as it was felt that they might prove good indicators of future trends. They discovered, however, a tentative swing back to asymmetrical roles. The pressures towards occupational success are such that the whole family has to be mobilised in support of the husband's career and the wife is very much the junior partner. As one director stated, 'the whole of my career has been based on partnership rather than togetherness. My whole family is geared to this. I let my wife know where I am going.'[27]

This may indicate less of a swing away from symmetrical conjugal roles than an illustration of the extent to which family relationships are in a large number of respects strongly influenced by position in the labour market. We should also recognise that people may subscribe to different sets of values, switching between them at appropriate moments. Edgell suggests that work values and leisure values are in fundamental conflict for the spiralist, although he is likely to subscribe to both.[28] He sees occupational success as the key variable, for one response to a 'blocked' career is to re-emphasise the importance of family and leisure.

The Pahls, as we noted in Chapter 3, have charted the cross-pressures of home and work in their study of managers and their wives and point to the existence of competing value systems. The paradox at the heart of the lives of the couples in their study was that husbands threw themselves into work in a manner that was often detrimental to family life, but the family happiness was the very thing for which they were working so hard. It was 'all for the wife and the children'. The wives were painfully aware that a less dedicated and whole-hearted approach to work by their husbands would be very much to the family's benefit.

The wives invariably had been involved in career decisions and were recognised as having the right of veto, although this was rarely used. Younger wives tended to mind moving less than older ones, but class background was found to be the crucial factor. Once a wife from a working-class family of origin had moved away she seemed happy to move again. They were generally more contented with the role of junior partner and were more home-centred than their middle-class counterparts. Many had experienced hardships as children and put a premium on their current life styles. They also lacked the confidence and feeling of being secure socially that would have enabled them to become involved in the communities to which they moved. The wives from middle-class backgrounds were much more likely to be involved in the local church, voluntary organisations and have some employment in the area. This was particularly so if they themselves had experienced higher education.

The Pahls note that friendships and social networks in these circumstances are far more important for the women. Where a man's identity derives from his work role his family is seen merely in terms of support. For the woman, if her family role is not to be the sum total of what she is as a person, involvement in networks outside the family is essential. However, the Pahls detect signs of resistance and opposition to the demands made by firms on their managers, particularly in the attitudes of educated wives from middle class backgrounds. They suggest that future managers, educated in the universities and more sensitive to issues like personal liberation and feminism, may be even more resistant in the 1980s.[29] Similarly, the Rapaports propose that one of the major advantages of 'dual-career' families is that high levels of affluence can be achieved without either partner being totally committed to their career. In effect both are 'less than fully engaged in the rat race'.[30] Dual-career wives come from higher social class backgrounds and tend to have had mothers who had occupations or who were perceived as being unhappy and frustrated as housewives. The only distinguishing feature of the husbands was a tendency for them to have had a warm, close relationship with their mothers, and the Rapaports suggest that this lays the foundation for an empathic and responsive attitude to the needs and aspirations of their wives.

There are strains of course. The dual-career family is distinctly overloaded. As one respondent put it, 'there is very little play in the system', and the stress falls disproportionately on the wife. There is little evidence in any of the families that the men were more involved in traditional female domestic labour 'beyond what males do generally to help out even in conventional families'. The reapportioning of household labour appears a relatively simple matter, but in fact the Rapaports were surprised at just how 'touchy' was the subject; 'some of the dual-career couples studied felt that this was an issue that would take at least another generation to be solved, and some of them concentrated on teaching their children to share domestic labour in a non-stereotyped way'. Another area of strain concerns 'normative dilemmas' and again it is the wife who is the most vulnerable. It is she who breaks the rules in terms of common beliefs about the sexual division of labour. Typical of the sanctioning comments made by neighbours and friends were remarks like,

'Oh, well, I suppose you won't mind when the baby doesn't recognise its mother.' Such tensions spilt over into 'social network' dilemmas and relationships with the wives of husband's colleagues who were not themselves pursuing careers could be extremely difficult. In spite of the problems, the Rapaports report that on balance the gains outweigh the losses. There was no evidence of disturbance among the children of these couples; on the contrary, the Rapaports thought them unusually resourceful and independent. The largest gains, however, were undoubtedly the self-realisation and fulfilment achieved by the female partner. The strains highlighted by these studies have not given rise to any marked instability in middle-class marriages, at least as measured by divorce rates. Unskilled manual workers are the most divorce prone group but after them come upper-working class and lower non-manual workers.[31]

Children in the middle-class family

Child-centredness, as we have seen, is one of the distinctive characteristics of the middle-class family, and as we noted in Chapter 1 when discussing Parkin's reference to the increasing importance of 'credentialism' or the gaining of educational qualifications in attaining access to scarce resources, including well-paid employment, the passing on of educational opportunities and attitudes has become essential for a successful middle-class career. It is this stress on providing the maximum support for each child that is held to explain the tendency for smaller families in the middle class. Cartwright's research into the way families take decisions about size supports the view that financial considerations are especially important. Middle-class families have a small number of children in order that the ones they do have may receive all the resources at the family's disposal, although there is a tendency for upper-middle-class families to contain more children.[32]

Middle-class children are undoubtedly more likely to succeed in the educational sphere. Research at all stages shows their educational attainments to be superior to those of their working-class peers, and this becomes more marked when we look at the higher levels of the educational system as around 71 per cent of undergraduates come from middle-class families.[33] This continues the trend detected by Douglas et al. at the lower levels, as 'over half the lower manual working class pupils of high ability have left school before they are sixteen and a half years old'.[34] Exactly how this superiority is to be explained is the subject of much acrimonious debate. It is suggested that educational institutions are essentially middle class and that their children are favoured within schools. Others have maintained that methods of socialisation in middle class homes are somehow superior and, coupled with the existence of abundant material resources, accounts for the fact that middle class children develop intellectual and social skills which enable them to perform well in schools.

Other research into the relationship between educational attainment and socialisation has tended to stress the importance of achievement motivation. The idea that society is a ladder which is there to be climbed is a familiar one to middle-class children; they are, moreover, likely to have learned that the rewards which life offers are consistently related to their own efforts.[35] Research by the Newsons, for example, has shown that middle-class parents are more likely to use rewards as incentives and use physical punishment only rarely, in comparison with working-class parents, with the result that middle-class children grow up viewing the world as a place to be mastered through their own activities.[36]

The Newsons' research is the most comprehensive so far available on class differences in socialisation. On a number of measures they show middle-class mothers to be more 'child-centred', including whether or not the child is ever apologised to, whether his artistic efforts are displayed, and whether the child is given any choice in the matter of meals, clothes, or activities. In other words they indicate the level of parental response to the child's individual characteristics, how far the child's own activities initiate events, and the extent to which they are responded to and taken seriously by parents. One of their most important findings related to the respective notions of 'independence' held by working-class and middle-class parents. 'Independence' for working-class parents means being able to survive in the world of other children without running for help, and their children play unsupervised over wide areas, with parents reluctant to arbitrate in disputes between children. They are encouraged instead to stand up for themselves and fight their own battles. For middle-class parents, 'independence' means being able to handle the adult world; and their children are much more closely supervised and rarely play outside their own street. They are much more likely, however, to stay overnight with friends and to undertake long journeys by public transport.

Evidence on child-rearing suggests important ways in which the childhood experience of middle-class children gives them an approach to life conducive to educational and occupational success. Some theorists would go further and say that this experience actually leads to superior intellectual development, certainly in so far as this is related to formal educational performance. One of the most controversial explanations of the superior educational performance of the middle-class child in comparison to working-class children has been put forward by Bernstein. He argues that the middle-class child is not simply better motivated through having acquired a set of values appropriate to educational success, but that his very use of language provides an educational advantage. The middle-class child, he claims, learns two distinct language 'codes'. There is a 'private code', also available to working-class children, which is used with family and friends. This is 'restricted', informal and particularistic in that it is tied to the concrete situations in which it is used. It is full of 'catch phrases' and has a simple sentence structure. Often sentences do not need to be finished. Everyone knows what is being said. Frequent use of phrases such as 'Oh, you know' set up 'sympathetic circularity' and meanings can be left implicit because everyone is on the same wavelength.

The middle-class child also learns a 'public code'. This is 'elaborated', formal and universalistic in that it can be understood outside the context in which it is spoken because meaning is explicit and enables the child to deal with situations outside the world of family and friends. It is the language of formal organisations and, more importantly in this context, it is the language of the school. By necessity formal educational knowledge can, in Bernstein's view, only be presented in terms of the 'elaborated code'. Its most fundamental characteristic is the articulation of explicit meanings. A child whose language experience in the home includes this will be at a clear advantage in the school.[37]

Bernstein's work has been supported by studies of class differences in early language use. Wooton, for instance, contrasts the ways in which middle-class and working-class mothers speak to their children. While most of the language of the working-class mothers studied had to do with control and took the form of commands directed at the child, middle-class mothers used less control speech and employed language much more to extend the child's play. This involved getting the child to describe and elaborate activities through speech, a strategy self-consciously adopted by the mothers in order to develop the child's verbal skills, for their conception of the child's development included the idea of themselves as manipulators of its environment. Working-class mothers, whilst concerned with the behaviour of their children, did not see themselves as affecting intellectual development: a child was either bright, or he was not.[38] Bernstein and Young report similar class differences in the preference for toys. Middle-class mothers had strong ideas about what they looked for in toys but for working-class mothers, as long as the child actually had toys, it did not matter what they were. Toys, quite simply, were not important.[39]

Ford, Young and Box maintain that the socialisation of middle-class children enables them to operate over a wide variety of social situations. In their terminology they have greater 'functional autonomy'. Whereas working-class children receive culture and learn to play roles, the middle-class child learns to interpret culture and to play at roles.[40] This point has been pursued by Witkin who suggests that the roles which middle-class children play are highly 'articulated', fitting coherently together in the child's experience. In school, for instance, they know exactly how to act and have definite expectations about what they want to receive from it. In the case of an 'expressive' English lesson, Witkin found them more critical than their working-class peers because this kind of lesson violated those expectations.[41]

In Bernstein's later work, the emergence of more child-centred, activity-based, pedagogic techniques in primary education is connected to the more personalised values found among sections of the new middle classes, especially 'the expanding major and minor professions concerned with the servicing of persons'.[42] This represents a significant departure from the traditional middle-class view that educational knowledge is a set of well-defined ideas to be learned and accepted. The newer approach emphasises the child as an active learner and entails the weakening of the boundaries between subjects as children are encouraged to make their own connections. The 'new mathematics', with its stress on the child's understanding of numbers and consequent de-emphasis of mechanical techniques, like rote learning of the multiplication tables, serves as a good example of the new approach. Bernstein's work has received serious criticism for both underestimating the power and vitality of working class language and overestimating the significance of the 'elaborated code' in the school.[43] Much of this criticism, however, is based on the mistaken assumption that Bernstein is denigrating working-class culture and providing educationalists with a rationale for the relative failure of working class children, but Bernstein successfully repudiates this in his own critique of the notion of 'compensatory education'.[44]

Another related area, which is almost as controversial, concerns the relative absence of middle-class children from official delinquency statistics. Self-report studies, which investigate the crimes that people will admit to, certainly show a diminution of these differences although they do not disappear completely. Box and Ford go so far as to argue that the whole of class differences in official criminal statistics can be explained in terms of the differential action of law enforcement agencies and class-biased definitions of crime.[45] Other criminologists violently disagree.[46] There can be little doubt, however, that the middle-class child's ability to negotiate formal situations and present himself in a favourable light makes his confrontations with social control agents, be they teachers, policemen or magistrates, less likely to end in the application of formal sanctions.

The picture that emerges of the child in the middle-class family is fairly consistent. The home provides material, intellectual and motivational resources, deliberately provided by parents to further the development of the child, which grows up with a belief in its own potency, a positive attitude towards school and the expectation of educational and occupational success.

Education and the middle class

Modern education, like the contemporary family, has its roots in the historical emergence of the middle class. The pattern of education in pre-industrial England was commonly that of apprenticeship, although that term had a much wider meaning than its modern equivalent.[47] Children from all classes would be sent to other houses to serve and to learn a trade or set of skills through practical experience. The earliest educational institutions were ecclesiastical, training monks and teaching Latin. But in the commercial and merchant classes the need for numeracy and literacy led to a demand for separate and practical schooling, although most schools developed from religious institutions. From its beginnings the moral and academic components of British education have been inextricably linked.

The exact significance of education in contemporary societies is a matter of considerable debate. Some educational theorists follow Althusser in seeing education as part of the 'ideological state apparatus' which functions primarily to reproduce the 'relations of production' in capitalist societies; education in this view has taken over from the Church as the primary means of state control and educational values are regarded as mere ideologies which disguise the real nature of the educational system.[48] Others, following Habermas, have argued that education, particularly at the higher levels, can be a forum for critical 'rational discourse', an area where criticism can be developed from which social change can emanate.[49] Student radicalism is often interpreted in this vein. K. Roberts et al. note, for example, that 'anyone wishing to find support for ideologies to the left of Labour, Gay Lib, or equality between rich and poor nations, is better advised to visit a university than a trade union branch meeting'.[50] The emergence of student radicalism is explained in terms of the increase in higher education and a corresponding expansion of the radical intelligentsia.[51] Parkin's study of young CND supporters found the majority to come from liberal, intellectual backgrounds and far from rebelling against parents they were in fact carrying on family traditions.[52] American research similarly has shown that many campus radicals have parents sympathetic to their values and reveals the extent to which the public overestimated levels of radicalism amongst young people in the 1960s.[53] Student radicalism should properly be viewed as the continuation of a tradition within the intellectual middle class and not as a necessary consequence of higher education, and despite the publicity, radicals remain a small minority in the student body. This was so even at the height of radical student activity. The sit-in at the London School of Economics in 1967 involved only 17 per cent of students,[54] while the strongest political organisation on American campuses at that time was Young America for Freedom, a right-wing Goldwater group.

The middle class continues to benefit disproportionately from the educational system in spite of reforms, such as the introduction of comprehensive schools, which were intended as egalitarian measures. This is not, of course, to deny that the education system provides an extremely important avenue for working-class mobility. We noted in Chapter 1 that Goldthorpe and his colleagues suggest that most social mobility is into the expanding non-manual and managerial sector. However, rates of *relative* class immobility persist, ensuring that the grip of the established middle class is not weakened and enabling them to ensure that their own children are not downwardly mobile.[55]

Social mobility need not weaken class inequality, as it may be regarded as a crucial aspect of the reproduction of class relations. Bordieu writes that, 'the controlled mobility of a limited category of individuals, carefully selected and modified by and for individual ascent is not incompatible with the permanence of structures . . . it is even capable of contributing to social stability in the only way conceivable in societies based upon democratic ideals'.[56] In his influential work on the relationship between education and social mobility in Britain and the United States, Turner suggests that differences in the educational systems of the two countries may be characterised in terms of a distinction between 'sponsored' and 'contest' mobility. Writing specifically of selective secondary schooling, he contrasts the British method of early selection leading to separate kinds of education with American 'contest' mobility where all children are kept in the same 'race' until 'selection' at the end. In Britain, talented children are selected and then undergo anticipatory socialisation into the middle class. Grammar school education was not simply about the teaching of an academic curriculum, but more importantly it was concerned with the dissemination of middle-class values, for 'under sponsored mobility schooling is valued for its cultivation of élite culture'.[57]

Each system has its drawbacks. Contest mobility creates problems of 'hotting up' and 'cooling out'; children must be motivated for the race but towards the end of it most of them have to be reconciled to failure. American children, Turner claims, are far less realistic about their capabilities than their British counterparts because of the pressures put on them to succeed. Sponsored mobility may deny opportunity to late developers and those talented children who, for one reason or another, are overlooked at the point of selection, while the conflicting loyalties and pressures on the working-class grammar school child and problems of adjustment are common themes in both educational and imaginative literature.[58] The impact of comprehensive schooling on this pattern is still not clear. It is obvious, however, that to the extent that comprehensive schools stream their intake into 'O' level, CSE and non-examination bands, as many do, they are effectively continuing a modified form of sponsored mobility. It still remains for us to establish, however, exactly how important education is for entry into middle-class occupations.

Educational attainment and occupation

The expansion of educational provision has disappointed many who thought that education could prove to be an agency for social change, for educational expansion has probably benefited the middle class more than any other group. Children from independent schools, as a result of the expansion of higher education, now have a better chance of going to university than they did before the Second World War. Although educational qualifications are now more widely available, there is little sign of an appreciable 'tightening of the bond' between educational qualifications and occupation, for 'new qualifications appear to buy the same amount of status as the old'.[59]

An important attempt to unravel the complex relationship between educational opportunity and social mobility is made by

Boudon. He argues for a two-tier model which distinguishes between 'primary' and 'secondary' effects: primary effects relate to the child's social background and basic disposition in so far as these affect his motivation and intellectual capacity; secondary effects relate to the perceived costs and benefits associated with any particular course of action. Thus, for a lower-class child a prestigious academic course may be perceived as a risk, as a 'pay-off' is by no means certain and the opportunity costs, such as forfeiting 'income', are likely to be high. Higher-class families are less likely to be deterred by these costs; indeed, not to take such a course would risk demotion for their children.[60]

On the basis of a large-scale investigation of educational careers in Britain between 1932 and 1972 Halsey and his colleagues find little to substantiate the importance of Boudon's 'secondary effects'. They report that children from the 'service class' (higher grade administrators, managers and professionals) had the best chance of selective secondary education. The longer children from other classes stayed in education, however, the greater the probability that their education would continue. The chances of a working-class child who had stayed in education to the age of seventeen then staying on until eighteen years of age, were roughly equal to those of a child from the 'service class'. The rates at which children from different classes drop out of education thus tend to converge rather than diverge, suggesting that in the 'sponsored mobility' context 'primary effects' are of much greater significance. Unfortunately their study confines itself to educational careers and does not explicitly deal with the direct relationship between education and occupation. Their general conclusion is that educational expansion in this period initially increased educational inequality by benefiting the 'service class' more than any other, but, by extrapolating into the future, they claim that further expansion will eventually reduce inequality, although this would be jeopardised by a period of educational retrenchment. Halsey and his colleagues also throw doubt on the importance of 'cultural capital' in determining educational outcomes, although it is doubtful whether the rather crude measure which they use, parental experience of secondary schooling, actually captures the complexities implied in that notion. They correctly point out, however, that the majority of pupils in grammar schools were the first generation of their families to experience selective secondary education and that 'the twentieth-century history of secondary school expansion, at least in Britain, draws attention to the accumulation and dissemination of cultural capital as much as to its preservation and concentration'.[61]

Education expansion, then, is associated with a certain amount of upward mobility. This is certainly one important reason for the fragmentary nature of the contemporary middle class. The effects have not, however, been as dramatic or as far-reaching as supporters of egalitarian education reform hoped, or their opponents feared. One reason for this is undoubtedly the continued existence of the independent sector of education which provides a privately purchased education for some members of the middle class. Thirty per cent of the Registrar General's class I and 15 per cent of class II children attend these schools.[62]

Independent schools

As we might expect the vast majority of children who attend independent schools are middle-class.[63] In Chapter 2 we showed how the famous public schools took their present form in the early nineteenth century. Gaythorne-Hardy also indicates in his history of the Public Schools that far from being schools providing education for a broad spectrum of middle-class groups, they became schools exclusively for the education of the British élite. While the school list of Eton in 1678 shows a high proportion of boys whose fathers were local tradesmen, between 1753 and 1790 these account for only 38 out of 3,000 pupils, with also a much higher number of pupils from titled families.[64]

There is clearly a 'pecking order' among independent schools. At the top are the Headmasters' Conference schools whose prestige is as substantial as their fees and who retain strong preferential links with the leading Oxford and Cambridge colleges. These schools, as we noted earlier, are still extremely influential in the education of the British élite. Out of the 339 Conservative MPs elected in 1979, 229 went to public schools, and 50 to Eton alone. They also continue to dominate the higher echelons of the civil service, while, in Kelsall's study in the early 1970's,

66 per cent of industrial directors and 70 per cent of financial directors were found to have been educated at public schools.[65]

The demise of the public schools has often been predicted but they have shown an enormous tenacity and the capacity to adapt to changing conditions. The demand for private education is high and is estimated to have risen during the 1970's. Large multinational companies, whose executives are expected to be internationally mobile, now offer education for children at prestigious public schools as part of their 'attractive remuneration packages'. As new sections of the middle classes consider private education, so the rigours and privations traditionally associated with the public schools have declined. Boarding is decreasing, a sign of the greater emphasis on personal relationships in the middle-class family, and fagging and cold baths are also disappearing. The classics-dominated curriculum has given way to a wider curriculum, and smaller classes are more the norm than in state schools.[66]

Below the top public schools are the old direct grant grammar schools, most of whom opted for independent status in 1976 and which still continue to be recognised as centres of academic excellence. Further down exists a 'second division' of independent schools that are recognised as efficient by the Department of Education, followed by a rump of around 2,250 independent schools without such recognition and about which virtually nothing is known.[67] It is likely that they are supported by lower-middle-class parents who do not trust their local state schools and who cannot afford more prestigious establishments. These fears are probably misplaced. As we will see, middle-class children are likely to do very well in state schools.

School experience and the middle-class child

As we have seen in our consideration of social mobility, education involves far more than simply the transmission of academic knowledge. There is a 'hidden curriculum' implicit in the presentation of knowledge. Values, attitudes, beliefs and a whole way of looking at the world underlie everything that happens in classrooms.[68]

Jackson and Marsden suggest that in the old grammar schools there was an essential continuity for the middle-class child between home and school experience. In their classic study of the Huddersfield area they note that local middle-class families saw the grammar schools very much as 'our schools' and 'in a host of small but telling ways the middle-class families had an educational inheritance with which to endow their children'.[69] The working-class child, however, experienced a 'culture clash' between the values and expectations of the school and those of the home, and those who succeeded in grammar schools were found to come disproportionately from families who had been downwardly mobile in the depression (the 'sunken middle class'), and from socially aspiring groups like foremen.

This notion of 'culture clash' has been more widely applied by some sociologists. School, it is argued, is a middle-class institution where middle-class values are transmitted to middle-class children and brighter working-class children, while the rest are bored, alienated and doomed to emerge with no qualifications and no real benefit. This is clearly an extreme view, but there is considerable evidence that middle-class children not only perform better educationally, they are also rated more highly by teachers on other dimensions, such as behaviour. Studies of teachers' perceptions of pupils and their effect on education found that favourably perceived children were assumed by the teachers, often erroneously, to be from middle-class families. Nash shows that children once perceived as bright, intelligent and lively by teachers, are able to negotiate interactions with teachers in such a way as to confirm this identity. Children who are less favourably perceived find it difficult to renegotiate their identities. These interactions are extremely subtle; when favourably perceived children are acting in a disorderly manner the whole class is told to quieten down, but when unfavourably perceived children are the culprits, they are sanctioned by name.[70]

Children who are similarly perceived by their teachers are likely to group together and constitute distinct subcultures in the school. Lacey, in his study of pupil subcultures in a grammar school, found that middle-class children stayed on at school longer, were placed in higher streams, and attained more qualifications. He argued that academic sifting and grading within the school led to the polarisation of pupils into two distinct subcultures, a highly pro-school subculture which valued school success, and an anti-school subculture which was vehemently opposed to everything for which the school stood. Hightown Grammar took the top 15 per cent of eleven-year-olds in the area. All arrived at school well motivated and of proven ability and most had been in the top ten of their junior school. Yet within two years the lower streams were forming an anti-school subculture, building up the reputation of being 'difficult to teach', and the headmaster was remarking that, 'of course, the 'D' boys shouldn't really be here'.[71]

Lacey's thesis is that the formation of pupil subcultures is the outcome of educational differentiation. The separation and ranking of pupils by staff inevitably means that many of them suffer a violation of the expectation they have of themselves as 'best pupils'. Drawing on American subcultural theory, Lacey suggests that such pupils reject the values of the school on which this judgement is made and embrace a set of delinquent values which are an inversion of school values. Hence activities which are highly valued by the school, like academic work, are despised, while outlawed activities, such as smoking, become highly symbolic acts of rebellion. The middle-class children in the school are less likely to be part of the anti-school subculture. The advantages they bring to school make them more likely to be in higher streams and they are more able to cope with the problems created by differentiation. A similar process of subcultural polarisation is revealed by Hargreaves's research in a secondary modern school. The class bias here is less apparent as only 6 per cent of pupils come from non-manual backgrounds and membership of the upper streams, hence the pro-school subculture, is associated with small family size and 'families orientated towards middle class values'.[72]

In his study of the participants in anti-school groups in secondary schools Willis draws attention to the continuity between working-class culture generally, particularly shop-floor attitudes, and the counter-cultures within schools. Both share a stress on group loyalties and function to carve out personal space in organisations which are viewed as oppressive and alienating. The relative weight which should be attached to internal school factors and external factors within working-class culture need not concern us here but Willis's thesis certainly suggests that the values associated with nonconformist groups within the school will be less attractive to middle-class children.[73]

Research in comprehensive schools reports no dramatic change in earlier findings. Middle-class children are placed in higher streams and may even do better than under the old grammar school system. Ford notes as a result of her intensive study of a comprehensive school that, 'at the same ability level the middle-class child stands a greater chance of placement in the 'grammar' stream of a comprehensive school than a working class child'.[74] This point is echoed by Bellaby, who states that, 'it is common to find that when comprehensive schools stream their intake they inadvertently fill the top streams with the middle-class children and the bottom with the sons and daughters of the skilled and semi-skilled workers'.[75]

Sociologists have not yet uncovered all the subtleties and nuances that underlie these processes. Sugarman suggests that social class in this context should be seen as 'a shorthand way of referring to a complex set of factors that are sometimes correlated with occupation'. His own research found that while a child's values and behaviour in school are related to his class position, they are even more closely related to his academic success in school and hence his future class position.[76] The question of how far the middle-class child's superior performance is determined by home values and motivations or simply the development of intellectual skills which make school success possible and thus lead to a personal investment in school values is still unclear. In any case, there are probably dangers in too glibly accepting the thesis that schools are straightforwardly middle-class institutions. After all, one half of teachers are themselves from working-class families.[77]

Middle-class children undoubtedly do well in school. The reasons for this are complex, but they certainly include the following: that the child's early experience and family life prepare him for school; that cognitive and intellectual skills laid down in the home prepare him for school success; and that the child's parents are both interested in and capable of intervening in his school experience in order to influence the outcome in a favourable direction. These facts may or may not make schools middle-class institutions; they certainly reflect, however, the ability of the middle classes to negotiate formal organisations of all kinds. The next section will explore this parental support more fully.

Middle class parents and the school

One of the most consistent research findings in the investigations of class differences in education is the much greater contact with and greater involvement in school and school-related activities by middle-class parents. Douglas found, for example, that in his study 32 per cent of middle-class fathers regularly had contact with school compared with only 12 per cent of manual fathers.[78] The middle-class parents in Bynner's study were also more likely to be involved in and to send their children to organisations and clubs of all kinds. Parental involvement does not indicate that the middle classes are more favourably disposed towards school; in fact, the reverse is quite probably the case, for working-class parents are generally more satisfied with the school which their child attends than middle-class parents.[79] Working-class parents usually see education as the prerogative of the school and are willing to let the staff get on with it. Middle-class parents, on the other hand, appear to place less trust in educational 'experts', are more confident of their ability to intervene effectively, and have a greater awareness of educational priorities. Both Douglas and Bynner report that middle-class parents are more likely to insist on seeing both the headmaster and the class teacher in their visits. They also visit on unscheduled occasions and not simply on those evenings set aside for parents by the schools, and are also prominent in other aspects of school life, such as parent-teacher associations.[80]

Goldthorpe and Lockwood, in their study of 'affluent workers' in Luton, note that these workers placed a high priority on the education of their children, although in comparison with a middle-class sample they were still less involved in school and had rather different educational priorities. When asked to rank school subjects in order of importance, they consistently placed 'useful' subjects like metal work and woodwork for boys, and domestic science and needlework for girls, at the top of their lists. The middle-class parents, with equal consistency, placed the emphasis on English and Mathematics.[81] In this respect, of course, the priorities of the middle-class parents mirror those of the school. Middle-class parents are quite simply 'in tune' with what goes on in school. The most important point to stress in any discussion of the relationship between the middle-class parent and education concerns their ability to manipulate successfully the symbolic meaning system of the school. In less technical language, they know which arguments count and which do not.[82]

Some revealing examples of effective and ineffective parental intervention are provided in Lacey's study. Two are particularly interesting, and follow the result of boys' having been placed in the lowest stream. Lacey contrasts the respective reactions to this of a working-class and a middle-class mother. The middle-class mother came to school and suggested that her child was an 'under-achiever' and was academically misplaced in the lowest stream, and that he had the capacity for greater attainments, needing only the impetus of top-stream boys to draw him along. Her son was duly placed in the 'express' stream. The other mother objected on the grounds that her son was a 'respectable' boy who would not fit in with the 'roughs' in the bottom stream. This fear may have entered the thinking of the middle-class mother as well, but if it did it was left unstated. The headmaster retorted that his school contained no 'roughs' and that the child had been placed in the stream to which he was academically most suited. The child stayed in the 'D' stream. This serves as a good example of how middle-class parents are able to intervene effectively through superior knowledge of the 'rules of the game'. For those who are less sure of these rules than the lady in Lacey's study there are a number of books available, like Burgess's guide through the educational world which contains one chapter aptly titled 'Who to chivvy'.[83]

Conclusion

Throughout this brief overview of middle-class child-rearing, education and family life, a complex picture emerges which reinforces the claims made in previous chapters that the middle class is an increasingly heterogeneous grouping. Many middle-class women for example, retain a fairly traditional female role, but others, particularly those exposed to higher education, are in the forefront of innovations in family life designed to give women an equal opportunity of a satisfying career. The stress on a 'good' education continues to be a central middle-class value, but many middle-class parents would include in that an emphasis on the child's self-development and its opportunities to fulfil itself as a person. The work ethic still looms large for middle-class groups, but it may no longer be considered legitimate in its own right. It is only accepted in terms of the benefits which accrue to the family and it is recognised, if only as a theoretical possibility, that a point may be reached where losses outweigh gains.

In conclusion, middle-class family networks provide significant flows of support and aid, despite widespread geographical mobility. The middle classes' hold on local schools is as strong as ever, while their children are well prepared to take their opportunities and highly likely to achieve at least the same social position as their parents.

6
LEISURE

Introduction

In the previous chapter we considered the influence of socialisation in the family and in educational institutions in shaping attitudes to work and career. Our discussion emphasised the crucial part played by home and school in the continuing contrast in middle- and working-class access to valued jobs. In this chapter we explore middle-class leisure patterns and again we locate the necessity of connecting these to both work experience and family and educational histories. Each of the various sectors of middle-class social existence, while requiring separate analytical treatment, are thus shown to be clearly and irredeemably woven together.

Traditionally sociologists have paid little attention to the analysis of leisure, although in the last decade or so, there has been a growing interest in the area[1] and considerations of leisure feature markedly in current debates about the central trends and changes taking place in the structure of advanced industrial societies. Dumazedier, for example, emphasises that leisure is the most distinctive characteristic of 'post industrial society' and that leisure values stressing self-fulfilment have replaced work ethics as dominant social values.[2] As we shall see, this view is contestable, for although leisure is important it does not constitute the sole feature of the central life interests of the middle classes. Our analysis of the role of leisure in middle-class life outlines the growth of, and time available for, leisure and draws on data from three levels of analysis: individual, role and institutional, and societal.

Most sociologists writing about leisure stress the difficulties in arriving at an adequate distinction between it and 'non-leisure'. Building upon Parker's[3] attempt to deal with this complex problem, Roberts[4] points out that it is now agreed that a satisfactory definition of leisure should incorporate at least a time and an activity dimension: leisure is time free from work and also encompasses activities that are self-determined and characterised by a feeling of (comparative) freedom. Dumazedier argues that the major characteristics that constitute leisure are the outcome of the development of industrial society. In pre-industrial society there were no clearcut distinctions between work and the rest of life: leisure formed part of an interrelated wholeness where 'work, play, worship and education were all blended as part and parcel of community life'.[5] Dumazedier suggests that two preliminary conditions are necessary for the emergence of the possibility of the majority of 'workers' gaining leisure. First, activities in society are no longer regulated as a whole by ritual obligations prescribed by the community; individuals become free to decide how to use their 'free time'. Second, paid work becomes segregated from other activities. These two conditions only exist in industrial and post-industrial society. Thus a distinctive feature of leisure is that it is time free from work, occupying an important part of our non-work life.

All social groups have benefited from the 'containment of work'[6] which is the outcome of a long gradual process. The biggest decline in the working week occurred between the middle of the nineteenth century and the First World War when the average basic working week declined from seventy to forty-eight hours although since then for manual workers the length of the working week and hence time available for non-work has not changed very much, currently averaging forty-five hours (basic time plus overtime). The average basic working week for non-manual workers is 37.3 hours. Paid overtime is not a significant feature of middle-class occupations and statistics indicate that members of the middle class work considerably fewer hours a week than manual workers and so theoretically have more time available for leisure.

There are, however, significant differences within the middle class. The New Earnings Survey shows a sizeable minority (18

TABLE 23 *Average weekly and annual working hours (main sample: married men working full-time)*

	Professional and managerial	Clerical	Skilled	Semi-skilled and unskilled	All
Total hours at work in the week	48.2	44.7	47.8	47.6	47.4
Hours worked at home	2.2	0.8	0.1	0.0	1.0
Hours on second job	0.4	0.3	0.3	0.3	0.3
Hours spent in journey to and from work	6.1	5.6	4.1	3.5	4.7
Total hours working and travelling to and from work in week	56.9	51.4	52.3	51.4	53.5
Bank holidays in year (in weeks)	1.2	1.2	1.2	1.2	1.2
Paid holidays in year (in weeks)	3.4	2.6	2.5	2.1	2.6
Total weeks worked in year	47.4	48.2	48.3	48.7	48.2
Total hours working and travelling to and from work in year (weekly hours x weeks)	2,697	2,477	2,526	2,503	2,564
Total number of people	173	71	240	110	594

Source: Young and Willmott, *The Symmetrical Family*, Penguin, 1975, p. 139.

per cent) who work forty hours a week or more, whilst the working week of some managers is reported as between forty-two and forty-four hours.[7] Similarly, Young and Willmott show that if 'travelling time' is added to 'working time', the class differences in the distance between home and work (greater for the middle class) ensure little difference between amounts of manual and non-manual leisure time (see Table 23). Non-manual workers have nonetheless traditionally received a greater paid holiday entitlement than manual workers, for whom it remained virtually non-existent until after the First World War, although they took unpaid holidays. In recent years manual workers have made greater gains and differences with non-manual workers have been gradually reduced.

Leisure activities and the middle class

What then can be said about the leisure activities of the middle class? The following section discusses middle-class leisure and recreational activities with data mainly derived from recent national surveys[8] together with some smaller scale studies. Roberts suggests that recreation, including sport, is a narrower concept than leisure and is best approached through the notion of play, so that recreation can be seen as 'activities that are socially recognised as playful, fundamentally divorced from the serious business of living'.[9] The method most surveys use to find out about people's leisure and recreational activities takes two forms: either asking people to tick off from a pre-determined list a number of 'leisure and recreational activities' that they have participated in, or the use of time budgets where people are asked to record in a diary their various activities for a specified period of time.[10] These surveys are measures of an individual's rates of participation in a variety of leisure activities, which are then linked to variables such as age, sex, income, occupation, education and also car ownership.

The middle class (as measured by occupation) participates in a much wider range of leisure and recreational activities, particularly non-home-based leisure, than do working-class people, although a majority of all leisure activity and leisure time is centred on the home, irrespective of social class.[11] Watching television is by far the major leisure activity and constitutes the nub of a family and home-centred pattern of leisure. Within this general pattern middle-class adults watch television on average around sixteen hours a week in winter and twelve in summer, three hours a week less than working-class adults. There is also evidence of class differences in viewing choices: more working-class people regularly watch ITV than do middle-class people.[12]

While most leisure time centres on the home, the middle class are proportionately more likely to read and garden and engage

TABLE 24 *Home-based activities*

Proportion in class doing activity 12 times or more in previous year	Professional and managerial %	Clerical %	Skilled %	Semi-skilled and unskilled %
Watching TV	95	99	98	95
Gardening	70	62	66	50
Playing with children	59	63	66	59
Listening to music on radio or tape recorder/record player	65	70	52	44
Home decoration or repairs	52	55	56	45
Car cleaning	55	44	51	35
Reading	67	53	33	28
Car maintenance	30	25	38	25
Collecting stamps or other objects	14	24	11	8
Technical hobbies	10	7	10	4
Playing cards or chess	9	14	8	4
Playing an instrument	10	8	5	4
Handicrafts	5	6	7	7
Model building	6	4	5	4
Average number of activities done 12 times or more in previous year	5.8	5.9	5.2	4.2
Total number 588	171	70	237	110

Source: Ibid., p. 212.

in house repairs and 'Do-it-Yourself'.[13] However, the latter refers to non-work activities that are difficult to classify; although it may be a freely chosen activity, it can be seen also as part of non-work obligated activity.[14] The major class differences in leisure centre on 'out of home' activities where the middle class spends more of its leisure time and participates in a much wider range of activities than the working class. Participation in cultural activities such as visiting the theatre, opera, ballet and historic buildings, is predominantly a middle-class pastime.

There is also higher middle-class participation in voluntary organisations; Young and Willmott's survey showed that the managerial and professional sectors are more likely to hold office in a voluntary organisation than any other part of the population. Social class differences also emerge in the extent of participation and preference for certain types of sport. The middle class generally plays more sport, typically swimming, squash, badminton, tennis, golf and sailing while participation in open air outings, too, is a more significant feature of middle class leisure, although possessing a car makes a major difference here, as it does to a whole range of leisure activities.[15] Young and Willmott point out that other than being single, owning a car makes the biggest difference to increasing the number of leisure activities participated in. A BBC survey into leisure activities showed that the major weekend activity is going out for a drive and visiting friends or family; the peak time for getting out and about is Sunday afternoon in summer when up to a third of the population are out of their homes (though not all in cars).[16]

Surveys show that higher levels of education and income are also associated with higher rates of participation in leisure and recreational activities. Young and Willmott refer to a 'trigger effect',[17] suggesting that one leisure activity may trigger off another; thus someone who has several leisure interests is likely to add to them. However, this does not adequately explain class differences, for the middle class has greater financial, educational and cultural resources to draw on in their use of leisure.

TABLE 25 *Proportion of different socio-economic groups taking holidays, 1976, (percentages)*

	AB	C1	C2	DE
1 holiday	50	47	47	35
2 holidays	23	12	10	9
3 holidays	10	6	5	4
No holidays	17	35	38	50

Source: *Social Trends*, Central Statistical Office, HMSO, 1977.

As outlined above, holidays[18] are one of the preferred means of reducing working time and constitute a major block of time for leisure. The number of holidays taken away from home has increased in the last thirty years from 27 million to 44 million a year. The most significant change has been the huge growth in holidays taken abroad, from 2 million in the early 1950s to an average of 7.5 million a year throughout the 1970s. Historically, taking a holiday was a characteristic of the leisurely life style of the upper classes, and the spa towns of the eighteenth century and the seaside resorts of the early and mid-nineteenth century were associated with the practice of 'taking the waters'. Walton suggests that the early 'leisure' resorts functioned as means for the wealthy leisured class to differentiate their status and life style from those below them. This was reflected in a 'pecking order' amongst the spa towns and seaside resorts with Bath and Brighton the preserve of the aristocracy. However, the 'vogue of taking a holiday by the sea' was emulated by and became the accepted habit of the growing middle class, facilitated by the growth in transport. There was a steady 'percolation' downwards of the seaside holiday habit through the lower reaches of the middle class, reaching the working class with the introduction of 'Bank Holidays' and Wakes weeks.[19]

By the end of the nineteenth century the pastime of taking a holiday away from home became an important feature of middle-class life styles. Newman suggests that the middle class defined holidays as a reward for effort expended, whereas the Wakes Week or day trip of the working class were collective affairs emphasising having a good time.[20] In Chapter 2 we outlined the growth of various coastal towns as enclaves for the retired middle class. In a study of the development of Scarborough as a seaside resort, Walvin shows that its growth from the eighteenth century onwards has developed along social class lines with the different social classes congregating in spatially separate parts of the town.[21] Nowadays holidays are a mass consumption industry. Class differences persist, however, and the middle-class still take more holidays per year, and increasingly a second and third holiday, and are more likely to go abroad. Newman suggests that the type of holiday experience sought is a reflection of social class images of the world. The middle classes are more likely to have a privatised and active approach to their holiday, which is reflected in a higher rate of participation in motorised caravanning, camping and self-catering holidays.

Surveys illustrate the diverse range of leisure and recreational activities which feature as aspects of middle-class life styles, but they do not capture the distinctive social dimensions affecting leisure, nor the interrelationships between leisure and other social institutions and roles. We now turn to these dimensions, especially the significance of work, life cycle, family and social networks for leisure.

Work, leisure and the middle class

An important feature of leisure is that it is 'time free from work'. Not surprisingly a traditional sociological interest has centred on the relationship between work and leisure. A seminal paper by Dubin,[22] using the concept of 'life sector', found that non-work rather than work was the central life interest of industrial workers. On the other hand, Orzack's[23] research on a sample of (professional) nurses found the reverse. This suggests that people in middle-class occupations are more likely to be work-centred than manual workers and that this will affect their attitudes to leisure and general life styles. Parker has refined this approach and constructed a typology which shows three types of work – leisure relationships.[24] In the 'extension' pattern work extends into and influences leisure and much of non-work time, including leisure, is used for work-related purposes, such as reading professional literature and meeting colleagues. This is the work – leisure configuration typical of social workers, for example, and may be common in other occupations where there is a high degree of involvement in and identification with the work role. The 'opposition' pattern, however, involves a sharp demarcation between work and leisure and is characteristic of occupations such as coalmining and trawling where leisure is used to compensate for the damage inflicted by alienating work roles. In between these two is the 'neutrality' pattern; this is the characteristic work – leisure relationship of many routine non-manual occupations and most manual occupations. Work is not experienced as particularly alienating or rewarding; work and leisure are seen as different spheres of life, giving rise to different experiences and satisfactions. We can use this typology for examining studies that have focused on the work – leisure relationship amongst certain non-manual occupations.

Work and leisure relationships of managers and professionals

Managers Parker's typology suggests, along with our discussions in earlier chapters, that this sector of the middle classes exemplifies the extension pattern and that work will have a major impact on leisure. Data on working hours of managers certainly show that managers have greater demands made on them by their work role and consequently have less time available for leisure and family life. Young and Willmott found that managers and professionals have an average 'true' working week of around fifty-seven hours, which compares with an average working week of forty-four hours for manual workers. In a comparative study by Child and MacMillan it is suggested that British managers do not appear to fit the common stereotype of 'organisation men' who hardly have any leisure, at least in contrast with their American counterparts who have an average working week of sixty-two hours and for whom work is clearly a central life interest. American managers devote much of their leisure time to improving their work performance and enhancing their career prospects, but British middle and lower management appear to display a more neutral than an extension work–leisure relationship.[25] These findings are based on survey or time budget methods which ask people to record or tick off from a list their activities and which can often overlook and minimise the unobtrusive ways in which work influences the consciousness and thinking of people who are supposedly at leisure. It is not only sociologists who solve complex theoretical problems while relaxing at home. As one of Young and Willmott's respondents so aptly puts it, 'I think about work continually when I am at home. If you are digging a flower bed for a couple of hours you can have a marvellous think about some problems of organisation. You are not necessarily trying to think something through at high pressure, you are just mulling it over.'

The Pahls[26] found that the activities engaged in on Saturdays by their sample of managers differed little from those of skilled manual workers; going shopping in the morning, watching sport on TV in the afternoon and spending the evening watching TV or with friends. Sport is an important out-of-home leisure activity for managers who display a more varied and greater degree of participation than many other occupations.[27] Young and Willmott suggest this may reflect an important aspect of recuperation from work by relaxing in a non-relaxed way and actively engaging in something in which they could absorb themselves.[28] Patterns of managerial leisure suggest that it is more concerned with enjoyment and self-fulfilment and is not significantly related to or affected by work.

It would be stretching the evidence too far to conclude from this that the central middle-class values of achievement and career advancement are no longer major forces amongst this section of the middle class. Despite ambiguities, 'career commitment' was still the central life interest of the managers studied by the Pahls, for example. The managers were relatively 'willing slaves to the system' and not unhappy at paying a price for maintaining their middle-class status and life style, although they experienced tension between commitment to work and responsibility to the family. Managers thus appear to fall somewhere between an extension and a neutral work–leisure relationship. Although work and leisure appear to be compartmentalised, it is clear that work is often regarded as interfering with leisure and family life.[29] Child and MacMillan suggest that due to the increase in multinational corporations and American controlled companies British managers may be increasingly obliged to take on a similar degree of work commitment to that of American managers. If this proves to be the case then the conflict between the two value systems we outlined in Chapters 3 and 5 may be heightened.

Further up the greasy pole, Young and Willmott's data on managing directors portrays a much higher degree of work commitment and demands made on leisure time than is the case for managers. Work was very clearly their major priority in life and leisure and family took a back seat. Sport, however, was a prominent feature of the little leisure that was taken, even more so than for managers, although Young and Willmott point out that the same qualities of discipline and assiduousness are applied to leisure activities as to work.

Professionals We have already seen in Chapter 3 that the commonly held stereotype of independent, 'gentlemanly' professional work is often misleading and that members of professions are today more likely to be employed in large bureaucratic organisations. Further research suggests that members of professional occupations have a variety of professional orientations which may affect their leisure activities, although they generally exhibit a higher degree of work centrality and commitment than for other occupations.[30] Parker's survey of professional life and leisure in Islington clearly portrays the extension pattern of work–leisure relationships. For the majority of his sample the qualities of autonomy and satisfaction experienced in work were also experienced in leisure. Work was a central life interest and many of the sample found it difficult to differentiate between the two spheres.[31]

An 'occupational community' most vividly exemplifies situations where work is the central life interest and has a major impact on leisure. Salaman's research on railwaymen and architects suggests an occupational community consists of three interrelated elements: members' identities and self images are based on the occupation, they share an occupationally based value system and associate with members of the same occupation. Members of an occupational community tend to be 'affected by their work in such a way that their non-work lives are liable to be penetrated by their work relationships, interests and values'.[32] Friends and leisure associates are chosen from work-based colleagues and members frequently talk 'shop' in non-work time. Work-connected reading (at home) – particularly for the architects – hobbies, and being a member of work societies or clubs indicates the 'convergence of work and non-work'. K. Roberts has also shown that being a member of an occupational community is associated with a higher degree of out-of-home leisure activities and a broadening of members' life styles away from preoccupation with family, home and television. However, he is critical of the work centrality explanation of leisure: although agreeing that being a member of an occupation community affects leisure habits, he argues that its influences are much less than those of the family influences or of the stage reached in the life cycle. It is to these factors that we now turn.[33]

The family, life cycle, social networks and leisure

The Rapaports emphasise the necessity of relating specific uses of leisure to individuals' broader life styles and relating these to the unfolding of the life cycle. Peoples' lives develop within three major life strands: work, family and leisure. These three strands intersect so that a person's involvement along one of these 'career' lines has implications for the others. Major status transitions such as entering a career, or getting married, lead to the 'unfreezing and reform of patterns of life'. There are four phases of the life cycle: adolescence, young adulthood, establishment and retirement, each having specific preoccupations which lead to variations in particular uses of leisure. This approach enables us to see why the family is the major social milieu in which the majority of leisure time and activity is centred. Marriage leads into the establishment phase of the life cycle and focuses leisure interests and participation primarily on the home and within the family network.[34]

Roberts has taken this life cycle approach to leisure a stage further by linking life styles to personal social networks. Most of our leisure time involves social relationships and for Roberts the most important feature of leisure behaviour is social intercourse which enhances the solidarity and quality of people's primary relationships. The important question research into leisure should ask is 'Who were you with?' rather than 'What do you do?' Social networks refer to 'the total systems of social relationships by which individuals are surrounded; relationships that can have many bases including family, work, education and neighbourhood'.[35] It is Roberts' view that individuals' life styles are built on these networks and that their interests and leisure activities are expressed within these frameworks. The family has the major influence on leisure because of its central position in structuring social networks. The middle class tends to rely less exclusively on members of the extended family network as their major source of leisure associates than the working class and to have more broadly based social networks and friendship patterns drawn from educational, work and neighbourhood contacts. There is some evidence for an 'independent convergence' towards a privatised and home-centred life style between 'affluent manual workers' and the lower middle class. However, middle class patterns of sociability and widely based friendship patterns are not a prominent feature of the leisure activities of privatised workers.[36]

Bell and Healey suggest that leisure is a direct function of family structure and that the now more typical middle-class egalitarian family structure has increased the leisure time available to women. This is not just a question of greater domestic involvement by men but more importantly of changing norms and values stressing more equality and less rigid role segregation and shared leisure within the family.[37] The dual career family is at the apex of the trend towards a more symmetrical family structure, although, as we noted in Chapter 5, the evidence still shows that married women have less time free from domestic involvement and household obligations and participate in a much lower range of leisure activities than their husbands.[38] There are, however, varying combinations of jointness and segregation within middle-class families which affect leisure. A 'companionate' style of marriage characterised by domestic togetherness is associated with home-based leisure, while a 'colleague' style, where husband and wife treat each other as equals, is associated with joint participation in a wider range of non-home-based leisure activities.[39] A conventional marriage pattern, with differentiated productive roles – husband at work, wife at home, with some sharing of leisure and domestic roles – is still an important feature of many middle-class families. This is characteristic of the early stages of the establishment phase of the family life cycle, especially in those middle-class families where the male is primarily concerned with career development as his major life investment. Concentration on the career reduces the time available for leisure and the family which, as we have seen, may lead to strain and tension in attempting to reconcile the competing claims of different spheres of the life cycle. Recent research suggests that the more egalitarian marital and leisure relationships characteristic of the dual career family structure is not particularly suited to the career demands of managers.[40]

Society, leisure and the middle class

In this final section we come back to the theme raised in discussing the growth of leisure, and the view that it is essentially associated with the development of industrial society. The complex question that is posed here concerns the direction of change in the advanced industrial societies and the role of leisure in this process. The French sociologist Dumazedier is one of the major advocates of the view that advanced technology and productivity have sufficiently reduced working time to make society for the majority of the population increasingly leisure-based. A new culture based on leisure values stressing self-fulfilment allegedly replaces the 'protestant ethic', and identity, meaning and purpose in life is sought and achieved through leisure, not work.

A second approach challenges this depiction of society as leisure-centred. The varying criticisms can be incorporated under the title the 'anti-leisure thesis' which asserts that working time has not paled into insignificance nor has a 'work free' Utopia been achieved.[41] For many occupations, including those in the higher echelons of the middle class, both the time devoted to and demands made by work are considerable and curtail time available for leisure. Linder has put forward the thesis that a major feature of advanced industrial society is a 'time famine': time has become a scarce resource. Far from there being an increase in leisure time the American middle class do not have enough time for leisure and constitute a 'harried leisure class'.[42] The gadgets and consumer durables that are used to save time, paradoxically require more time for maintenance and servicing and time to earn the money to pay for them. In fact 'the time it takes to get an appliance ready for use or to clean it after use may exceed the time it would take to do the job by hand'.[43]

The principles underlying an industrial economy, especially the use of rational planning and speeding up the uses of time, have penetrated leisure itself. The essential features of leisure may be described as 'anti-leisure': activity which is undertaken compulsively as a means to an end, involving a sense of necessity and a high degree of time consciousness, with a minimum of personal autonomy, and which avoids self-actualisation, authentification or finitude. An amusing example given to illustrate anti-leisure and time-famine is the claim that the pastime of taking a mistress has disappeared, largely because it takes too much time, and has been replaced by the 'one nighter'.[44]

Leading British sociologists who have specialised in research into leisure conclude that we are neither a 'society of leisure' nor of 'anti-leisure' but a 'society with leisure'.[45] Work has not been replaced by leisure as the pivotal process either in society or in people's lives. The growth of leisure has had an important effect on the quality of life but is not, certainly for the majority of the middle class, the whole of life. Roberts claims that the social relationships and networks within which leisure occurs are acquiring a leisurely quality with greater scope for variety and choice. These leisure qualities and values are one of the factors responsible for changes taking place in social institutions, in particular the family.

Approaches to analysing leisure in terms of its relationship to work provide little evidence for the view that leisure is the major central life interest of the middle class. As we have seen for those sections of the middle class in professional and higher management occupations, work remains the central life interest and extends into leisure often with little differentiation between the two spheres. Lower levels of management and routine white collar occupations are typified by a neutral relationship between work and leisure with the two spheres being kept separate. When leisure is related to other social features, especially to overall life styles, family life cycle and social networks, we see that some middle-class occupations, especially for managers, involve strain in reconciling the demands and values of work roles with those of the family and home, and at the establishment phase of life cycle, the latter become the focal point for leisure.

These strains and tensions can be placed in the context of a wider approach which characterises advanced (capitalist) society as beset with legitimation crises and cultural contradictions.[46] This suggests that work values and leisure values conflict rather than that one or the other is necessarily dominant. In the early stages of capitalism the 'protestant ethic' provides a value system covering both an appropriate work and non-work ethic; the latter is characterised by thrift, self-control and frugality, and the former by achievement, hard work and delayed gratification.

Bell argues that modern culture has since separated from its close tie with the economy and, with the rise of mass consumption and a rising standard of living, is characterised by hedonism, consumption and instant pleasure. Thus culture no longer legitimates work and occupational roles as the essence of achievement or as ends in themselves, but reinforces spending and enjoyment. Yet the contemporary business enterprise still emphasises the protestant work ethic: it wants its members, particularly managers and executives, to work hard, to pursue a career and accept delayed gratification. Contradictorily, however, in order to prevent 'overproduction', corporate advertisements draw on the new culture and advocate a life style based on consumption and self-fulfilment. 'One is to be straight by day and a swinger by night. This is self-fulfilment and self-realisation'.[47]

Some sections of the middle classes are at the centre of these cultural contradictions. The research on managers has focused on the tension experienced between work and a leisure-centred home and family life. However, the data on professionals does not indicate as yet any great conflicts involving contradictory values. Work is their major life interest and the basis of their identity. Their leisure is characterised by the same qualities experienced in work with no apparent conflict or contradiction between the two. A more marginal section, such as routine white-collar workers, may be more acutely affected by different values in their work and leisure situations. Their work–leisure relationship has been characterised as segmented and neutral, perceived as two different spheres. As work, market and status differentials traditionally enjoyed by this sector gradually erode and career prospects become more limited, work may become less a central life interest and routine white-collar workers may feel modern cultural contradictions more acutely than other sections of the middle class. However, the importance of achievement via an occupation, or a 'career', is still a key feature of the middle-class value system, and features prominently in middle-class attitudes to education and aspirations for their children. Work and career advancement is still the crucial base on which middle class life styles are erected. A small minority of the middle class is at the forefront of changes leading to more flexibly based life-styles centring on both work and leisure, with no apparent contradictions between the two spheres. Dual career families display a low degree of sex role differentiation with values emphasising autonomy and self-fulfilment through both work and leisure. A variant of dual careerism which may lead to a life style increasingly characterised by leisurely qualities is the albeit very small minority pastime of 'job sharing' where a couple share the same job.[48]

Finally, young people have generally benefited from the growth of leisure which features prominently in their life styles, and the development of a 'youth culture' is a manifestation of this. Murdoch and McCron suggest that successful middle-class pupils and students particularly are faced with the problem of reconciling a crucial feature of adolescence: the search for 'expressivity', which is allegedly devalued at school, and the demand for deferred gratification in pursuit of examination success and achievement.[49] This dilemma is partially resolved by participating in the alternative culture at the weekend. At the moment the evidence suggests that their stake in the system and maturation into the next stage of the life cycle wins out. Perhaps it is those sections of middle-class youth and young adults undergoing extended periods of full-time education who most acutely experience the cultural contradictions of capitalism.

7 POLITICS

Introduction

A major theme in previous chapters is that the middle class does not exist as a single, coherent entity with clearly circumscribed boundaries but is composed of different sections or fragments that frequently exhibit quite contrasting beliefs and practices. Thus, there is no one pattern of middle-class leisure, no single set of middle-class family practices or middle-class orientations to education. Similarly, in this chapter, as we consider middle-class politics, we must register our suspicions at too-simple comparisons in the political behaviour of the two classes, and be sensitive to both conflicts as well as alliances within the middle class. But first, of course, we need to consider the term 'politics.'

'Politics' may be considered as those activities and arrangements that involve the articulation of competing demands on governments and attempts to resolve them. In Britain, as in most western societies, these arrangements are normally described by political scientists and others as 'democratic'; that is, British politics is seen as conducted more or less along the lines formulated in theories of 'liberal pluralism'. Central to this theory are the following assertions: the state functions independently of special social interests; if individuals feel strongly about a matter they will get together and press their claims on governments; public policies reflect the pressures of varying demands made on governments; and, crucially, elections ensure that political leaders are accountable to public opinion. Political parties and pressure groups are key organisations in this scheme for they aggregate and articulate interests, while political parties also develop policies that are placed before the people and which are implemented if a party wins an election.

Although the theory of liberal pluralism is criticised as an appropriate prescription of how 'democracies' ought to operate, the severest criticisms are aimed at it as an accurate description of how they actually function. Two important and connected propositions are usually advanced in support of claims that liberal democracies do not operate as depicted in the theory. First, it is suggested that key political institutions are not neutral but serve certain class interests, and this is at least partly explained by 'class skewness' in the composition of those who generally articulate demands (the leaders and members of pressure groups and political parties) and those who respond to them (political leaders). The middle class, it is argued, is better able than the working class to organise more effectively the articulation of its demands, which are then received sympathetically by middle-class élites with broadly similar views. A second criticism focuses on the assumption that a group's 'interests' are necessarily indicated by expressed wants and preferences. An approach that emphasises 'action' and which seeks to locate 'power' by observing which demands are successfully carried through in the face of competing demands in concrete decision processes ignores those situations where interests are not articulated. The poor, or the 'eccentric', for example, anticipating that their demands will inevitably fail, may consider political activism to be not worth the effort; or, if they do militate, they may find that their demands are deflected from the political agenda by decision-makers defining their aims as illegitimate. In some cases exploited groups may not perceive their 'true interests' and thus remain inactive because of the ideological dominance exercised over them by powerful rulers who control crucial socialisation agencies such as schools or the media. Conversely, the advantaged or politically 'legitimate', the middle class, for example, may not have to 'act' to ensure that their interests are safeguarded or advanced by political leaders whose 'definition of the situation' is the same as theirs. Indeed, the need to exert 'pressure' may be regarded as a means of last resort.[1]

We may usefully consider the 'middle class in politics' in

terms of three roles: voter, activist and governmental decision-maker, although as we have just noted, this emphasis on political action does not exhaust consideration of middle-class interests in politics. Two further caveats should also be lodged. First, as we have continually stressed throughout the preceding chapters, the middle class is not of a piece, and many members of the 'marginal' middle class, for example, may feel as powerless in the face of 'middle-class' political dominance as the working class – perhaps more so. Secondly, political conflicts are not inevitably reflections of occupational class cleavages and 'middle-class' political activity should not be considered necessarily as the pursuit of narrowly defined class interests. This last point is particularly relevant for accounts of voting behaviour.

Voting

Voting behaviour in Britain has long been regarded as primarily reflecting class position, which in turn is held to be signified by occupation. Butler and Stokes, noting that 'in contemporary interpretations of British voting behaviour class is accorded the leading role', and although detecting a diminution in the class–party relationship, agreed with the general consensus following their impressive trawl of the forces shaping electoral choice in Britain in the 1960s. Their evidence reveals that 'occupation is the most important of the elements that characterise the classes in the public's mind' and that there is a 'continuous fall of Conservative strength down the occupational scale'.[2] Alford's comparative survey[3] of electoral behaviour in Britain, Canada, Australia and the United States in the early 1960s shows party allegiance to be more closely correlated with occupational position in Britain than in the other countries, while Westergaard and Resler's more recent study of class in Britain, *Class in a Capitalist Society*, published in 1975, does not challenge these earlier interpretations, for they conclude that 'support for rival political parties is divided on class lines' and argue that all other influences on voting are 'of a very secondary kind'.[4]

These studies support the familiar picture of British electoral politics as consisting of two major parties, Labour and Conservative, divided on manual/non-manual lines, but with just enough 'deviant' class voters to ensure that governments regularly change party hands. Voting on class lines is regarded as quite rational; the two major parties pursue different class policies, the Labour Party advancing working-class interests and the Conservative Party those of the middle class, and individuals thus vote on rational, self-interested grounds for their class party.

The association between occupational class and political alignment in the post-war years is well grounded. Table 26 indicates that the higher you are in the occupational structure the more likely you are to vote Conservative. Nor does the model appear inappropriate for local council elections. Electors appear to base their voting decision less on a careful appraisal of candidate competence in local matters than on national party identification. Gyford has remarked that the steady 'nationalisation' of British local politics this century now ensures that 'As a determinant of party loyalty social class is an influence which is not seriously weakened by local conditions . . . . It thus provides

TABLE 26 *Class differences in voting behaviour, 1970–74*

	1970 %	**February 1974** %	**October 1974** %
Middle class (A/B)			
Conservative	65	66	62
Labour	27	18	19
Liberal	8	16	19
Lower middle class (Cl)			
Conservative	52	55	47
Labour	42	27	29
Liberal	6	18	24
Working class (C2D)			
Conservative	35	33	29
Labour	57	51	55
Liberal	8	16	16
Very poor (E)			
Conservative	29	32	35
Labour	64	56	53
Liberal	7	12	12

Source: Gallup (1976); contained in R. Rose, *Studies in British Politics*, 3rd edn, Macmillan, 1976, p. 207.

the bedrock of local party support, and in simple terms explains why, for example, the Royal Borough of Kensington and Chelsea is very unlikely ever to have a Labour council.'[5]

Unlike the cataclysms expected by Marx the strong relation between class and political identity has been regarded by many non-Marxists as having a benign influence on the British political system. Lipset, for example, in *Political Man*, published in 1960, suggests that class issues are essentially economistic and bargainable; they involve competing claims on national economic resources which are resolved by regular adjustments. Class bargaining and compromise reinforce both the legitimacy and the effectiveness of capitalist societies, thus enabling working-class demands to be met out of increasing productivity. In contrast, 'traditional' conflicts between, say, religious or linguistic or ethnic communities involve clashes of 'ideology', or world views, which are characterised by moral intensity. Such conflicts demand either complete victory or total defeat if they are to be resolved, rather than accommodation and pragmatism.[6]

Whatever the merits of this approach the inability of Britain's economy in the last two decades to sustain the growth required to 'buy off' working-class demands has ensured that class conflict cannot be considered as somehow functional for the economic and political systems but may lead to them being severely disrupted. Furthermore, the relationship between occupational class and party alignment is shakier in the 1970s and 1980s than it was in the 1950s and 1960s. The 'troubles' in Northern Ireland and the development of vociferous nationalisms in Scotland and Wales have emphasised the 'Englishness' of class-related party loyalties and highlighted a tendency for some political scientists to equate Britain with only part of the United Kingdom. But even in England the association between occupational class and voting behaviour is declining. Although it has long been recognised that around one-third of manual workers vote Conservative (thus preventing a succession of Labour governments) an increasing tendency for the middle class to vote Labour has led a number of writers to describe British electoral behaviour in terms of its declining partisanship. Rose, for example, notes that in the two general elections of 1974 'the parties that saw their vote rise – the Liberals and Nationalists – drew their support from approximately a cross section of the electorate' and concludes that the relationship between occupational class and party allegiance, always 'significant but limited', may be declining further.[7]

Crewe et al. also point to the 'accelerating refusal of the electorate to cast a ballot for either of the two governing parties.' They calculate that while the Conservatives were taking 47.8 per cent of the votes cast in 1951, this had declined to 36.7 per cent by October, 1974. In the same period Labour's share also fell, from 48.3 per cent to 40.3 per cent. Crewe et al. suggest that the combined drop in support for the two class-based political parties, from 96.1 to 77.0 per cent, is associated with a diminution in the class alignment. Using the ratio of Conservative to Labour party identifiers within manual and non-manual occupational categories as their measures they show that class alignment (the percentage of non-manual Conservatives minus the percentage of manual Conservatives) declined from 43 to 22 over the decade 1964–74 (see Table 27). Furthermore, despite a return by politicians in the 1970s to the language of class conflict the proportion of respondents prepared to assign themselves (even after being pressed) to a social class 'fell sharpl̸y' (from around 50 per cent to just over 40 per cent). Crewe et al. propose that their findings reflect an improvement in standards of living, reduced occupational inequalities and a consequent 'blurring' of class lines.[8] K. Roberts et al. offer a similar explanation to

TABLE 27 *Occupational grade and party identification, 1964 to October 1975.*

	1964		**1966**	
	Occupational grade		**Occupational grade**	
	1–4	**5–6**	**1–4**	**5–6**
Conservative	75^{a}	32^{b}	72^{a}	28^{b}
Labour	25	68	28	72
	a – b = 43		a – b = 44	
	1970		**1974**	
	Occupational grade		**Occupational grade**	
	1–4	**5–6**	**1–4**	**5–6**
Conservative	70^{a}	35^{b}	65^{a}	33^{b}
Labour	30	65	35	67
	a – b = 35		a – b = 32	

Source: Crewe et al., p. 169

account for the virtually identical 'erosion of partisanship' found in their Liverpool study. They suggest that the hidebound two-party system has failed to adjust to the fragmentation of the British class structure and argue that the expansion in non-manual occupations and accelerated mobility from the working class increases middle-class Labour voting as substantial numbers of the upwardly mobile retain their Labour loyalties, thus leading to a decline in a simple class-party axis.[9]

These accounts of the decline in the long-established association between occupational class and political partisanship are particularly interesting, for they do not seriously question the primacy of class related electoral behaviour. Rather, the weakening of class differences in party alignment is thought to reflect changes in class structure, the blurring of class divisions or the fragmentation of class identities. There is little suggestion, as Dunleavy notes, of new cleavages that may replace the salience of occupational class.[10] Instead, Rose, for example, looks to social influences other than occupation, such as housing or trade union membership, as a means of identifying 'pure' or 'core' classes – those with a high level of class-specific attributes – to provide greater predictiveness for class explanations of voting behaviour. Thus, non-manual workers with good academic qualifications, who do not belong to trade unions and who own their house are more likely to vote Conservative than non-manual employees without these characteristics. Subjective class identification is similarly helpful in improving prediction as 'the higher the self-rating a person gives himself, e.g., upper middle class rather than middle class, the more likely he is to favour the Conservatives'. Yet, as Rose points out, even this approach has diminishing utility for: 'In 1959, differences in occupation, housing and trade union membership could explain 21.9 per cent of differences in party choice,' but by 1970 this was down to 12 per cent.[11]

However, factors other than occupational class may have an increasing significance in British electoral behaviour. Two approaches that take this view, and which do not regard these factors as simply derivative of work positions, are recent Weberian and Marxist interpretations of urban political processes.

Weberian urban sociology

As we noted in Chapter 1 Weber identifies objective classes as those groups possessing similar life chances by way of their economic power in the market. A central distinction is drawn between those social formations whose market power derives from their possession of property, which enables them to realise income ('property classes'), and non-propertied or 'acquisition classes' whose economic power derives from the possession of marketable skills. Unlike Marx, Weber maintains that classes arise in any market situation and that property classes do not consist simply of those who control industrial property but consist also of those possessing any form of property that enables them to materially benefit, including domestic property. Although in practice the two types of ownership are generally closely linked, it is possible for the propertyless in the sphere of production to occupy a different class situation in relation to the distribution of domestic property by, for example, owning a house.

In recent years a number of writers have sought to justify 'housing classes' theoretically as significant political agents. Rex and Moore in their study of immigrant groups in Birmingham in the 1960s identified up to seven housing classes based on types of tenure, from owner-occupiers in select areas at the top to private tenants in poor lodgings at the bottom. These classes competed for scarce and desired housing resources and could be distinguished by their unequal chances of achieving them. Of crucial importance in governing access to valued housing was, on the one hand, possession of an adequate income to secure a building society advance for owner occupation, and, on the other, the ability to meet local residential qualifications for council housing. Without these the alternative was private rental in seedy, run-down areas, but this form of housing provision was regarded as undesirable by both owner-occupiers and council tenants who constantly sought to restrict its development.[12]

Rex and Moore's theory of housing classes has been widely criticised, and a particularly effective critique is offered by Haddon. He argues that housing tenure groups are housing status groups not housing classes; tenants and owner-occupiers do not conform to Weber's concept of class for they are unable to generate returns on entering the housing market but simply seek access to accommodation. In Weber's definition only those with the ability to sell and buy land and developments, and thus possessing the ability to realise disposable income, constitute a propertied class. However, Haddon's argument that owner-occupiers are not in a position to generate returns from the possession of their houses is surely debatable.[13] Saunders has cogently argued that housing is unlike most other forms of consumption (e.g., cars, stereos) which are literally 'consumed', that is, the exchange value of the commodity is either lost or severely depreciated; housing is property usable for returns (even if it is not necessarily used in this way), and owner-occupation provides the possibility denied other forms of tenure of large capital gains. Three crucial factors furnish the means for real wealth accumulation from the ownership of domestic property: tax subsidies, effectively negative interest charges levied by the building societies in periods of high inflation, and a higher rate of house price inflation than general inflation. The domestic property market thus gives rise to a threefold class division, consisting of those who seek housing solely as a means of accumulation (the suppliers of housing), those to whom it is both a source of accumulation and a place to live (owner-occupiers), and those to whom it is simply a source of accommodation (tenants).

Saunders maintains that cleavages between the housing classes are reflected in political action. Owner-occupiers, for example, may combine against both land developers and tenants; in Croydon, when domestic property values were threatened by proposals from builders to erect housing on green belt land and their plans to construct higher density estates, owner-occupiers organised themselves in fierce resistance against the construction industry. At the same time owner-occupiers are ready to kick out against council tenants, by opposing proposals to increase the number of council dwellings in an area or fighting plans to raise the rates rather than increasing council house rents.

There is little doubt that owner-occupation provides the basis for distinctive voting alignments, particularly at the local level where, unlike most other European societies, local property taxes are a major source of local authority income. Perhaps the clearest signs of distinctive 'owner-occupation' voting are to be discerned in the electoral interventions of ratepayers' associations. Ratepayers' associations inevitably seek to minimise rates rises and constantly complain about 'funding' what they regard as 'artificially low' levels of council rents. Resentment at the freezing of council rents at a time of unprecedented rates rises was a major factor behind the 'ratepayers' revolt' described by King and Nugent that occurred in Wakefield (and elsewhere) in 1974 and 1975. The letter from a local building contractor to the *Wakefield Express* which led to the formation of the Wakefield City Ratepayers' Association complained that it was 'high time that the people in the middle-class income bracket, who pay the bulk of the rates and taxes in this country, decided to band together to fight this waste of money. Council house rents have been frozen and it would appear that once again we are asked to foot the bill.'[15]

Council house rents provide around 7 per cent of local government income, but comprises a much larger proportion of locally derived income. Consequently, variations in levels of council rents have significant and immediately recognisable consequences for rates charges. Although council house tenants also pay rates, it is the owner-occupier who is supremely conscious of his role as ratepayer, and fierce political battles in local councils over both rates and rents charges tend to reflect the opposing interests of domestic property owner and council tenant.

King and Nugent indicate that ratepayers' candidates in Wakefield achieved impressive electoral success in areas which contain a higher than average proportion of owner-occupiers, and these findings are replicated in Grant's study of ratepayers' association in Walsall. His data suggest that the owner-occupier vote is not simply a reflection of occupational class; the ratepayers' share of the ballot is substantially stronger among owner-occupiers than it is amongst the non-manual electorate generally (see Table 28).[16]

As well as clashes within the housing market between domestic property owners and the suppliers of domestic capital, conflict may also occur between types of property owner. For example, Grant's account of a ratepayers' association in a Devon seaside resort highlights conflict between domestic and commer-

TABLE 28 *Ratepayer share of the vote and ward socio-economic composition in Walsall (ranked by non-manual heads of household)*

Ward	Percentage owner-occupied households	Non-manual heads of households	Non-manual persons	Ratepayer Vote 1975	1976
Paddock	82.7	67.2	65.3	19.1	—
Streetly	93.5	63.4	66.0	50.9	47.4
Aldrige	66.6	46.2	48.1	53.6	55.0
Hatherton	38.5	36.3	36.7	34.1	33.3

Source: Grant, op. cit., Ch. 7, n16 p. 99.

cial property interests. In the 1960s, a number of mainly retired residents in Seaton, through the ratepayers' association, opposed attempts by local traders to expand the town's tourist trade, which would have boosted the shopkeepers' returns but, the residents argued, would also turn their quiet retreat into a 'Blackpool of the South' (in their eyes not a complimentary description). The dispute resulted in the ratepayers' association, although not putting forward its own candidates, endorsing those from other parties who were prepared to resist the expansionary powers of the local traders. They met with some success. In the 1970 Urban District Council elections the only unsuccessful candidate 'was a shopkeeper who had not received the endorsement of the ratepayers' association'.

These examples lend credence to claims that housing is a significant source of electoral cleavage, at least at the local level. However, do we need a conception of 'housing classes' to account for this? Instead of regarding housing groups as classes, could they not be considered as status groups and variations in partisan alignment as simply reflecting status differentials, not class differences? Some Marxists (e.g., Castells[17]) argue that home ownership, and attempts to extend it to the working class, are 'ideological' means of fragmenting the non-capitalist class, a way of cloaking the basic lines of class cleavage. Yet it is difficult to comprehend the persisting and often fierce electoral dog-fights between the representatives of owner-occupation and those defending the council tenant simply in terms of differing 'styles of life'. As Saunders asserts, it is 'precisely because owner-occupiers do collectively constitute a group with distinct material interests to defend [that] their significance is felt at both the local and national level of British politics, and thus provides strong grounds for arguing that their tax subsidies could not be withdrawn without a prolonged political battle'.[18]

However, there are a number of difficulties with Saunders's notion of 'housing classes' which he himself recognises. One centres on the contingent nature of those factors that provide the possibility of real capital gain from owner-occupation. It is not inconceivable that house price inflation could fall below the level of general inflation, or that tax subsidies will be severely truncated, or that building societies may be forced to charge 'real' interest rates to borrowers to protect the interests of their savers. One or more of these occurrences would severely threaten the economic basis for the conception of 'housing classes'.

An alternative approach to Weberian 'housing class' theories, which while similarly maintaining that housing (and other consumption variables) provides the basis for electoral alignments that are not reducible to occupational class differences, but which seeks to explain these in terms of different modes of consumption rather than the operation of the domestic property market, is sectoral consumption theory.

A theory of consumption sectors

This position derives from the work of Castells and his important distinction between individualised and collective forms of consumption,[19] and is successfully employed by Dunleavy in his account of the influence of housing and transport locations on political alignment from an analysis of data drawn from February 1974 Gallup surveys.[20] Individualised forms of consumption (purchases in shops and stores, for example) are directly determined by market forces and involve the commercial or private organisation of goods. Location in these consumption processes is determined by the amount of income earned by a household in employment, and, consequently, political struggles over individualised consumption tend to be expressed in bargaining over wages and salaries at the workplace. In contrast, collective consumption processes usually refer to state-provided services, such as housing, education or transport, and usually reflect demands for governmental intervention following the inability of the market to provide these services. Collective consumption processes are inevitably 'politicised' by the assumption of state responsibility for them in a way that does not occur with the control exercised over individual commodity consumption by the 'invisible market'. This is reinforced by the large-scale provision and management of state services which 'creates favourable conditions for the emergence of collective consciousness and action'. Finally, because location in collective consumption processes is less directly determined by market forces, and thus by income and work position, they 'constitute an independent basis for the development of social cleavages, standing outside those originating in production relations'.

Although the idea that some consumption locations are relatively independent of occupational class position is well established in Marxist urban sociology, an additional element in Dunleavy's formulation is the notion of 'consumption sectors' which refers to those areas where consumption processes are fragmented between individual and collective modes. For example, the existence of an individual/commodity/private mode alongside a collective/service/public mode in housing and transportation provides the basis for the constitution of electoral cleavages that are relatively independent of occupational class locations. Thus, 'voters involved in collective modes of consumption are aligned to the left, while those involved in individualised modes are aligned to the right, relative to the underlying alignment of their social class locations'. As a result, in areas like housing there should be salient political cleavages between home-owners and public housing tenants.

Dunleavy is insistent that cleavages in consumption patterns cannot be regarded as simply mediated aspects of occupational class, for his survey data indicate that half of skilled manual workers are owner-occupiers, while a similar proportion of all manual workers have access to a car. This is not to underestimate the fundamental importance of occupational class interests, but to suggest that consumption influences, such as housing or transport, may be more 'immediate' and 'visible' to individuals and thus provide a vital influence on political alignment.

Dunleavy's analysis of the Gallup samples lends credence to his approach. For example, he convincingly illustrates that when the joint effects of housing and transport variables on electoral partisanship are calculated there is a 'clear tendency' for the Conservative lead over Labour to decrease as one moves from the most private to the most public mode of consumption (see Table 29). Dunleavy argues that the sectoral approach 'generates very different predictions about the patterns of consumption cleavages and about consumption influences on political align-

TABLE 29 *Consumption category effects on voting within social grade*

(a) **Conservative percentage of the two party vote**

Consumption category		Social grade A/B	C1	C2	D	E	All	N
Home owners	2 cars	89	78	64	61	*	78	462
	1 car	80	74	50	52	63	65	1,860
	No car	91	68	49	42	54	56	726
Private tenants	1 car	79	57	54	39	*	55	261
	No car	*	68	29	33	46	41	329
Council tenants	1 car	48	50	32	31	47	32	842
	No car	50	49	25	21	40	29	1,056
Total		81	67	41	47	47	52	5,536

(b) **Conservative lead over Labour, as a percentage of all votes**

Consumption category		Social grade A/B	C1	C2	D	E	All
Home owners	2 cars	67	46	23	18	*	50
	1 car	50	39	1	3	24	25
	No car	77	29	−1	−13	7	10
Private tenants	1 car	44	11	6	−19	*	7
	No car	*	31	−37	−27	−7	−15
Council tenants	1 car	−4	−1	−30	−33	−5	−24
	No car	0	−1	−44	−48	−17	−36
Total		45	31	−14	−27	−6	3

* Less than 20 respondents in the cell. Private and council tenants with two cars are excluded from the table because their cell sizes fall below this limit.

Source: Dunleavy op. cit., Ch. 7, n10, p. 436.

ment' from the Weberian approach. Certainly Table 29 indicates that the effects of private tenancy on voting behaviour is much more distinctive than would be expected from an approach that regards all tenants (council and private) as comprising one category and characterised by their lack of domestic property ownership than one which divides them by their different modes of consumption.

Yet differences in the political predictions of the two perspectives are easily exaggerated; both approaches suggest that housing groups provide the basis for electoral cleavages that cut across class alignments. The major contrast lies in the manner in which housing groups are theorised. While Saunders sees housing cleavages as constituted by the conflicts of material interest between the suppliers, owners and non-owners of domestic property, Dunleavy regards home-owner/council tenant conflicts as revolving less around capital accumulation than around the relative state subsidisation of the two tenures, that is, the different modes of housing consumption.

We have noted some of the difficulties associated with Saunders's Weberian analysis, and the 'collective consumption' approach also has its difficulties. Particularly, as Pahl points out in another context, it is not at all clear that at the actual point of consumption the distinction between 'commodity' and 'collective' forms of provision is especially salient for most people. Goods provided by the market are used in the same way as those provided publicly.[21] As Saunders suggests, state-provided resources such as council housing are still consumed individually, by relatively isolated family units, and this may reduce rather than enhance the possibilities of 'collective consciousness' amongst council tenants.

Middle-class Labour voting

The decline in the relationship between occupational class and party choice in Britain in the 1960s and 1970s is largely accounted for by the increase in the number of middle-class Labour supporters. Crewe et al. calculate that while 'in 1964 the ratio of Conservative to Labour partisanship in the middle classes was 3:1, by October 1974 it had narrowed to less than 2:1' as the proportion of middle-class Labour identifiers increased from

17 per cent to 27 per cent.[22] At the same time, there was little change in the number of working-class Conservatives. Jary's estimate of the number of non-manual socialist voters by the mid-1970s is somewhat higher. Using data from the Butler and Stokes's surveys as well as Crewe et al.'s samples, Jary calculates that in percentage terms the middle-class Left now matches the number of working-class Conservatives, with both slightly in excess of 30 per cent.[23]

Explanations for the increase in middle-class Left voting usually start from the recognition of two distinct types of middle-class Labour identifier, the 'proletarian' and the 'altruist', who are held to support the party on different grounds.

'Proletarian' middle-class Left The 'proletarian' Labour voter is drawn from the 'marginal' middle class and is so described because he possesses an employment status and level of rewards similar to those of manual workers and tends to subjectively identify with the working class. Left voting is hardly 'deviant' for this section of the middle class as the 'underdog' appeal of the Labour Party fits well with their own low status. The increase in middle-class Labour voting, therefore, may be regarded as a reflection of the increasing proletarianisation of routine non-manual occupations. A rather different interpretation attaches more explanatory weight to social background than work experience. Goldthorpe et al., for example, suggest that with the expansion of non-manual positions there is an increase in the number of upwardly mobile individuals from manual families, and these have a tendency to retain their original Labour sympathies.[24]

'Altruistic' middle class left This type of middle-class Labour voter is found among the 'lower professionals' or the established middle class, especially in public sector jobs such as teaching and social work. They tend to be highly educated with a principled, well-articulated radicalism. This image derives primarily from Parkin's study of those involved in the Campaign for Nuclear Disarmament in the late 1950s and early 1960s, who exhibited these characteristics. They are described as 'altruistic' because of their disinterest in the material rewards of political success in comparison with the psychic satisfaction to be derived from 'expressive politics.'[25]

However, there are dangers in drawing general conclusions about established middle-class support for the Labour Party from a study of a rather special pressure group. The Labour Party periodically forms a government with attendant powers to change patterns of resource distribution and its comparatively stronger commitment to public expenditure than the Conservatives serves well the career prospects of that section of the middle class working in the public sector. Labour voting by them may be considered 'altruistic' only if we slavishly follow the class–party axis and ignore that pattern of partisanship constituted by cleavages between public and private sector employment.

Nonetheless, quite plausible empirical data has been marshalled to support claims for two types of middle-class Labour voter. Rallings, using data taken from four Gallup polls carried out prior to the 1970 general election (which provides a sample of 1,078 non-manual Labour voters) found that '70.7 per cent of Labour supporters are classified "Cl", with 58.3 per cent subjectively working class'. Compared to middle-class Conservative voters, Labour identifiers were less likely to be owner-occupiers and drawn from the highest white-collar occupations, and they were also more likely to be a council tenant or belong to a union. Rallings concludes that 'the more the middle class resemble the working class sociologically, the more likely they are to vote Labour'. However, 42 per cent of the Labour sample regarded themselves as middle-class and these were much more likely to be owner-occupiers, professional workers, or to have received higher education than those who subjectively identified with the working class.[26]

Other data substantiates the 'two types of Labour voter' thesis. In K. Roberts et al.'s Liverpool survey around one-quarter of white-collar workers were found to be Labour voters, but this number increased dramatically among those with 'proletarian' self-images. At the same time, however, the percentage of Labour voters among well-educated white-collar respondents with a 'ladder' imagery – the 'new radicals' – was only slightly less than among the 'proletarians'.[27] Similarly, while Jary detects a greater likelihood of Labour voting within the lower middle class than among the upper middle class, the size of the latter is still substantial (43 per cent and 29 per cent respectively in 1970). Furthermore, the upper-middle-class Left display greater radicalism in their attitudes to public ownership, social service provision, trade unionism, and opposition to big business, and to 'manifest greater detachment from traditional bases of legitimacy, such as the Monarchy and the Church'.[28]

There appears to have been a weakening in the solidity of the Conservative hold over the political hearts and minds of sections of the established middle class in recent years, which suggests that the 'proletarianisation' thesis is only a partial explanation for the increase in non-manual Labour voting. Between 1964 and October 1974 Crewe et al. indicate that while the Conservatives lost support in all non-manual grades, the loss was 'proportionately greater in the upper and middle echelons of the middle classes' than among the 'marginal middle class of clerical and other routine office workers, and among lower administrative and managerial employees, the lower-status professions, and small entrepreneurs, the fall was 'dramatic'.[29]

The implications for the political system of a swelling in middle-class Labour support are the object of two contrasting interpretations. One, associated with Marxism, asserts a definite shift to the left in the political centre of gravity as a result of a twofold process: firstly, as a consequence of the increasing 'proletarianisation' of the 'intermediate classes', manifested in loss of authority, job security, income and status; secondly, a heightening radicalism by well-paid professional and intellectual employees whose opposition to existing patterns of power is engendered by the dissemination of critical thinking in higher education and the growth of public service occupations which foster hostile attitudes to the market individualism of competitive capitalism (see Habermas[30] and Gouldner[31]). A contrasting interpretation, put forward by Lipset, and by Crewe et al., for example, posits a more benign possibility for liberal democracy. An increase in middle-class Labour voting is regarded as symptomatic of a general erosion of partisanship which may lead to a less ideological form of politics in which electoral behaviour is characterised by increasing 'instrumentality' and the political parties judged in terms of their efficiency and effectiveness, particularly on economic issues. Both interpretations have some support in the electoral data although, as Jary notes, statements about future political developments are inevitably 'inconclusive' given the indeterminancy of human action.

Party Political activism

Labour Party

It is reasonable to expect middle-class support for the Labour Party to be more pronounced when we turn from the relatively passive act of voting to forms of political involvement that are more demanding, such as belonging to and being active in a party. The working class is generally less participative than the middle class in political and other associations for they usually lack those resources, such as time or verbal skills, that are often prerequisites for successful involvement in organisations. Trade unions are an exception for they provide individual and material pay-offs for their members and are the major agencies for the defence of working-class interests where it really matters, at the workplace. But where the returns for involvement are less immediate or direct, activism and leadership tend to be the prerogative of, particularly, the educated middle class, even in 'working-class parties', for they possess both the resources and the preparedness to accept other than pragmatic returns for their activity although, as we have noted, the latter are not necessarily lacking, particularly for public sector workers.

This is not to deny that the growth of the Labour Party and its entry into mass politics provided a means for greater working class participation in the political system. In 1906, for example, all twenty-nine Labour M.P.s had a working-class background, although by 1935 this had fallen to 64 per cent (from a much larger number).[32] At the local level the rise of the Labour Party ensured that the class composition of council chambers became less skewed against manual employees. In places such as Sheffield,[33] Wolverhampton[34] and Newcastle-under-Lyme[35] the proportion of Labour councillors with manual occupations reached as high as 40 per cent in the inter-war years, while

Elliott, McCrone and Skelton's review of Edinburgh politics over the last century indicates that 52 per cent of Labour councillors had manual occupations in 1955, although this had dropped to 41 per cent by 1975.[36]

A recurrent theme in recent analyses of the Labour Party, however, is the claim that the organisation has experienced a 'middle-class takeover' and that its working-class activists have steadily been forced out of the party. This is most explicitly argued by Hindess in his book *The Decline of Working Class Politics*, published in 1971. In this work, based on a study of the Liverpool City Labour Party in the late 1960s, Hindess argues that the party's middle-class activists have wrested control from the party's traditional manual supporters with the result that party policies no longer reflect working-class concerns. Dividing the Liverpool constituency into 'working-class' and 'middle-class' wards, Hindess maintains that the former have declined in activity and influence while the latter have correspondingly become more powerful, with the result that the long-standing loyalty of the working class to the party has been virtually dissipated. Consequently, 'the close association between party and class has itself declined'.[37]

Although there are doubts about the representativeness of Hindess's study (the Liverpool constituency party may not be typical of other local Labour parties, while the late 1960s was a period of especially strong disaffection with a Labour administration), his argument is worth considering at length. The book may be identified as containing two major propositions: first, that there has been a decline in working-class membership and activity within the Labour Party; second, that a middle-class takeover of the Party's leading positions has resulted in policies that are abstract and technocratic rather than suited to the personal needs of the working class. We examine each proposition in turn.

'Decline of working-class politics' A consideration of the party at national level appears to support Hindess's position strongly for, as Forester notes, 'the Labour Party does indeed appear to be less of a working-class party than at any time in its history'. This is exemplified by the changing occupational backgrounds of Labour members of parliament; between 1955 and 1970, for example, the proportion of those entering the House of Commons from the professions, mainly lecturers and lawyers, increased from 49 to 61 per cent, while the number of manual workers fell from 35 to 25 per cent.[39] However, two qualifications must be entered. First, these figures in part reflect a general expansion in non-manual and professional positions in the post-war period; it is worth noting that a relatively large number of middle-class members have working class parents (around 40 per cent) which suggests that yesterday's manual member is, as the result of social mobility, often today's non-manual M.P. Secondly, the 'exclusion' of the working class from the Labour Party is less novel than Hindess infers. Forester points to the disproportionate influence of middle-class Fabians in the early days of the movement and the repeated complaints ever since that it is easier to recruit white-collar employees to the party than genuine proletarians.

The thrust of Hindess's argument is that it is at local constituency level that the attenuation of working-class Labourism is most marked – 'at the level of grass roots politics, beginning with the relationships between the political structure and the ecology of the city'.[40] Yet, in places other than Liverpool at least, this is problematical. If we take trends in membership, it is undoubtedly the case that the Labour Party has suffered a severe drop in subscriptions since the early 1950s, 'probably more than half' according to Forester, from around an estimated 700,000 to about 400,000.[41] But falling support is not confined to the Labour Party. The Conservatives also have experienced a sharp drop in membership, which suggests a general erosion in rates of party participation. Furthermore, the level of Labour membership over the last thirty to forty years is characterised by sharp short-term fluctuations. Gould's study of 'Riverside' constituency Labour Party indicates only a couple of hundred members in the 1930s, but over 2,000 in the early 1950s.[42] Similarly, Bealey et al.'s account of the development of the Party in Newcastle-under-Lyme reveals a large increase in membership in the late 1940s, only for it to subside again by the late 1950s.[43] Thus Hindess's account of the haemorrhaging of support from the Party in a period of heightened disillusion with a Labour government has to be treated with care as an indication of long-term levels of membership.

'Middle-class takeover' The decline in Labour Party membership is not necessarily symptomatic of an emerging middle-class predominance in the local constituencies as Hindess argues. A number of studies (e.g., of Sheffield, [44] Glossop,[45] and Wolverhampton[46]) indicate that the middle class has always been over-represented in leadership positions at the local level. Birch's account of the Labour Party in Glossop in the 1950s reveals that while almost four-fifths of members were industrial workers, only one-third were in leadership positions. A survey of local Labour leaders in thirty-six constituencies carried out by Janosik in the 1960s shows 26 per cent to be manual workers and around one-third to be businessmen or professionals.[47]

Similarly the middle class has long appropriated a disproportionate share of Labour's council seats. In Edinburgh, despite the comparatively high percentage of manual councillors on the Labour side in 1955 (see above), ten years later the proportion of non-manual councillors was clearly higher than that drawn from the working class (44 per cent and 34 per cent respectively, not including 17 per cent who were housewives and likely to possess middle-class backgrounds).[48] Hampton, in his analysis of Sheffield politics, found a similar predominance of non-manual Labour councillors to that contained in the Edinburgh survey,[49] while Sharpe's study of the 1961 London County Council elections revealed that 52 per cent of the successful Labour candidates were in non-manual occupations and only 21 per cent had manual jobs.[50] It may be that the social composition of Labour councillors outside northern industrial towns is even more weighted towards the middle class. Saunders notes that in Croydon in 1973 around 70 per cent of Labour councillors were drawn from professional and managerial groups while 14 per cent were skilled manual workers, although over half the local population was working-class.[51]

The 'ecological' shift in influence from working-to middle-class wards detected by Hindess is not replicated in other studies, including one by Baxter which also looks at Liverpool's Labour politics. He argues that the disproportionate influence of middle-class wards in the local constituency parties is a well established phenomenon, for 'the organisation of the Labour Party in Liverpool has always been bad apart from occasional exceptions', especially in working-class constituencies.[52] Forester's researches into the Labour Party in Brighton in the early 1970s similarly found 'no overall obvious shift in power towards the middle-class areas' in recent years. Although Forester details the disproportionate activism of middle-class members this does not appear to have debilitated working-class wards; indeed, he remarks that 'it is the working-class wards which are more likely to have a higher than average percentage of active and very active members'.[53]

Although Hindess exaggerates the scale and dimensions of change within local Labour parties his work offers several valuable observations on the relationship between middle-class party activists and the working class, and he particularly questions the extent to which the former adequately represent the latter. This point is taken up by both Saunders and Forester in their respective studies. They refer to the tendency in Croydon and Brighton for predominantly working-class wards to be represented by middle-class Labour councillors who live some miles away from their constituents, and whose links with the local community are inevitably 'somewhat tenuous'. In both towns middle-class Labour councillors tended to operate with a political outlook quite foreign to that of their working-class supporters. In Croydon, for example, well-educated socialists were much less concerned than working-class activists with concrete housing provisions and more with the 'development of a humane and rational housing programme'; for example, tenants' associations broadly supported a Conservative scheme to sell council houses to sitting tenants and to provide help with mortgages, a plan which Labour councillors vehemently opposed. Saunders records the 'evident tension' between what he describes as 'the idealism, universalism and principles of the Labour group and the materialism, parochialism and pragmatism of the representatives of the town's council tenants'.[54] Forester, in comparing members in working- and middle-class wards in Brighton, also discovered a 'much more materialistic' orientation to socialism among the former, although, unlike Hindess and Saunders, he has little evidence that they are less interested in general principles than specific issues.[55] If there is increasing working-class alienation from the Labour Party, contrary to Hindess's assertions, it is likely to lead to more rather than less socialism, for young, well-educated Labour councillors are much more committed to socialist ideals than their manual supporters. Or at least they possess different conceptions of socialism.

Conservative Party

We have seen that the Conservative Party continues to attract a lion's share of the middle-class vote despite the emergence of a middle-class Left as a significant electoral force. That the Party remains a natural habitat for the middle class is even more apparent when we consider membership of Conservative constituency associations. In comparison with Conservative voters, Conservative members are more heavily located in the Registrar-General's social grades I and II; furthermore, the higher the level within the national organisation the greater the proportion belonging to the upper middle class (see Table 30). This 'social pyramid' is well illustrated by Pinto-Duschinsky's analysis of the occupations of Conservative chairmen and M.P.s, which indicates that 65 per cent of the former and 73 per cent of the latter were either substantial executives or proprietors, or 'professionals'.[56] We lack detailed accounts of Conservative memberships in local constituencies, although what evidence we have paints a picture of middle-class predominance. Bealey et al.'s 1960s sample of Conservative members in Newcastle-under-Lyme, a mainly working-class town, found that 64 per cent were drawn from the top two social groups (as then defined by the official census) while 14 per cent were skilled workers.[57]

TABLE 30 *The social pyramid: the percentage belonging to the upper middle class (social grades I and II) at different levels of the Conservative organisation.*

Total electorate	16
Conservative voters	24
Conservative Party members	40
Conservative Party workers	42
Conservative constituency chairmen	85
Conservative Members of Parliament.	97

Source: M. Pinto-Duschinsky, op. cit., Ch. 7, n56, p. 288.

Tappin's recent study of Conservative activists in forty-six Scottish constituencies reveals 75 per cent in non-manual occupations, a figure that does not include categories such as housewife or retired which could be expected to contain a further middle-class element.[58]

There are few studies, however, that look closely at the amount and type of support at local level given by businessmen, particularly by smaller proprietors. This is unfortunate, for a common interpretation of Conservative economic policy in recent years rests on a set of assumptions about the business composition of local Tory activists and their influence on Conservative leaders. We may call this the theory of petit-bourgeois Conservatism.

Petit-bourgeois Conservatism Conservative economic policy has been characterised in the post-war period as comprised of distinctive 'corporatist' and 'liberal' episodes. A recognition by Conservative administrations of the need for economic planning by the state in close cooperation with leaders of the major employers associations and the trade unions, exemplified by formal incomes policies since the early 1960s, is contrasted with the dominance of 'free market' ideas – highlighted by calls for less state 'interference' and lower levels of public expenditure – when the Party is in opposition. An explanation for these oscillations suggests that, out of office and removed from the 'collectivist' influence of the civil service, big business and the trade unions, Conservative leaders become more responsive to the demands of their predominantly small business activists who compel the adoption of 'laissez-faire' policies. Gamble, for example, argues that, in government, Conservative leaders recognise the 'realities' of power in modern industrial societies, particularly the constraints imposed by demands for state regulation of the economy from both trade unions and large employers. In opposition, however, party policies 'emphasise the needs and plight of the small businessmen in deference to the pressure from the rank-and-file'.[59] Similarly, in discussing Conservative economic policy between 1945 and 1964, Harris asserts that 'liberalism', despite its steady diminution as a powerful doctrine in the Conservative Party, remained influential within the ranks of its political supporters although 'small business had very little to look forward to in the new *étatiste* corporatist world'.[60] The actions and statements of Conservatives themselves have lent credence to the theory, particularly since 1974, as Conservative leaders such as Thatcher, Joseph and Howe have asserted the vital role to be played in Britain's new 'social market economy' by the small entrepreneur.

However, the theory of petit-bourgeois Conservatism is rarely considered in the light of empirical evidence. For example, the little empirical work that is available on Conservative activists does not support the proposition that Conservative activists are drawn predominantly from the small business sector. Pinto-Duschinsky's survey of the occupations of constituency chairmen shows that while 41 per cent were either company directors or relatively large proprietors, only 16 per cent were small proprietors or shopkeepers.[61] This relative disinterest in local party leadership is also indicated in Bechhofer and Elliott's study of Edinburgh shopkeepers that we looked at in Chapter 4. These were overwhelmingly Conservative in voting intention (66 per cent), but it was a 'grudging Conservatism' that lacked real commitment. Bechhofer and Elliott remark that 'many of them are reluctant Tories, voting for the party which is the lesser of two evils', and up to two-fifths thought it would make little difference which party was in government, including as many as 43 per cent of the male respondents.[62] These findings suggest that whereas small businessmen are predominantly Conservative voters, they are less likely to be Conservative members and even less likely to be Conservative activists. Certainly Bechhofer and Elliott 'found no evidence of a sizeable minority being actively engaged in politics, organising and working for their party'.

Secondly, the proposition that small business activists in the Conservative Party are committed to 'free market' economic policies is difficult to substantiate directly given the lack of specific studies of Tory small business activists. There is, however, indirect support for them. As we have seen, autonomy and independence are highly prized commodities in the petit-bourgeois world investigated by Bechhofer and his colleagues. Their work highlights the 'economic individualism' of small retailers, the feeling that individuals should stand on their own two feet and make the best of their skills. This is accompanied by a strong anti-collectivism, vigorous opposition to state intervention in the economy, and a belief in individual mobility. This shying away from large organisations was also a feature of the small manufacturers in the Home Counties studied by Curran and Stanworth.[63] As we noted in Chapter 4, their work indicates how petit-bourgeois 'individualism' is also expressed in 'idiosyncratic' practices in the selection of staff, notably a general disregard of formal qualifications, a point made too by Newby et al. in their work on small farmers.[64]

These investigations at least suggest that small businessmen possess a constellation of attitudes consonant with a 'market economy' ideology, although, as we have already noted in connection with the Edinburgh study, these attitudes may also serve as a brake on activism; the more strongly they are held, the less likely they are to be pursued in collectivities. Yet before we accept this part of the theory of petit-bourgeois Conservatism we should note certain difficulties. For a start, the petit-bourgeoisie have not been slow in defending their own restrictive market practices or in constructing arguments to justify them. In the 1930s retail associations tenaciously prevented legislative attempts to abolish resale price maintenance; trade associations continued to act as guilds, maintaining prices and profit margins as competition intensified between retailers during the depression. Resale price maintenance was finally abolished only in 1964, and then after considerable resistance by the retail trade.[65]

Thirdly, the view that small business activists compel 'market economy' policies on Conservative leaders in opposition also appears doubtful given that there is a long-established tradition of deference and loyalty to party leaders by the Conservative rank-and-file, apparently confirmed by the evidence from the admittedly few studies of local Conservative parties that we have which indicate a remarkable disinterest by activists in policy matters.[66] Two possible indicators of petit-bourgeois pressure for 'market capitalism' in the constituencies are the selection of parliamentary candidates and resolutions submitted to the annual conference. If we take the first indicator, it could be argued that small business influence at the local level is manifested in selection committees who choose candidates sympathetic to the 'market individualism' of small businessmen. However, they certainly do not do this in the most direct fashion, by choosing small businessmen, for their number in the ranks of Conservative M.P.s is small. Nor is there much sign, despite the greater autonomy for local selection committees in the Party since 1945, that 'free market' candidates are especially favoured, for as Butler and Pinto-Duschinsky conclude, 'in the great majority of cases, an aspirant's personality matters more than his position within the political spectrum'.[67] Analysis of resolutions from the constituencies at annual Conservative conferences does not support the view of a small business dominated rank-and-file pressing 'free market' policies on leaders, either. Wilson's consideration of motions since 1945 reveals few signs of a congruous petit-bourgeois ideology of individualism, but rather a range of disparate ideas.[68]

One of the major reasons for the advocacy of 'competitive capitalism' by leading Conservatives on removal from office in 1974 lay in the so-called 'middle-class revolt', which characterised the early years in opposition. As we outlined in Chapter 1, between 1974 and 1976 there were clear signs of widespread disaffection and belligerency by sections of the middle class who could traditionally be counted on for their Conservatism. This found expression in a host of new, militant ratepayers' and self-employed associations, as well as more general organisations, such as the Middle-Class Association (MCA) and the National Association for Freedom (NAFF). Although these groups responded to specific legislative measures introduced by an incoming Labour government, particularly a special national insurance levy on the self-employed, but also trade union and taxation measures, they also displayed a marked disenchantment with the Conservative Party. Heath's 'collectivism', the collapses before the trade unions, particularly the miners, the introduction of VAT, and local government reorganisation all contributed to the avowedly 'non-partisan' stances of these new groups. Consequently, a number of Conservative leaders, notably Joseph, Biffen and Boyson, argued that the 'middle of the road collectivism' of the Heath administration had alienated traditional supporters who could only be reassured by distinctive libertarian policies.

The sight of widespread petit-bourgeois disaffection with the

Party, and the hostility of groups such as the National Federation for the Self-Employed (NFSE) and the Association of Self-Employed People (ASP), clearly set the alarm bells ringing for many Conservatives and by 1976 a Small Business Bureau (SBB) had been set up at Central Office within a revamped Department of Community Affairs. The SBB has sought to forge closer links with the small business sector, especially the new small business groups, by establishing SBB branches in local constituencies and holding regular consultative conferences; its creation marked increasing public encouragement of small businesses by the Party leadership after 1974. However, these developments were less the result of compelling pressure from small business activists outside the Party. It was petit-bourgeois disaffection with the Party, the absence of internal petit-bourgeois pressure and the search by small businessmen for other forms of representation that led to a calculated attempt by the leadership to recover lost voters among Conservatism's traditional supporters. The growth of new militant small business associations clearly posed a threat to the Party's claim to speak for the small sector; leaders felt that the Party could only be weakened if large numbers of 'natural Tories' campaigned in 'non-party' organisations. Furthermore, the creation of the SBB was part of a wider electoral effort to establish links with sections of the community previously ignored or alienated by the Conservatives. Although the new leadership from 1975 was clearly appealing to the small business sector for support, it also wanted better relations with other groups. The Department of Community Affairs thus included a reinvigorated Conservative Trade Unionists Section, the revived Federation of Conservative Students and new Anglo-West Indian and Anglo-Asian divisions, as well as the Small Business Bureau.

Finally, if we consider the claim that, once in office, the Conservatives ditch the small sector in favour of big business, it would be surprising if governmental economic policies did not reflect the interests of large capital; the British economy is dominated by about fifty large multinational companies and it would be odd if they did not punch their weight politically. It is not easy, of course, to be sure what are the 'interests of large capital'. One method is to look at actions by Conservative governments that elicit strong protest from the small entrepreneur but, as far as we can tell, very little from large firms. The abolition of Resale Price Maintenance by the Conservatives in 1964 is a case in point. So are a number of actions undertaken by the Heath administration. It virtually abandoned the Industrial Relations Act (used only by small employers); introduced a formal incomes policy (loathed particularly by small firms); replaced Selective Employment Tax with multitiered VAT (noted for the administrative burdens it imposed on small businessmen but less of a problem for larger concerns with specialised taxation departments); brought in proposals for an additional national insurance contribution for the self-employed (which sparked off a self-employed 'revolt' when finally implemented by the next Labour government); and expensively reorganised local government (bitterly opposed by local traders for bumping up the rates). The present Conservative government, despite the rhetoric of opposition, has largely pursued an economic course that favours (or is less harmful to) big rather than small capital, such as reducing high rates of personal taxation, increasing interest rates to a record level, and granting large public subsidies to Rolls Royce and British Leyland.

There is a danger, however, in assuming that the interests of small and large business inevitably conflict, for they may converge and make it even more difficult to label specific policies as either in the interests of one or the other. Big business protestations of support for the small businessman are not simply rhetorical chimes in a now fashionable 'small is beautiful' chorus, but symptomatic of a harder-nosed recognition of common business interests. We detailed a number of reasons for the 'functionality' of big–small business alliances in Chapter 4, for small businesses may maintain areas of low profitability, produce new commodities, and provide training and employment for young and unskilled workers, all of which can be taken advantage of by larger concerns. Bechhofer et al. note, too, that threats to small enterprises imperil 'sacred' bourgeois values. Calls for the safeguarding of small business are a way of reasserting the rights of private property more generally.[69]

Finally, despite the current dominance of economic individualism within the Conservative Party, 'collectivist' sentiments still wield considerable authority. Ian Gilmour, Peter Walker and James Prior are among leading Conservatives who have publicly reacted to what they fear may be a return to the 'bolt-holes' of narrow, traditional middle-class politics, arguing that the Conservative Party is not a 'class party but a national party' based on middle-of-the-road opinion. These differences in part reflect a continuing dilemma in Conservative circles over electoral strategy which follows from recognition of the changing nature of the middle class. The traditional, but steadily declining entrepreneurial classes offer a shaky basis for a party engaged in mass politics, and an awareness of this has encouraged many in the Party leadership in the last few decades to call for a more vigorous pursuit of the expanding new middle class of managers and administrators. Efforts to broaden its middle-class appeal are reflected in the changes in Tory rhetoric. Gamble, for example, observes that a 'good' word like 'independence' now has a rather different meaning than strictly economic independence, 'in order to attract support from the mass of clerks and professional workers who staffed the great bureaucracies of state and industry'.[70] It has come to mean more than a stand-on-your-own-feet philosophy in occupational contexts, but refers to wider consumer and citizenship roles. The civil servant, if less open to calls for a return to a new entrepreneurial age, may still respond to the rhetoric of 'individualism' if it is interpreted as supporting owner-occupation (the property-owning democracy), or encouraging selectivity in the field of welfare provision, or if it is construed as a barb at irritating trade unionists who refuse to empty the bins or run the trains.

For the present, however, the Conservative Party is under the influence of the 'New Right' rather than the 'Progressives', and the emphasis in Tory ideology remains on ensuring that traditional middle-class supporters do not experience the severe disillusionment with the Party that occurred during the Heath administration. To arguments that this unnecessarily narrows the Party's electoral base the response is that 'traditional' self-help values are not class-based, but are also firmly rooted in the working class. There is some justification in this argument, for the result of the May 1979 general election, when substantial numbers of working class people supported the Conservatives, and when the Labour Party held its own among the middle class, suggests that the electoral divide between the two major parties is increasingly resembling less a manual/non-manual cleavage than one centred on public and private sector employment and consumption.

Non-party activism

A feature of pressure group politics in Britain in the post-war period has been the tendency under both the Conservative and the Labour administrations for the major economic groups, the CBI and the TUC, to be incorporated into the very heart of the political and administrative machinery so that they are regularly consulted by governments and closely cooperate in the formulation of economic policy. For those sections of the middle class not represented by the large producer groups, either in strong trade unions or by the CBI (which, as Grant and Marsh indicate, is predominantly influenced by big business),[71] the growth of the 'corporate state' has resulted in the feeling that their interests were being constantly ignored and affronted, even by their political allies in the Conservative Party. The small businessman as we have earlier indicated, in particular formed the hub of several campaigns in the 1970s that aimed to correct, in their view, the overweening power of the trade unions and the predispositions of governments to favour larger concerns at the expense of the small entrepreneur.

'The revolt of the middle class'

It is often pointed out that the middle class dominate our social and political institutions. It provides the leadership of the major parties and possesses an unequal share of those resources – time, energy, money and verbal skills – that are a prerequisite for successful and sustained pressure group activity. Yet, as we have argued in preceding chapters, unless the term 'middle class' is analysed, statements about 'its' role and influence tend to be meaningless. The middle class contains a variety of occupational groups and its political influence is largely limited to a distinct middle-class élite while the rest are often as powerless as any other group. In recent years sections of the middle class have defended more militantly interests they believed to be ignored by economic and political leaders. This may be seen in the expansion of non-manual trade unionism and the preparedness of 'professional' groups such as nurses and teachers to go on strike, outlined in Chapters 3 and 4. At the same time, the 'marginal' entrepreneurial class has also been less reluctant to employ 'direct action' strategies outside the formal channels of party politics, and in the 1970s this was reflected in a number of highly vociferous campaigns by newly formed ratepayers' and self-employed associations. These groups eschewed the niceties of conventional pressure group politics and opted instead for a strategy of belligerency and public confrontations with authority. The National Association of Ratepayers' Action Groups (NARAG), formed in June 1974, and the National Federation for the Self-Employed (NFSE), created in October 1974, epitomised the spirit of direct middle-class activism. Although naturally differing in many respects these two groups shared important features: each presented a 'non-party', 'non-political' and 'non-class' stance, and both attracted considerable public support. Within six months NARAG claimed an affiliated membership of 350,000 while NFSE claimed 45,000 members within a year.[72]

The National Association of Ratepayers' Action Groups

Formed as a coordinating body for the 'ratepayers' revolt' of 1974–5, NARAG's creation owed much to the reluctance of the existing national ratepayers' organisation, the National Union of Ratepayers' Association (NURA), to adapt to the anger and militancy of the many new ratepayers' association spawned by rates increases in 1974 that nationally averaged 30 per cent but were much higher in some areas. It gave expression to the search by ratepayers for immediate and sensational ways of voicing anger and did so as a deliberate political tactic. As a member of NARAG's committee and later chairman stated, 'The fact is, you've got to be a little bit sensational to attract attention. If you act sensibly and reasonably – having meetings and quiet lobbying – they don't want to know. If, however, you march on London with banners, etc, then everyone listens.'[73]

Although, as a result, NARAG did not establish close regular contact with Whitehall, for a short period it was clearly accepted by élites as a spokesman that had to be listened to. The Conservative opposition enthusiastically took up the rates issue, defeating the government in the Commons on the matter in June 1974, and forcing the Labour administration to set up an official committee (the Layfield Inquiry) to discuss the rating system. During the October 1974 general election the Conservatives promised eventually to abolish the rating system and in the meantime to transfer the cost of teachers' salaries from the local authorities to the central exchequer. The impression left by NARAG on the Labour government was also forceful: a massive £350 million subsidy for domestic ratepayers was announced in July 1974, and was followed by a record rate support grant in October.

NARAG was operating in favourable circumstances in 1974: Tory leaders felt the rates issue could prove a rallying point for disaffected Conservatives, while the Labour government could not afford to ignore the groundswell of ratepayer discontent in an election year. Yet, as Nugent chronicles, within a few months the organisation was internally divided. At local level ratepayers' associations quarrelled over whether they should fight local elections and perhaps jeopardise Conservative chances, or remain a 'non-party' pressure group, while some members wanted the association to take a wider interest in local government than simply the rates issue. At national level NARAG was also spent by efforts to turn it into a wide-ranging right-wing pressure group (urging the cessation of social security payments to strikers and their families, for example). Combined with the gradual decline in the animus over rates increases, these factors ensured that by the late 1970s, 'all the signs were that NARAG was experiencing the sort of difficulties that have long plagued ratepayers' associations at local level: waning enthusiasm, declining funds and an excessive reliance on the activity of a few'.[74] Few NARAG associations attained the permanence of the older ratepayers' associations under NURA's wing gained by focusing on a range of local grievances. Many who were drawn into ratepayers' associations at the height of the 'revolt' were what Dowse and Hughes call 'sporadic interventionists'[75] – they lacked political experience and were soon disappointed when original, naîve expectations were not realised. Their onrush into the political arena was thus brief and attracted little support outside their own particular point of attention. Yet some of the 'new' associations remain, in some cases broadening out into environmental/community groups and seeking a closer, more serious-minded relationship with politicians and officials. In this, and also their history of internal turbulence, they strongly resemble the NFSE.

The National Federation of the Self-Employed

The self-employed 'revolt', spearheaded by NFSE, involved similar organisational developments to those of NARAG. Specific tax grievances following the introduction of VAT in 1973, and proposals in the same year for additional Class Four National Insurance contributions from the self-employed, fuelled general small business disenchantment with the advance of 'collectivism': the extension of state involvement and control in the economy, the concentration of resources into larger units in the private sector, and the increasing power of trade unionism. NFSE rapidly expanded as it demonstrated a willingness to engage in combative and direct forms of political action, such as a threat to call a VAT strike. This may have alarmed established business representatives in the CBI and the National Chamber of Trade but it undoubtedly reflected grass roots impatience with orthodox political lobbying.

In the months following its formation in 1974, NFSE adopted a more radical posture than staider business organisations such as the CBI, the Association of British Chambers of Commerce, or the Small Business Association. Despite the anger of many small businessmen over the Class Four national insurance proposals, the issues surrounding VAT provoked the most militant threats. Differential rates charged on different categories of goods and services were loathed for exacerbating the severe administrative burden placed on the small trader by the tax. They added further heat to the argument that the small entrepreneur was becoming 'an unpaid tax collector', a burden particularly onerous to the small man without the administrative resources of the larger concerns.

In May 1975 NFSE advised its members to withhold VAT

payments to the Customs and Excise after 1 July. This threat of illegality had the effect that may have been intended. It resulted in a Federation delegation meeting the Financial Secretary to the Treasury and senior officials at Customs and Excise to put their case. In addition, the Department of Health and Social Security responded to NFSE's demands for an earnings related system of contributions and benefits that would accommodate the self-employed by setting up an investigation. Admittedly, this enquiry later ruled out such a scheme on the grounds of prohibitive administrative costs, but these developments encouraged the Federation to tread the path of 'respectability'. Leading political figures, such as Peter Walker, were approached for advice and NFSE were told of the importance of establishing a responsible image as a prerequisite for securing legitimation from government.

Consequently, the Federation's militancy and bellicosity diminished towards the end of 1975. Unlike NARAG, this did not reflect declining support for the organisation – membership remained about 40,000 – but involved a deliberate change of strategy. Four examples of this search for credibility may be cited: NFSE pressed strongly for government aid and training schemes for the self-employed, implying an acceptance of the desirability of pursuing self-employed interests within the prevailing political context; the threat of direct action over Class Four was withdrawn and instead moves to secure tax relief on the contributions became policy; involvement in broader right-wing issues was avoided and in December 1976 the Federation severed all connections with the right-wing National Association of Freedom (NAFF) 'because of NAFF's extreme political views;' and the NFSE refused to join in the furore created by the government's tightening of tax procedures in the use of sub-contract labour in the building industry.

This change in approach did not go unchallenged. Attempts to establish a closer relationship with government took place against a background of internal unrest, including charges of financial mismanagement. Furthermore, some of NFSE's leaders preferred a 'dirty tricks' campaign which would create official chaos to an incremental approach. These arguments were strengthened by the implementation of a series of Acts passed by the Labour government which appeared especially to threaten the small employer. The Trade Union and Labour Relations Act 1974 and the Employment Protection Act 1975 provided the trade unions with greater opportunities to increase membership and secure closed shop agreements. Employer's rights to dismiss employees were also restricted.

As a consequence the leadership's strategy has been constantly criticised by members unhappy at the Federation's low profile, and their point of view has steadily gained the ascendancy. In 1977 the NFSE's first Annual Conference empowered the leadership to take the Class Four issue to the European Court at Strasbourg, while in July leaders succumbed to demands for an emergency meeting of Council made by members furious at the refusal of the Executive to support a demonstration and rally against the closed shop. The meeting, held in September, resulted in a number of leadership changes, including the resignation of the Chief Administrative Officer following a vote of no confidence and criticism of his plans to build up NFSE's administrative structure.

This return to 'belligerency' gathered pace in 1978. In February, for example, hostility to the Employment Protection Act boiled over in the promise to begin sacking 250,000 workers in small businesses at 50,000 a month. The complete abolition of Class Four was re-adopted as Federation policy and it began to attract wide media coverage with repeated accusations that the VAT inspectorate asked children of suspected tax evaders to spy on their parents. NFSE attacks on the Arbitration and Conciliation Advisory Service (ACAS) as 'politically biased' have become increasingly vituperative, and it has set up its own rival body.

The switch back to an aggressive strategy by NFSE is not noticeably the result of élite disregard. All shades of establishment opinion now enthusiastically lauds the small businessman and several measures to aid the small entrepreneur have been introduced by both governments. Yet this has not prevented the Federation veering unsteadily between a strategy of responsibility and a strategy of bellicosity. Its tactical vacillations are reinforced by at least three factors. First, the occupational diversity of the self-employed sector may result in governmental policy outraging some groups while others may be largely unaffected.

The Trade Union and Labour Relations Act and the Employment Protection Act have consequences for small employers, but few for sole traders or those employing only close relatives. The Class Four national insurance proposals hit the self-employed, but have had less impact on employers. Thus, one part of a small business organisation's membership may scream for direct action, while the rest may be relatively unconcerned over a particular issue.

Secondly, small businessmen remain distrustful of élites, despite their courtship by government. Their ambivalence is understandable. A Labour government faces restrictions on the extent to which it can meet the demands of smaller concerns. Trade union leaders are seeking ways of accelerating the unionisation of small business employees, and strongly oppose demands from the small sector that they should be exempted from recent 'social' legislation, particularly the Employment Protection Act, arguing that as a result workers in small organisations would become 'second class citizens'. Despite the rhetoric of opposition, the attitude of Conservative governments to the small entrepreneur has done little to alleviate their suspicion of Conservatism's close relations with big business. Indeed it is reinforced by the party's reluctance to rescind most of Labour's legislation on the closed shop. It is possible that the tensions marking NFSE relations with government may even intensify if a Tory administration is regarded as reneging on early promises.

Thirdly, although the self-employed may continue to be wooed by the establishment – to help revivify the inner-city areas and to provide employment – they are likely to remain disaffected by the apparently inexorable process of 'collectivism'. Inasmuch as small business militancy is a response to these wider societal developments, demands for direct action to combat the 'palliatives' of specific government measures will probably continue.

Middle-class political identity

The long-standing difficulties in organising the variegated middle class that we have referred to in earlier chapters are exemplified by John Gorst's Middle Class Association which was founded in November 1974, to 'save the middle classes' from the militancy of trade unionists, the 'spiteful' tax measures of a Labour government, and the 'corporatism' of Edward Heath's Conservatism.[76] Unlike NARAG and NFSE it attracted mainly disaffected Tories from the established middle class, particularly doctors, accountants and architects, despite its aim to unite 'professional, managerial, self-employed and small business occupations'. The Association although it quickly attracted 5,000 members (from 214 occupations) was short-lived. Supporters quarrelled over the term 'class' – many disliked its 'socialist' connotations – and the organisation folded by early 1976 after a period in the hands of a militant anti-communist who had organised a coup against Gorst's leadership.

Thus a distinguishing feature of this form of 'middle-class politics' is its internal divisiveness, fragmentation, and the brief existence of groups. King notes that 'there is little sign of a common class consciousness, an awareness of belonging to a class with specific interests'.[77] Independent political action by the middle class outside the Conservative Party on the scale of the 'Poujadistes' in France or the 'Mittelstand' associations in Germany has yet to be sustained in Britain. Garrard et al. suggest that this failure may lie in the historically highly amorphous, regionally varied and relatively open British class structure with its gradations of power and the early incorporation of the small employer into municipal politics and the major parties (first Liberal, then Conservative). An important constituency for middle-class pressure groups, as Bechhofer and Elliott point out, is the traditional small business stratum, for it has a long tradition of trade associations (such as those representing landlords and shopkeepers) on which to build these groups. Yet the ambiguous work situation of many small businessmen, often part owner and part worker and drawn from a variety of social backgrounds, plus their 'anti-collectivism' and belief in industrial effort, militated against a common basis for action[78]

However, it would be misleading to imply that only the 'marginal' middle class and the 'radical individualists' on the 'Right' of the political spectrum have become more politically active in recent years. Crouch argues that there has been a general movement 'away from established institutions of participation (primarily the political parties but also trade unions and other bodies) to various others: ad hoc community-level or unofficial groupings, special interest lobbies, new radical movements of urban protest and direct action'.[79] However, although radical students or motorway protesters may attract the headlines, not all newly emerged activism is bellicose. For example, numerous environmentalist organisations have developed which have generally preferred a strategy of responsibility rather than mass protests. Grant points out that they tend to attract relatively large proportions of well-educated members who have a fairly sophisticated appreciation of the way in which the political system works and recognise the importance of establishing credibility in the eyes of policy-makers. Local amenity societies, which seek to influence land-use planning by local authorities and which specialise in conservation matters, generally look with favour on local government planning officials, and this is reciprocated.[80] Barker and Keating's analysis of 635 registered amenity societies reveals that they are generally 'pro-planning' in outlook, regard the production of improvements and new developments as their central concern, and this 'interventionist' position reflects the fact that they often contain professional workers such as planners and architects within their ranks. Many are public employees and less antipathetic to the idea of planning than the 'older' sections of the middle class, particularly the petit bourgeoisie, who provided the bulk of support for the groups that comprised 'the middle-class revolt'.[81]

Middle-class political activism illustrates again that the middle class contains a variety of occupational groups with distinct interests. Some may combine politically on occasions because they can agree on what they oppose, but often this is articulated in the vaguest terms, for example they are against 'state control', 'militant trade unionism' and 'unfair socialist budgets'. They usually lack a coherent political philosophy and are opposed by other sections of the middle class, those wishing the state would plan 'better' not less, and those in public employment whose careers may depend on increasing not declining government expenditure.

Political leaders

A major criticism of pluralist theory is that its emphasis on the dissipation of power within a mesh of competing veto groups leads to an underestimation of the role of the state as a political force with huge power resources at its disposal. The idea of the state as a distinct locus of power is found in both Marxist and non-Marxist perspectives. Weber clearly has this in mind when he discusses the special interests and values of state bureaucrats whose shadowy and somewhat malevolent control of the administrative apparatus makes them a powerful stratum separate from social classes. Similarly, as Parkin observes, the classical liberal view of the state, still found in the writings of Hayek and 'Chicago' monetarist economists and influential within the leadership of the Conservative Party, regards the growth of the modern state as leading 'to the steady erosion of the moral core of bourgeois ideology, especially the ideals of self-help, market freedom, and individualism – ideals that are displaced by their very opposites: state welfare, central planning, and collectivism'.[82]

The Marxist critique of liberal pluralism, put forward most cogently by Miliband, views 'the state system' less as an independent source of oppression than as an instrument that operates to enhance the interests of the capitalist class. Capitalists rarely govern directly themselves (although their reluctance to do so is greatly exaggerated, according to Miliband), but there are powerful constraints on governments of whatever political persuasion in capitalist societies to tailor their decisions to match business sentiment. Not only are political leaders reliant on the capitalist class to produce a nation's wealth, but they share a 'common purpose' that stems from the similarity of their social backgrounds, 'for businessmen belong in economic and social terms, to the upper and middle classes – and it is also from these classes that the members of the state élite are predominantly, not to say overwhelmingly, drawn'.[83] For Miliband, therefore, social origin, education and class situation are factors creating shared social meanings and ideological dispositions among state élites, and the coherence that this provides is not disturbed by upward mobility from the subordinate classes for these become 'bourgeoisified': as they rise 'so they do become part, in every significant sense, of the social class to which their position, income and status gives them access'.

The extent to which the middle class, or certain sections of it, dominate Britain's political institutions is well portrayed by the excellent empirical analyses of the political élite by Guttsman[84] and Johnson.[85] Guttsman's data cover the period 1830–1955, while Johnson is concerned mainly with the years 1955–70. Examination of the social backgrounds of M.P.s and Cabinet Ministers throughout the period when the right to vote was extended to include most of the adult population (1832–1918) reveals that élite democratisation lagged behind that of the electorate. The middle class did not attain a majority in the cabinet until 1895, more than sixty years after they had achieved electoral predominance in the 1832 Reform Act (see Table 31).

TABLE 31 *Class structure of Cabinet personnel, 1868–1955*

	1868–1886	1886–1916	1916–1935	1935–1955	1868–1955
Aristocracy	27	49	25	21	93
Middle class	22	49	62	57	159
Working class	—	3	21	21	42
Total	49	101	108	99	294

Source: Guttsman, op. cit., Ch. 7, n32, p. 79.

This steady if slow progression up the political tree by the middle class, which we referred to in Chapter 2, is partly explained by its reluctance to create its own channels of élite recruitment. Existing routes were used, notably the major public schools, particularly Eton, and Oxbridge; these traditional channels actually increased in importance throughout the twentieth century despite the development of the Labour Party (see Tables 32 and 33).

Labour members of parliament

Perhaps nothing illustrates the grip that the middle class exercises on Britain's political life than its increasing monopolisation of leading positions in the major working-class party. In 1970 only a quarter of Labour M.P.s had been manually employed

TABLE 32 *Education and occupation of M.P.s, 1918–51 (in percentage).*

	1918–35 Cons	Labs	1945 Cons	Labs	1951 Cons	Labs
Education School:						
Elementary only	2.5	75.5	1.5	53.0	3.0	51.0
Grammar	19.0	15.5	13.5	24.0	14.5	26.5
Eton	27.5	1.5	29.0	2.0	25.0	1.5
Harrow	10.0	1.0	7.0	0.5	7.5	0.5
Other public schools	11.0	6.5	49.0	20.5	50.0	21.0
Nos.	348	153	215	401	321	296
Education University:						
Oxford	45.0	18.0	46.5	26.0	48.0	31.0
Cambridge	34.0	23.0	33.0	14.5	32.5	14.0
Other	21.0	59.0	20.5	59.5	19.5	55.0
Nos.	503	81	124	129	202	111
Nos. without university educ.	500	363	89	272	119	185
Occupation						
Employers and managers	32.0	4.0	32.5	9.5	32.5	9.0
Rank and file workers	4.0	72.0	3.0	41.0	4.5	45.0
Professions	52.0	24.0	61.0	48.5	57.5	45.5
Housewives	—	—	0.5	1.0	—	0.5
Unoccupied (rentiers)	12.0	—	3.0	—	5.5	—
Total Nos.	1003	444	215	401	321	296

Source: Ibid., Ch. 7, n32, p. 105. (adapted)

before their election, while the number with a professional background exceeded that found on the Conservative side (see Table 33). As the proportion of Labour members with higher education more than doubled between 1945 and 1970 (from about 20 per cent to over 50 per cent), the number of Oxbridge graduates increased from 12.9 per cent to 22.9 per cent.

The increasing 'middle-classness' of Labour M.P.s is largely accounted for by the candidate selection practices of constituency parties. Rush has shown that by 1966 they hardly ever nominated anyone with a manual background, while a second source of candidate nomination, the Cooperative movement, was similarly 'embourgeoisified'. Between 1955 and 1966 only one-

TABLE 33 *Education and occupation of M.P.s, 1955–70 (in percentage)*

	1955 Cons	Labs	1964 Cons	Labs	1970 Cons	Labs
Education						
School:						
Elementary only	2.3	34.0	1.0	31.2	0.6	20.6
Secondary	22.1	43.7	23.7	51.1	24.5	57.8
Harrow	5.8	0.3	5.6	—	4.2	—
Eton	22.7	1.4	22.4	0.6	17.9	0.7
Other public schools	47.1	20.6	47.3	17.1	52.8	20.9
Nos.						
Education						
University:						
Oxford	30.5	10.5	30.3	12.9	30.0	14.9
Cambridge	22.4	6.1	22.0	6.0	21.5	8.0
Other	10.5	23.2	10.8	23.3	11.5	30.8
Total university	63.4	39.8	63.1	42.2	63.0	53.7
Nos.	218	110	192	134	208	154
Nos. without university educ.	126	167	112	183	122	133
Occupation						
Employers and managers	36.3	9.0	37.2	8.2	39.7	7.7
Professions	60.2	49.1	59.8	52.7	58.8	61.3
Workers	3.5	41.9	3.0	39.1	1.5	31.0
of which						
(i) manual	0.3	35.0	0.7	32.5	0.6	25.1
(ii) non-manual	3.2	6.9	2.3	6.6	0.9	5.9
Total Nos.	344	277	304	317	330	287

Source: Johnson, op. cit., Ch. 7, n79. (1973), p. 46 (adapted).

sixth of their candidates were manual workers. Only trade union sponsorship ensures some working-class representation in the Commons; in the period 1950–66 just over 80 per cent of union candidates had manual worker origins, although this figure may have dropped since with the expansion of white-collar unionism. However, these candidates normally have a good chance of success; in 1970, for example, 112 out of a total of 137 union-sponsored candidates were elected.[86]

The expansion in middle-class positions only partly explains these changes. Johnson suggests that increasing demands within the party for 'ability' to constitute the criterion for candidate selection is a major factor in advantaging young middle-class graduates at the expense of older, less educated workers, for this 'puts a premium on education, professional qualification and articulacy'.[87] As the Labour Party has become a 'party of government', to be judged on its claim to manage the country more efficiently than its opponents, so has the tendency to select the 'brightest and the best' correspondingly intensified. There is a case, however, for classifying M.P.s not by parental or previous occupation but by their present occupation, that is as members of parliament. M.P.s should perhaps be considered as part of the professional middle class; to be a member of parliament is, like being a doctor or lecturer, to have an occupation to which entry increasingly requires a university education. Johnson notes, for example, that M.P.s now regard themselves in this way, basing claims for better pay and conditions on comparisons with groups such as civil servants and receiving severance pay if defeated in a general election.

Conservative members of parliament

In comparison with the Labour Party changes in the occupational backgrounds of Conservative members have been less dramatic. The major development is the displacement of landed aristocrats by the entrepreneurial middle class, and this has proceeded to the extent that it renders dubious the assertion that businessmen are reluctant politicians (and confirms that politicians are not reluctant businessmen!). Johnson calculates that in 1970, 218 Conservatives held 1,123 chairmanships and directorships between them, an average of five each. In comparison, '55 Labour businessmen had 104 such positions, an average of almost two each and made up 19 per cent of the Parliamentary Labour Party'. If we add to the total those 'professionals' who are really entrepreneurs selling services (e.g., lawyers), well over half M.P.s are businessmen.

Cabinet Ministers

A discussion of changes in the class compositions of Conservative Cabinets in recent years can be brief as the picture is one of remarkable stolidity. Between 1955 and 1972 the number of Ministers with a business background increased slightly, although this has diminished marginally in the present Conservative administration.[88] On the Labour side the changes that have occurred reflect, to a lesser degree, those that have occurred within the ranks of the M.P.s, although they appear to speed up during the course of a government. For example, few manual Ministers survived for long in the 1966–70 Labour administration, and by 1970 all had disappeared. Johnson points out that by 1970, of the twenty-three middle-class members: ten were public school products, thirteen of them had been to Oxford (five of them, indeed had been Oxford dons), one had been to Cambridge and seven to other universities.

As has happened in the selection of candidates, this reflects the displacement of 'politics' by technical criteria in the construction of Cabinets as the administration proceeds. While Prime Ministers are initially concerned to pay-off accumulated political and personal obligations and to ensure ideological and social balance in their ministerial teams, this soon changes to a perceived requirement for managerial 'competence' and the executive ability to handle a government department; inevitably, this results in more graduate, professional Ministers.

Interests and influence

How important are social origins for an explanation of 'interests'? The suggestion that the middle class, or parts of it, is substantially advantaged by the political system does not rest necessarily on demonstrating that political leadership positions are filled by those with middle class backgrounds, although this surely helps such an argument. Poulantzas, for example, criticises Miliband for conceiving the state and social classes as entities reducible to the actions of individuals. Individuals are to be regarded instead as 'expressions' of their position in the class structure. The state in capitalist societies is thus theorised as providing both ideological legitimation and the conditions of material production for the domination of one class by another, irrespective of the class characteristics of the individual participants.

However, individuals should not be considered simply as 'carriers' of their structural position for individuals have the capacity to act differently under apparently similar objective circumstances. In the face of a requirement to cut its expenditure one local authority may prefer to raise the rates rather than cut back on nursery education while another may prefer to take the opposite course. This is not to deny the existence of structural constraints (the local authorities have to take some action) but to argue that their influence on action are only properly deduced from, for example, a comparative, empirical analysis of government policy-making. Furthermore, while Miliband may overemphasise the congealing influences of family networks and social milieux in the reproduction of class differences and ideological predispositions, their existence helps us account for the shared definitions of reality that characterise the interactions of political élites and some middle-class activists, not least at the local level.

Property and local politics

We earlier discussed middle-class penetration of local Labour parties and its reflection in the social composition of Labour councillors, but we have yet to consider changes in the occupational background of non-Labour councillors. This is best approached by looking at the relationship between property and the local council, and we draw on the excellent historical accounts of two major British cities, Birmingham and Edinburgh, for this purpose.

The studies by Hennock,[90] and Morris and Newton[91] provide a continuous profile of the local political élite in Birmingham from the first town council in 1839 until the mid-1960s, and they are particularly instructive on the role played by businessmen as community decision-makers. The most general feature outlined by Hennock of the period up to the first world war is the gradual decline in the number of small businessmen on the council, apart from a brief resurgence in the late 1850's. Although they made up 54.7 per cent of the councillors in 1839, mainly in the penny-pinching 'Economy Party,' by 1896 they comprised only 15.3 per cent. At the same time the number of large businessmen on the council steadily increased, from 7.8 per cent in 1862 to 22.2 per cent in 1896, while the 'professional' group also grew until it was almost as large as the big business group by the end of the century. From around 1870 until the creation of the Greater Birmingham council in 1911 these last two groups dominated the council from within the Liberal Party.

Most studies of local politics in the twentieth century indicate a reversal of the process of big business involvement in the council chamber largely as the growth of large concerns predisposed owners and managers to influence national rather than local decision-makers (Bealey et al.[92] Birch,[93] Jones,[94] Lee[95]). Parish pump politics are thus left to smaller businessmen, primarily in the Conservative Party, and the increasing number of manual and lower professional workers to be found in the burgeoning Labour Party. However, the pattern of business withdrawal observed by Newton and Morris in Birmingham, although steady, appears less rapid than elsewhere; in 1966 businessmen still comprised 35 per cent of councillors, outnumbering both professional and manual workers, while their control of major committee chairmanships meant that they were 'powerful out of all proportion to their numbers'.[96] The use of the sweeping category 'businessman' may cloak changes in the type of business representation on the council. Newton and Morris draw particular attention to the 'striking' expansion of building interests in the chamber since the 1920s as the council became more involved in the city's housing plans and thus became a source of considerable attention for local developers.

A similar picture emerges in Elliott et al.'s account of local politics in Edinburgh over the period 1875–1975. They note that the character of 'property interests' have changed as local economies have come to be dominated by independent small businesses rather than by large firms, often with headquarters many miles away, as well as the local council which controls large amounts of public property. Elliott et al. explore the impact of these changes on Edinburgh politics by looking at three periods: 1845–1918, 1919–39; and 1940–75.[97]

In the first period the great proportion of councillors were property holders, including 80 per cent who were Edinburgh landlords, while the largest single group was made up of businessmen, including a quarter who were small shopkeepers. These belonged primarily to the Liberal Party, while the Conservatives attracted professional groups, especially lawyers, although the party structure remained underdeveloped and most candidates stood as individuals. Increasing support for the Labour Party in the inter-war years helped to structure the party system as an anti-socialist Progressive Association was formed to counteract Labour's organisation. The period also marked an extension of local authority responsibility for such matters as housing and transport and meant that 'Housing became a major issue in local elections and it directly affected property and building interests. Landlords were threatened by an increase in the supply of modern council houses and local builders by plans to use direct labour to build them.'[98] However, estate agents gradually replaced builders as the largest building interest and this change was reflected in the chamber. The final phase is characterised by the resurgence of a Conservative Party more attractive to the new professional 'servicers' of the building business, such as surveyors, mortgage brokers and lawyers, than the owners and managers of property. The Tories gradually emerged as the main opposition to Labour, and 'as the hold of Progressives with its parochial and petit-bourgeois character weakened, so the shopkeepers or small business candidates withdrew in favour of Tory challengers, who frequently came from rather different backgrounds'. By 1974, of the thirty strong Conservative group of councillors, 30 per cent were professionals, 37 per cent were businessmen and 20 per cent were white-collar workers.

We conclude with three final points on the relationship between property and local politics. First, although both small and larger property holders may have given ground to the new established middle class in the council chamber, they retain their political influence through their membership of a network of powerful local bodies, such as the Chambers of Commerce and Trade, the Rotary Club, the magistrate's bench and local school governorships. Secondly, the 'over-representation' of particular types of property on the council does not necessarily lead to these interests being favoured by council policy. In Croydon, for example, Saunders documents how the town centre redevelopment scheme, which harmed the local bourgeoisie and benefited incoming, usually larger businessmen was undertaken by a council composed predominantly of the former.[99] Finally, a consideration of the relationship between property and local politics must consider the influence wielded by domestic property owners. We have referred to the 'ratepayers' revolt' of the mid-1970s as an example of political action when owner-occupiers are especially enraged, but owner-occupiers exert political leverage in less dramatic ways. Saunders refers to the 'fundamental and underlying consensus of values and interests' between suburban middle-class groups and the local political élite which helps the former to present their demands (when they have to go as far as taking action) as 'non-political' and non-contentious. There are close personal relationships in Croydon between councillors and officials on the one hand, and the leaders of the staggeringly well supported and well organised ratepayers and residents associations on the other (the Federation of Southern Croydon Residents' Association has an active membership of 17,000 families). The local authority's persistent refusals to increase housing densities in the leafier parts of the borough to accommodate 'overspill' families from other parts of the Greater London Council Area exemplifies how council policy can reflect the interests of its middle-class residents without the need for the latter's 'mobilisation'. It explains why owner-occupiers, at least in Conservative dominated local councils in the south, manifest a passionate belief in the efficacy of 'non-political' local government, for who needs 'politics' when one's interests are so well catered for by political élites?

8

CONCLUSION

Despite the view that sociologists tend to ignore the middle class the previous chapters cover a remarkably wide range of literature on particular sections of the middle class. A major theme that recurs is that we should beware of over-simple contrasts between 'the middle class' and 'the working class'. There are two reasons for this warning. First, there appears to be increasing convergence by substantial sections of both classes on a variety of indicators – authority, working environment, status, family and political practices. Among the 'marginal' middle class, for example, we are likely to find individuals who identify with the working class, belong to trade unions, have little chance of advancement from routine, powerless work situations, vote Labour, and spend their leisure and family time in ways that even the sharpest-eyed sociologist would find difficult in distinguishing from that of the proletarian. Second, while the middle class has never comprised a coherent unity, even in the classic bourgeois age of the nineteenth century, it is even more of a heterogeneous grouping today. Not only do we need to distinguish between the entrepreneurial, independently professional middle class and the employed middle class, a cleavage that gives rise to smouldering resentment and occasionally flares into 'middle-class revolts' that are explained as much in terms of conflict within the middle class as antipathy to the working class, but we may also note signs of an increasing disparity in material and non-material rewards between the established and marginal middle class. Mix in, too, such factors as the increase in female employment and the post-war expansion in social mobility and we discover a less unified and more complex middle class than ever before.

We may briefly consider middle-class heterogeneity as indicated by three areas: occupation, values and politics. To take occupation first, while it is still possible to discern a 'break' in the reward system between manual and non-manual employment, its significance for class analysis is less clear than it was. Not only do we have difficulty in knowing to what the terms 'manual' and 'non-manual' refer, but the sexual division of labour also obscures the picture. For example, are typists to be regarded as 'middle-class' because they work in offices and wear white blouses although their working conditions may be drab, their pay poor, their authority non-existent and their hopes for advancement small? Does it matter for class analysis if a typist's husband is a coal-miner or an insurance agent? That is, to what extent does class refer to family or individual position, and if the former, who gives it its class identity?

Furthermore, even if the 'proletarianisation of the middle class' thesis is exaggerated, one reason for the advance of middle-class unionisation lies in the levelling and homogenisation of working conditions for many white-collar employees. It is not that these positions have necessarily been 'de-skilled', but that loss of authority to a smaller, more powerful group of top executives is reflected in the weakening of claims to special status and income differentials in comparison with the working class. This affects even parts of the solid middle class, particularly those managers who have worked their way up to middle management from the shop floor and who, if not yet especially attracted to trade unionism, show signs of bewilderment and disaffection with corporate 'rationalisation' schemes. The growth of state employment, too, also serves to obscure traditional conceptions of starkly contrasting fates for manual and non-manual employees, for in the public sector the latter frequently have no manual workers to order and are themselves increasingly subject to stringent financial and bureaucratic control.

These occupational changes are reflected at the level of values. We observed that the old bourgeois or 'protestant' ethic of hard work, thrift, independence, civility and 'gentlemanliness' helped to accommodate new thrusting parvenus with a patrician, feudal, political order in the nineteenth century. While we doubt whether these values have been as irredeemably eroded as some commentators maintain – family, work, educational and leisure patterns suggest that these values are still rooted within the middle class, particularly its 'traditional' sections – it is clear that public and large-scale organisational employment, the inclination to trade unionism, the growth of the 'consumer society', and developments towards 'symmetrical' and 'dual-career' families are among factors that have jolted established bourgeois norms and values. In particular, we find it increasingly difficult coherently to disentangle middle-class and working-class worlds in terms of contrasts between 'collectivism' and 'individualism'. Instead, it may be better to move away from notions of class-based value dichotomies and regard both classes as characterised by competing value systems – the cross-tugs of group or individual action, work or leisure, for example – whose influences depend on varying circumstances and conceptions of self-interest.

Finally, we note disparities of political power within the middle class, and while recognising middle-class political dominance, suggest that we should not overlook the sense of powerlessness and dispossession felt at the growth of corporatism, trade unionism and monopoly capitalism by several middle-class groupings; the small owner, the well-educated student activist and the ratepaying home-owner. The growth of the state is important, too, in locating the decline in the association between occupational class and party loyalty, for the increase in middle-class Labour voting to match a long-standing and continuing working-class Conservatism is to a large extent explained as the effect of both public sector employment and publicly organised consumption (housing, education, transport). But all this may disguise a seeping disenchantment with party politics and a move by the middle class towards non-party organisations. While a central task for the Conservatives is the reassurance of their traditional middle-class supporters, particularly the petite bourgeoisie, that for the Labour Party is to capture the hearts and minds of the new protestors – environmentalists, feminists, for example – to sustain its claim to be the party, not only of the working class, but of the middle-class radical, too.

REFERENCES AND FURTHER READING

Chapter 1 Concepts and issues

1 H. Newby et al., *Property, Paternalism and Power*, Hutchinson, 1978.
2 D. Lockwood, *The Blackcoated Worker*, Allen & Unwin, 1958.
3 F. Bechhofer et al., 'Structure, consciousness and action: a sociological profile of the British middle class', *B.J. Sociology*, December 1978, p. 411.
4 R. King and N. Nugent, *Respectable Rebels: middle class campaigns in the 1970s*, Hodder & Stoughton, 1979.
5 D. Webb, 'Some reservations on the use of self-rated class', *Sociological Review*, Vol. 21, 1973, pp. 321–30.
6 Kenneth Roberts et al., *The Fragmentary Class Structure*, Heinemann, 1977, p. 170.
7 P. Hutber, *The Decline and Fall of the Middle Class: and how it can fight back*, Associated Business Programmes Limited, 1976, p. 122.
8 R. Lewis and A. Maude, *The English Middle Classes*, Phoenix House, 1949.
9 A. Giddens, *The Class Structure of the Advanced Societies*, Hutchinson, 1973, p. 111.
10 Newby et al., op. cit., p. 266.
11 R. Aron, *La Lutte des Classes*, Paris, 1964.
12 R. Dahrendorf, *Class and Class Conflict in Industrial Society*, Routledge, 1959, p. 51.
13 Giddens, op. cit., p. 73.
14 F. Parkin, 'Social stratification', in T. Bottomore and R. Nisbet (eds), *A History of Sociological Analysis*, Heinemann, 1978, p. 612.
15 J. Urry, 'Towards a structural theory of the middle class', *Acta Sociologica*, Vol. 16, 1973, 175–87.
16 F. Parkin, *Marxism and Class Theory: a bourgeois critique*, Tavistock, 1979, p. 17.
17 N. Poulantzas, *Classes in Contemporary Capitalism*, New Left Books, 1975, p. 270.
18 P. Baran, *The Political Economy of Growth*, Calder, 1957, pp. 32–3; see also A. Hunt, 'Theory and politics in the identification of the working class', in A. Hunt (ed.), *Class and Class Structure*, Lawrence & Wishart, 1977, pp. 81–112.
19 G. Carchedi, *On the Economic Identification of Social Classes*, Routledge, 1978.
20. See also R. Crompton, 'Approaches to the study of white collar unionism', *Sociology*, September, 1976.

21 Lockwood, op. cit., 15–16.
22 J. Garrard et al., *The Middle Class in Politics*, Saxon House, 1978, p. 1.
23 G. Bain and R. Price, 'Who is a white collar employee?', *B.J. Industrial Relations*, Vol. 10, 1972, 325–39.
24 Poulantzas, op. cit., p. 270.
25 E. Garnsey, 'Women's work and theories of class stratification', *Sociology*, Vol. 12, May 1978, pp. 223–43.
26 Parkin, op. cit., p. 12.
27 F. Zweig, *The Worker in an Affluent Society*, Heinemann, 1961.
28 J. Goldthorpe et al., *The Affluent Worker in the Class Structure*, Cambridge University Press, 1969.
29 F. Zweig, *The New Acquisitive Society*, Barry Rose, 1976.
30 Roberts et al., op. cit., p. 94.
31 F. Parkin, *Class Inequality and Political Order*, MacGibbon & Kee, 1971, p. 18.
32 Tables 1 and 2 are adapted from I. Reid, *Social Class Differences in Britain*, Open Books, 1977, p. 26 and p. 33 respectively.
33 Parkin, *Class, Inequality and Political Order*, op. cit., p. 56.
34 See Chapter 3.
35 G. Routh, *Occupation and Pay in Great Britain 1906–60*, Cambridge University Press, 1965.
36 J. Westergaard and H. Resler, *Class in a Capitalist Society*, Penguin, 1976, p. 75.
37 Bechhofer et al., op. cit., p. 424.
38 *National Analysis of Salaries and Wages*, Reward Regional Surveys Limited, 1979.
39 Giddens, op. cit., p. 108.
40 D. Wedderburn and C. Craig, *Men in Manufacturing Industry*, Cambridge, 1969.
41 *Bargaining Report*, Labour Research Department, 1979.
42 Roberts et al., op. cit., p. 32.
43 See Reid, op. cit.
44 W. Runciman, *Relative Deprivation and Social Justice*, Routledge, 1966.
45 J. Goldthorpe and K. Hope, 'Occupational grading and occupational prestige' in K. Hope (ed.), *The Analysis of Social Mobility*, Oxford, Clarendon Press, 1972.
46 Parkin, *Class Inequality and Political Order*, op. cit., 30–34.
47 Parkin, *Marxism and Class Theory*, op. cit., p. 14.
48 Roberts et al., op. cit., p. 33.
49 C. Bell, *Middle-class Families*, Routledge, 1968.
50 Newby et al., op. cit., pp. 73–145.
51 King and Nugent, op. cit.
52 See C. Rallings, 'Political behaviour and attitudes among the contemporary lower middle class', in Garrard et al. (eds), op. cit., p. 185.
53 Giddens, op. cit., p. 288.
54 Garnsey, op. cit.
55 J. Goldthorpe et al., 'Trends in class mobility', *Sociology*, Vol. 12, September 1978, pp. 441–68. See also J. Goldthorpe and C. Llewellyn, 'Class mobility in modern Britain: three theses examined', *Sociology*, Vol. 11, May 1977; and J. Goldthorpe, *Social Mobility and Class Structure*, Oxford University Press, 1980.
56 Bechhofer et al., op. cit., p. 412.

57 R. Bacon and W. Eltis, *Britain's Economic Problems: too few producers*, Macmillan, 1976.
58 King, op. cit., p. 33.
59 Bechhofer, op. cit., p. 422.
60 Roberts et al., op. cit., 123–60.
61 L. Benson, *Proletarians and Parties*, Tavistock, 1978, p. 38.
62 Giddens, op. cit., p. 107.
63 Parkin, op. cit., p. 45. (1979).
64 J. Goldthorpe, 'Comment' on Bechhofer et al., *B.J. Sociology*, op. cit.

Chapter 2 The development of the middle classes

1 For discussion on this see Asa Briggs 'The language of class in early nineteenth-century England' in A. Briggs and J. Saville, *Essays in Labour History*, Macmillan, 1960; and Asa Briggs, 'Middle-class consciousness in English politics, 1768–1846', *Past and Present*, 1956.
2 D. Macrae, *Ideology and Society*, Heinemann, 1961.
3 P. Laslett, *The World We Have Lost*, Methuen, 1965.
4 Gregory King, *Natural and Political Conclusions upon the State and Conditions in England* (1696), quoted in L. Stone 'Social mobility in England 1500–1700', *Past and Present*, 1966.
5 Laslett, op. cit.
6 W. J. Reader, *Professional Men*, Weidenfeld & Nicolson, 1966.
7 D. Mathew, *The Social Structure of Catholic England*, Oxford University Press, 1948.
8 Stone, op. cit.
9 F. Thompson, *English Landed Gentry in the Nineteenth Century*, Routledge, 1963.
10 G. Cole, *Studies in Class Structure*, Routledge, 1955.
11 E. J. Hobsbaum, *The Age of Revolution, 1788–1848*, Weidenfeld & Nicolson, 1962.
12 Briggs, 'Middle-class consciousness in English politics', loc. cit.
13 James Mill, *Essay on Government*, 1820.
14 David Ricardo, *Principles of Political Economy*, 1817.
15 James Mill, *Westminster Review*, 1826, p. vi.
16 Lord Brougham, *Speeches on Social and Political Subjects* (1857), quoted in Harold Perkin, *The Origins of Modern English Society, 1780–1850*, Routledge, 1969.
17 Perkin, op. cit.
18 Thompson, op. cit.
19 Thompson, op. cit.
20 C. Erickson, *British Industrialists, Steel and Hosiery, 1850–1950*, Cambridge University Press, 1959.
21 P. Deane, *The First Industrial Revolution*, Cambridge University Press, 1965.
22 G. Kitson Clark, *The Making of Victorian England*, Methuen, 1961; W. Bagehot, *Essays on Parliamentary Reform*, Methuen, 1883.
23 Perkin, op. cit.
24 John Biffen, Chief Secretary to the Treasury, in a speech to Conservatives, reported in *The Sunday Times*, 20 January 1980.
25 Thompson, op. cit.

26 W. Burn, *The Age of Equipoise*, Allen & Unwin, 1964.
27 K. Smellie, *One Hundred Years of English Government*, 2nd edition, Duckworth, 1950.
28 Quoted in Frank E. Huggett, *Victorian England as seen by Punch*, Sidgwick & Jackson, 1978.
29 See A. Marwick, *Class: image and reality in Britain, France and the United States since 1930*, Collins, 1980.
30 J. M. Keynes, *Economic Consequences of the Peace*, Macmillan, 1918, p. 9.
31 C. Booth, *Life and Labour of the People of London*, 1903.
32 S. Rowntree, *Poverty: a study of town life*, 1901.
33 See P. Thompson, *The Edwardians*, Weidenfeld & Nicolson, 1975, for an illuminating account of the Edwardian social structure.
34 C. Money, *Riches and Poverty*, 1905.
35 C. Masterman, *The Condition of England*, 1909; see also, S. Hynes, *The Edwardian Turn of Mind*, Oxford University Press, 1968.
36 T. Escott, *King Edward VII and His Court*, London, 1903.
37 K. Middlemas, *Pursuit of Pleasure: high society in the 1900's*, Gordon & Cremon, 1977.
38 A. B. Atkinson, *The Economics of Inequality*, 1975; see also, A. H. Halsey, *Change in British Society*, Oxford University Press, 1978.
39 G. Orwell, 'The English people', in *Collected Essays, Journalism and Letters 1943–1945*, Vol. 2, Penguin edition, 1970.
40 A. Bennett, 'Middle class', in *Essays*, 1909.
41 R. H. Gretton, *The English Middle Class*, 1909.
42 Thompson, op. cit.
43 H. J. Dyos, *Victorian Suburb*, Leicester University Press, 1961.
44 Booth, and Rowntree, op. cit.
45 Report of the interdepartmental committee on physical deterioration, 1904.
46 In A. Newton (ed.), *The Empire and the Future*, p. 3, quoted in A. Marwick, *The Deluge*, Macmillan, 1965.
47 A. Balfour, *Decadence*, Cambridge, 1908.
48 H. Belloc, *The Servile State*, 1912.
49 Masterman, op. cit., p. 58.
50 In R. Lewis and A. Maude, *The English Middle Classes*, Penguin, 1949; condensed by them from a report in *The Times*, 1907.
51 For the fullest account of the impact of the First World War on British social structure see Marwick, *The Deluge*, op. cit.
52 M. Abrams, *Conditions of the English People*, 1945.
53 Middlemas, op. cit., p. 177.
54 J. Ramsden, *The Age of Balfour and Baldwin*, Longman, 1978.
55 W. L. Guttsman, *British Political Elite*, MacGibbon and Kee, 1966.
56 B. Donoughue and G. W. Jones, *Herbert Morrison, portrait of a politician*, Weidenfeld & Nicolson, 1973.
57 C. F. G. Masterman, *England After the War*, 1922, quoted in Lewis and Maude, op. cit.
58 Ibid.
59 Middlemas, op. cit.
60 S. Spender, *The Thirties and After*, Macmillan, 1977; paperback, Fontana.
61 J. Stevenson and C. Cook, *The Slump: society and politics during the Depression*, Cape, 1977.
62 J. B. Priestley, *English Journey*, Heinemann, 1934.
63 P. Addison, *The Road to 1945*, Quartet, 1977.

64 J. Ramsden, *Trends in British Politics since 1945*, Macmillan, 1978.
65 G. Orwell, *The Lion and the Unicorn*, 1941, collected essays, journalism and letters, Vol. 2, 1970.
66 Addison, op. cit.

Chapter 3 Work: the established middle class

1 J. Goldthorpe, 'Comment' on Bechhofer et al., *B.J. Sociology*, December 1978; A. Giddens, *The Class Structure of the Advanced Societies*, Hutchinson, 1973, p. 108.
2 N. Poulantzas, *Classes in Contemporary Capitalism*, New Left Books, 1975, p. 285.
3 F. Bechhofer et al., 'The petits bourgeois in the class structure: the case of shopkeepers', in F. Parkin (ed.), *The Social Analysis of Class Structure*, Tavistock, 1974, p. 104.
4 K. Kumar, 'The salariat', *New Society*, October 1976, p. 127.
5 A. Berle and G. Means, *The Modern Corporation and Private Property*, New York, 1932, p. 9.
6 J. Child, *The Business Enterprise in Modern Industrial Society*, Collier-Macmillan, 1969, p. 45.
7 J. Burnham, *The Managerial Revolution*, London, 1962, 73–4; (repr. Greenwood Press, 1972).
8 R. Dahrendorf, *Class and Class Conflict in Industrial Society*, Routledge, 1959, p. 42.
9 G. Carchedi, *On the Economic Identification of Social Classes*, Routledge, 1978.
10 R. Crompton and J. Ubbay, *Economy and Class Structure*, Macmillan, 1978, p. 70.
11 T. Veblen, *The Theory of the Leisure Class*, New York, 1899.
12 A. Atkinson, *Unequal Shares*, Penguin, 1972, p. 21; T. Noble *Modern Britain*, Batsford, 1975, p. 175.
13 C. Harbury and P. McMahon, 'Intergenerational wealth transmission and the characteristics of top wealth-leavers in Britain', in P. Stanworth and A. Giddens (eds), *Elites and Power in British Society*, Cambridge University Press, 1974, pp. 123–43.
14 P. Stanworth and A. Giddens, 'An economic élite: a demographic profile of company chairmen', in Stanworth and Giddens (eds), op. cit., p. 86.
15 R. Whitley, 'The city and industry: the directors of large companies, their characteristics and connections', in Stanworth and Giddens (eds), op. cit., p. 79.
16 R. Pahl and J. Winkler, 'The economic élite: theory and practice', in P. Stanworth and A. Giddens (eds), op. cit., p. 116.
17 Whitley, op. cit., p. 66.
18 Kumar, op. cit., p. 128.
19 T. Nichols, *Ownership, Control and Ideology*, Allen & Unwin, 1969, p. 141.
20 C. Crouch, 'The ideology of a managerial élite: the National Board for Prices and Incomes 1965–70', in I. Crewe (ed.), *British Political Sociology Yearbook*, Vol. 1, *Elites in Western Democracy*, Croom Helm, 1974, p. 60.
21 Burnham, op. cit.
22 P. Drucker, *The New Society*, Heinemann, 1951.
23 J. Galbraith, *The New Industrial State*, Penguin, 1967.

24 J. Schumpeter, *Imperialism, Social Classes*, Cleveland, 1961.
25 T. Geiger, *Die Klassengesellschaft in Schmeltzigel*, Cologne, 1949.
26 Giddens, op. cit., p. 171.
27 *The Times*, 'The £400m League', in J. Urry and J. Wakeford (eds), *Power in Britain*, Heinemann, 1973, p. 61.
28 J. Scott, *Corporations, Classes and Capitalism*, Hutchinson, 1979, p. 118.
29 M. Barratt-Brown, 'The controllers of British industry', in Urry and Wakeford (eds), op. cit., p. 78.
30 T. Nichols and H. Benyon, *Living with Capitalism: class relations and the modern factory*, Routledge, 1977, pp. 47–53.
31 Child, op. cit., p. 42.
32 Nichols, op. cit., p. 226.
33 Scott, op. cit., p. 143.
34 J. Winkler, 'Ghosts at the bargaining table: the director and industrial relations', *B.J. Industrial Relations*, Vol. 12, July 1974, p. 197.
35 D. Clark, *The Industrial Manager: his background and career pattern*, Business Publications, 1966, p. 43.
36 R. Clements, *Managers: a study of their careers in industry*, Allen & Unwin, 1958, Appendix II, Table 17.
37 Stanworth and Giddens, op. cit., p. 83.
38 J. Goldthorpe, *Social Mobility and Class Structure in Modern Britain*, Oxford University Press, 1980.
39 Giddens, op. cit., p. 171.
40 Winkler, op. cit., p. 199.
41 Pahl and Winkler, op. cit., p. 109.
42 Scott, op. cit., p. 41.
43 Ibid., p. 103.
44 Nichols and Benyon, op. cit., p. 37.
45 D. Gallie, *In Search of the New Working Class*, Cambridge University Press, 1978.
46 B. Roberts et al., *Reluctant Militants*, Heinemann, 1972.
47 H. Braverman, *Labour and Monopoly Capitalism*, Monthly Review Press, 1974.
48 Crompton, op. cit., p. 421.
49 Roberts et al., op. cit., 168–200.
50 F. Hirsch and J. Goldthorpe (eds), *The Political Economy of Inflation*, Martin Robertson, 1978.
51 See, for example, R. Blackburn and M. Mann, *The Working Class in the Labour Market*, Macmillan, 1979, p. 57.
52 Gallie, op. cit., p. 183.
53 Ibid., p. 186.
54 K. Roberts et al., op. cit., p. 75.
55 R. Williams and D. Guest, 'Are the middle classes becoming work shy?', *New Society*, July 1971.
56 R. Pahl and J. Pahl, *Managers and their Wives*, Penguin, 1971, p. 33.
57 Ibid., p. 238.
58 Ibid., p. 38.
59 C. Sofer, *Men in Mid-Career*, Cambridge University Press, 1970.
60 Lewis and Maude, op. cit.
61 J. Raynor, *The Middle Class*, Longman, 1969, p. 41.
62 Pahl and Winkler, op. cit., p. 118.
63 Newby, op. cit., p. 18.

64 E. Durkheim, *Professional Ethics and Civil Morals*, Glencoe, Illinois, 1958.
65 A. Carr-Saunders and P. Wilson, *The Professionals*, Frank Cass, 1964.
66 P. Elliott, *The Sociology of the Professions*, Macmillan, 1972, p. 53.
67 J. Jackson, 'Introduction', in J. Jackson (ed.), *Professions and Professionalisation*, Cambridge University Press, 1970.
68 See, for example, T. Parsons, 'Professions', *International Encyclopedia of the Social Sciences*, New York, 1968.
69 D. Bell, *The Coming of Post-Industrial Society*, Heinemann, 1974.
70 P. Halmos, *The Personal Service Society*, Constable, 1970.
71 T. Johnson, 'The professions in the class structure', in Scase (ed.), op. cit., pp. 93–110.
72 N. Parry, 'Professionalism and unionisation among the middle class: a conceptual problem for sociology', in Garrard et al. (eds), op. cit., p. 222.
73 G. Millerson, *The Qualifying Associations: a study in professionalisation*, Routledge, 1964, p. 13.
74 W. Goode, 'The Theoretical Limits of Professionalisation', in A. Etzioni (ed.), *The Semi-Professions and their Organisation*, New York, 1969, p. 227.
75 C. Turner and M. Hodge, 'Occupations and professions', in J. Jackson (ed.), op. cit., pp. 19–50.
76 T. Johnson, *Professions and Power*, Macmillan, 1972.
77 N. Parry and J. Parry, *The Rise of the Medical Professions: a study of collective social mobility*, Croom Helm, 1976.
78 N. Parry and J. Parry, 'Social closure and collective social mobility', in Scase (ed.), op. cit., p. 112.
79 Ibid., p. 119.
80 Parkin, op. cit., p. 54.
81 Ibid., p. 103.
82 Op. cit.

Chapter 4 Work: the marginal middle class

1 *Report of the Committee of Inquiry on Small Firms*, Chairman, J. Bolton, Cmnd 4811, HMSO, 1971, p. 68.
2 Ibid., p. 79.
3 Ibid.
4 Ibid., p. 81.
5 F. Bechhofer and B. Elliott, 'Persistence and change: the petite bourgoisie in industrial society', *Arch. Europ. Social.*, Vol. 18, 1976, p. 89.
6 R. Brown, 'Work', in P. Abrams (ed.), *Work, Urbanism and Inequality*, Weidenfeld & Nicolson, 1978, p. 83.
7 D. Eversley, 'Landlords' slow goodbye', *New Society*, January 1978.
8 D. McCrone and B. Elliott, 'What else does someone with capital do?', *New Society*, May 1979.
9 N. Poulantzas, *Classes in Contemporary Capitalism*, New Left Books, 1975, pp. 142–4.
10 Bolton *Report of the Committee . . . on Small Firms*, op. cit.
11 J. Goldthorpe et al., *The Affluent Worker in the Class Structure*, Cambridge University Press, 1969.
12 C. Caplow, *Principles of Organisation*, New York, 1964, p. 267.
13 G. Ingham, *Size of Industrial Organisation and Worker Behaviour*, Cambridge University Press, 1970, p. 65.

14 M. Stacey et al., *Power, Persistence and Change: a second study of Banbury*, Routledge, 1975, p. 21.
15 Bolton Report, op. cit., 1–2.
16 J. Boswell, *The Rise and Decline of Small Firms*, Allen & Unwin, 1972, p. 15.
17 F. Bechhofer and B. Elliott, 'The voice of small business and the politics of survival', *Sociological Review*, February 1978, p. 61.
18 Ingham, op. cit., p. 29.
19 H. Newby, *The Deferential Worker*, Allen Lane, 1977.
20 H. Newby, et al., *Power, Property and Paternalism*, Hutchinson, 1978, pp. 134–40.
21 J. Curran and M. Stanworth, 'Some reasons why small is not always beautiful', *New Society*, December 1978, p. 627. See also J. Curran and M. Stanworth, 'Worker involvement and social relations in the small firm', *Sociological Review*, May 1979, pp. 317–42.
22 Bechhofer and Elliott, op. cit.
23 J. McHugh, 'The self-employed and the small independent entrepreneur', R. King and N. Nugent (eds), *Respectable Rebels: middle-class campaigns in Britain in the 1970's*, Hodder & Stoughton, 1979, p. 66.
24 Newby et al., op. cit., p. 25.
25 Rallings, in Garrard et al., op. cit., p. 184.
26 Westergaard and Resler, op. cit., p. 103.
27 K. Roberts et al., op. cit., p. 158.
28 D. Lockwood, *The Blackcoated Worker*, Allen & Unwin, 1958, p. 14.
29 F. Klingender, *The Condition of Clerical Labour in Britain*, Lawrence, 1935, p. 61.
30 H. Braverman, *Labour and Monopoly Capitalism*, Monthly Review Press, 1974, pp. 293–361.
31 B. Roberts et al., *Reluctant Militants*, Heinemann, 1972, p. 9.
32 Lockwood, op. cit., p. 89.
33 Ibid., p. 20.
34 Ibid., p. 22.
35 Ibid., p. 85.
36 See Braverman, op. cit., p. 325.
37 Lockwood, op. cit., p. 99.
38 H. Wainwright, 'Women and the division of labour', in Abrams (ed.), op. cit., p. 169.
39 Ibid., p. 170. See too, Westergaard and Resler, op. cit., pp. 97–106.
40 A. Giddens, *The Class Structure of the Advanced Societies*, Hutchinson, 1973, p. 183.
41 H. Davis, *Beyond Class Images*, Croom Helm, 1979, p. 153.
42 C. Jenkins and B. Sherman, *White-collar Unionism*, Routledge, 1979, p. 7.
43 G. Bain, 'The growth of white-collar unionism in Great Britain', *B.J. of Industrial Relations*, 4, November 1966.
44 G. Bain, *The Growth of White-Collar Unionism*, Oxford University Press, 1970, p. 73.
45 K. Prandy, *Professional Employees*, Faber, 1965, p. 31.
46 Lockwood, op. cit.; R. Blackburn, *Union Character and Social Class*, Batsford, 1967.
47 R. Carter, 'Class, militancy and union character: a study of the Association of Scientific, Technical and Managerial Staffs', *Sociological Review*, May 1979, p. 304.

48 T. May, 'Middle class unionism', in R. King and N. Nugent (eds), op. cit.
49 G. Bain, *The Growth of White-Collar Unionism*, op. cit.
50 A. Carr-Saunders and P. Wilson, *The Professionals*, Frank Cass, 1964, p. 319.
51 G. Millerson, The *Qualifying Associations: a study in professionalisation*, Routledge, 1964, 26–41.
52 G. Bain et al., *Social Stratification and Trade Unionism*, Heinemann, 1973. p. 72.
53 Ibid., p. 72, quoting Blackburn, op. cit., p. 24.
54 Ibid., p. 77.
55 See M. Hart, 'Why bosses love the closed shop', *New Society*, February 1979, pp. 352–4.
56 K. Roberts et al., op. cit., p. 129.
57 Ibid., p. 131.
58 May, op. cit., p. 107.
59 B. Roberts et al., op. cit., p. 323.
60 *The Guardian*, 24 January, 1979, p. 1.
61 May, op. cit., p. 111.

Chapter 5 Family and education

1 P. Abrams and A. McCulloch, *Communes, Sociology and Society*, Camb. University Press, 1976.
2 R. Rapaport and R. Rapaport, *Dual Career Families Re-examined*, Martin Robertson, 1976.
3 See D. Cliff, 'Religion, morality and the middle class', in R. King and N. Nugent, *Respectable Rebels: middle-class campaigns in the 1970's*, Hodder & Stoughton, 1979.
4 See M. Young and P. Willmott, *Class and Kinship in East London*, Routledge, 1957.
5 P. Laslett, *Households and Family in Past Times*, Cambridge University Press, 1972.
6 P. Aries, *Centuries of Childhood*, Penguin, 1962, p. 395.
7 Ibid., p. 390.
8 C. Harris, 'Changing conceptions of the relation between family and societal form in western society', in R. Scase, *Industrial Society: class, cleavage and control*, Allen & Unwin, 1977.
9 E. Shorter, *The Making of the Modern Family*, Fontana, 1977.
10 M. Poster, *Critical Theory of the Family*, Pluto Press, 1978, p. 167.
11 M. Young and P. Willmott, *The Symmetrical Family*, Routledge, 1975, p. 273.
12 W. Watson, 'Social mobility and social class in industrial communities', in M. Gluckman and E. Devons (eds), *Closed Systems and Open Minds*, Oliver & Boyd, 1964.
13 M. Stacey et al., *Power, Resistance and Change: a second study of Banbury*, Routledge, 1975, p. 29.
14 C. Rosser and C. Harris, *The Family and Social Change*, Routledge, 1966.
15 H. Newby et al., *Property, Paternalism and Power*, Hutchinson, 1978.
16 R. Firth et al., *Families and Their Relatives: kinship in a middle-class sector of London: an anthropological study*, Routledge 1969, p. 449.
17 Ibid., p. 458.

18 See Young and Willmott, *Class and Kinship in East London*.
19 V. Karn, *Retiring to the Seaside*, Routledge, 1977.
20 C. Bell, *Middle-Class Families*, Routledge, 1969.
21 C. Bell, 'Occupation, career, family cycle and extended family relations', *Human Relations*, Vol. 29, no. 10, 1976, pp. 463–75.
22 D. Bell, *The Cultural Contradictions of Capitalism*, Heinemann, 1976; see also E. Zaretsky, *Capitalism, the Family and Personal Life*, Pluto Press, 1976, p. 61.
23 R. Levitas, Unpublished research.
24 A. Rigby, *Communes in Britain*, Routledge, 1974, p. 9.
25 P. Abrams and A. McCulloch, *Communes, Sociology and Society*, Cambridge University Press, 1976, p. 127.
26 E. Bott, *Family and Social Network*, Tavistock Publications, 1957, p. 60.
27 Young and Willmott, *The Symmetrical Family*, p. 258.
28 S. Edgell, 'Spiralists, their career and family', *B.J. Sociology*, Vol. 21, 1970, pp. 314–23.
29 J. Pahl and R. Pahl, *Managers and their Wives*, Allen Lane, 1970.
30 Rapaport and Rapaport, op. cit., p. 305.
31 See I. Reid, *Social Class Differences in Britain*, Open Books, 1977, p. 133.
32 A. Cartwright, *How Many Children?*, Routledge, 1976.
33 I. Reid, op. cit., p. 193.
34 J. Douglas et al., *All Our Future*, Panther, 1968, p. 196.
35 See O. Banks, *The Sociology of Education*, Batsford, 1968, Ch. 5.
36 J. Newson and E. Newson, *Seven Years Old in the Home Environment*, Allen & Unwin, 1976.
37 B. Bernstein, *Class, Codes and Control*, Routledge, 1971, Vol. 1.
38 A. Wooton, 'Talk in the homes of young children', *Sociology*, Vol. 18, May 1974, pp. 277–95.
39 B. Bernstein, and D. Young, 'Social class differences in conceptions of the uses of toys', *Sociology*, 1, May 1967, pp. 131–40.
40 J. Ford, et al., 'Functional autonomy and role distance', *B.J. Sociology*, Vol. 18, 1967, pp. 370–81.
41 R. Witkin, 'Social class influence on the amount and type of positive evaluation of school lessons', *Sociology*, Vol. 5, 1971, pp. 109–89.
42 B. Bernstein, 'Class pedagogies, visible and invisible', in *Class, Codes and Control*, Vol. 3, Routledge, 1976.
43 H. Rosen, *Language and Class*, Falling Wall Press, 1972.
44 B. Bernstein, 'Education cannot compensate for society', in Open University Reader, *School and Society*, Routledge, 1971.
45 S. Box and J. Ford, 'The facts don't fit: on the Relationship Between Social Class and Criminal Behaviour', *Sociological Review*, Vol. 19, 1971, pp. 31–52.
46 W. Bytheway and D. May, 'On fitting the facts. A rejoinder to Box and Ford', *Sociological Review*, Vol. 19, 1971, pp. 535–607.
47 See I. Pinchbeck and M. Hewitt, *Children in English Society*, Vol. 1, Routledge, 1969.
48 L. Althusser, 'Ideology and ideological state apparatus', *Lenin, Philosophy and Other Essays*, New Left Books, 1971, pp. 123–73.
49 J. Habermas, *Legitimation Crisis*, Heinemann, 1976.
50 K. Roberts et al., *The Fragmentary Class Structure*, Heinemann, 1977.
51 See R. Flacks, 'Young intelligentsia in revolt', in D. Wrong and H. Gracey (eds), *Readings in Introductory Sociology*, Macmillan, 1972.

52 F. Parkin, *Middle-Class Radicalism*, Manchester University Press, 1968.
53 S. Lipset and P. Altbach, 'Student politics and higher education in the United States', in S. Lipset (ed.), *Student Politics*, Basic Books, 1967.
54 T. Blackstone, *Students in Conflict: L.S.E. in 1967*, Weidenfeld & Nicolson, 1970.
55 J. Goldthorpe et al., 'Trends in class mobility', *Sociology*, Vol. 12, 1978, pp. 441–68.
56 P. Bordieu, 'Cultural reproduction and social reproduction', in R. Brown (ed.), *Knowledge, Education and Cultural Change*, Tavistock Publications, 1973, p. 71.
57 See B. Jackson and D. Marsden, *Education and the Working Class*, Penguin, 1962.
58 D. Potter, 'Stand up Nigel Barton', in *The Nigel Barton Plays*, Penguin, 1967.
59 W. Tyler, *The Sociology of Educational Inequality*, Methuen, 1977, p. 43.
60 R. Boudon, *Educational Opportunity and Social Inequality*, John Wiley, 1974.
61 A. Halsey et al., *Origins and Destinations: family class and education in Modern Britain*, Oxford University Press, 1980, p. 88.
62 Reid, op. cit., p. 181.
63 Ibid., p. 183.
64 J. Gaythorne-Hardy, *The Public School Phenomenon*, Hodder & Stoughton, 1977, p. 49.
65 R. Kelsall, 'Recruitment to the higher civil service', in P. Stanworth and A. Giddens (eds), *Elites and Power in British Society*, Cambridge University Press, 1974.
66 P. Venning, 'Survival of the public schools', in R. Bell et al., (eds), *Education in Britain and Ireland: a source book*, Open University Press, 1973.
67 M. Dent, *Education in England and Wales*, Hodder & Stoughton, 1977.
68 See M. Young, *Knowledge and Control: new directions for the sociology of education*, Collier-Macmillan, 1971.
69 Op. cit., p. 56.
70 R. Nash, *Classrooms Observed*, Routledge, 1973.
71 C. Lacey, *Hightown Grammar*, Manchester University Press, 1970.
72 D. Hargreaves, *Social Relations in a Secondary School*, Routledge, 1975, p. 168.
73 P. Willis, *Learning to Labour*, Saxon House, 1977.
74 J. Ford, *Social Class and the Comprehensive School*, Routledge, 1969, p. 37.
75 P. Bellaby, *The Sociology of Comprehensive Schooling*, Methuen, 1977, p. 105.
76 B. Sugarman, 'Social class, values and behaviour in school', in M. Craft (ed.), *Family, Class and Education*, Longman, 1970.
77 See H. Entwhistle, *Class, Culture and Education*, Methuen, 1978, p. 46.
78 J. Douglas, *The Home and the School*, Panther, 1967, p. 82.
79 J. Bynner, *Parents' Attitudes to Education*, HMSO, 1972, p. 27.
80 See C. Benn and B. Swann, *Half Way There: a report on British comprehensive school reform*, Penguin, 1972, p. 381.
81 J. Goldthorpe et al., *The Affluent Worker in the Class Structure*, Cambridge University Press, 1969, p. 139.
82 Lacey, op. cit., p. 76.
83 T. Burgess, *Home and School*, Allen Lane, 1973, Ch. 12.

Chapter 6 Leisure

1 K. Roberts, *Leisure*, Longman, 1970; K. Roberts, *Society and the Growth of Leisure*, Longman, 1978; S. Parker, *The Future of Work and Leisure*, MacGibbon and Kee, 1971; S. Parker, *The Sociology of Leisure*, Allen & Unwin, 1976; J. Dumazedier, *The Sociology of Leisure*, Elsevier, Amsterdam, 1974.

2 Dumazedier, op. cit., Ch. 1.

3 Parker, *The Future of Work and Leisure*, op. cit., 18–32.

4 K. Roberts, *Society and the Growth of Leisure*, op. cit., 1–13.

5 Dumazedier, op. cit., p. 15.

6 K. Roberts, *Society and the Growth of Leisure*, p. 15.

7 J. Child and B. Macmillan, 'Managers and their leisure', in M. Smith et al., *Leisure and Society in Britain*, Allen Lane, 1973.

8 The first major large-scale national surveys were: British Travel Association/University of Keele; *National Recreation Survey*, 1967; K. Sillitoe, *Planning for Leisure*, HMSO, 1969; North West Sports Council, *Leisure in the North West*, 1972. A useful summary of the main findings of the above surveys is contained in J. Coppick and B. Duffield, *Recreation in the Countryside*, Macmillan, 1975. See also the *General Household Surveys*, HMSO, 1973, 1977. For a summary of the findings on leisure of these two surveys see F. Birch, 'Leisure patterns in 1973 and 1977', in *Population Trends*, Vol. 17, Autumn 1979.

9 K. Roberts, op. cit., p. 7.

10 M. Young and P. Willmott, *The Symmetrical Family*, Penguin, 1975, pp. 337–60.

11 See, for example, *Social Trends 1980*, HMSO, p. 226.

12 I. Reid, *Social Class Differences in Britain*, Open Books, 1977, p. 210.

13 This may reflect a higher degree of home ownership amongst the middle class – see *Social Trends, 1980*.

14 Such activities are also an important aspect of what has been referred to as the 'hidden economy'. See J. Gershuny and R. Pahl, 'Britain in the decade of the three economies', *New Society*, January 1980.

15 Young and Willmott, op. cit.; see also M. Elson, 'The weekend car', *New Society*, April 1974.

16 This BBC survey, 'The peoples activities and use of time' is summarised in 'What do people do when they are not working?', *New Society*, December 1978, pp. 683–5.

17 Young and Willmott op. cit., p. 218.

18 Holidays are defined by the British Tourist Authority as 'a period of four or more nights away from home which is considered by the respondent to be a holiday'.

19 J. Walton, 'Holidays and the discipline of industrial labour', in M. Smith (ed.), *Leisure and Urban Society*, Leisure Studies Association, 1978.

20 B. Newman, 'Holidays and social class', in M. Smith et al., op. cit.

21 J. Walvin, 'Down to the sea in droves', *New Society*, August 1976, pp. 440–2.

22 R. Dubin, 'Industrial workers' worlds', *Social Problems*, January 1956. This is also available in E. Smigel (ed.) *Work and Leisure*, College and University Press, 1963.

23 L. Orzack, 'Work as a central life interest of professionals', *Social Problems*, Autumn 1959.

24 S. Parker, 'Relations between work and leisure', in M. Smith et al., op. cit. See also S. Parker, 'Work and leisure, theory and fact', in J. Haworth and M. Smith (eds), *Work and Leisure*, Lepus Books, 1975.
25 Child and Macmillan, op. cit.
26 J. Pahl and R. Pahl, *Managers and Their Wives*, Allen Lane, 1971.
27 See Young and Willmott, op. cit., and Child and Macmillan, op cit., p. 115. A major problem with Young and Willmott's data is that they have combined managers and professionals. It is impossible to know if there were any significant differences between them and the way in which one group biased or affected the findings.
28 Young and Willmott, op. cit., p. 259.
29 Ibid., p. 166. Managers and professionals say work interferes with their home and family life to a greater extent than do manual workers; similarly they are more likely to be interrupted at home by work-related problems.
30 R. Lansbury, 'Careers, work and leisure amongst the new professionals', *Sociological Review*, November 1974, pp. 305–400.
31 S. Parker, 'Professional life and leisure', *New Society*, October 1974.
32 G. Salaman, 'Some sociological determinants of occupational communities', *Sociological Review*, February 1971, p. 31.
33 K. Roberts, *Society and the Growth of Leisure*, pp. 117–21.
34 R. and R. Rapaport, *Leisure and the Family Life Cycle*, Routledge, 1975.
35 K. Roberts, *Society and the Growth of Leisure*, p. 94.
36 Goldthorpe et al., *The Affluent Worker in the Class Structure*, Cambridge University Press, 1969, 85–115. See also K. Roberts, ibid., p. 119.
37 C. Bell and I. Healey, 'The family and leisure', in M. Smith et al., op. cit., pp. 195–70.
38 See K. Roberts, *Society and the Growth of Leisure*, p. 103, and Young and Willmott, op. cit., p. 217.
39 See K. Roberts, ibid., p. 105.
40 R. Rapaport, *Working Couples*, Routledge, 1978.
41 See K. Roberts, *Society and the Growth of Leisure*, p. 13.
42 See S. Linder, *The Harried Leisure Class*, Columbia University Press, 1970.
43 Parker, op. cit., p. 35.
44 See G. Godbey, 'Anti-leisure and public recreation policy', op. cit., pp. 46–52.
45 Parker, op. cit., p. 152, and K. Roberts, *Society and the Growth of Leisure*, p. 123.
46 See D. Bell, *The Cultural Contradictions of Capitalism*, Heinemann, 1975; J. Habermas, *Legitimation Crisis*, Heinemann, 1975. Though in many respects similar, Habermas's analysis goes beyond Bell's. He suggests there are three potential sources of crises: economic, political and social cultural. The crises can manifest themselves in different forms: as a system crisis of the economy or rationality of administration, or identity or social crises in the form of legitimation or motivation failures. Bell concentrates on analysing the contradictory value systems contained within contemporary culture.
47 Bell, op. cit., p. 72.
48 See W. Arkin and L. Dobrofsky, 'Job sharing', in Rapaport and Rapaport, *Working Couples*, op. cit., pp. 122–37.
49 G. Murdoch and R. McCron, 'Scoobies, skins and contemporary pop', *New Society*, March 1973, pp. 690–2.

Chapter 7 Politics

1 These points are found in several works, but see P. Bachrach and M. Baratz, *Power and Poverty*, Oxford University Press, 1970; R. Dahl, *A Preface to Democratic Theory*, University of Chicago Press, 1956; J. Habermas, *Legitimation Crisis*, Heinemann, 1976; S. Lukes, *Power: a radical view*, Macmillan, 1974; H. Marcuse, *One-dimensional Man*, Routledge, 1964.
2 D. Butler and D. Stokes, *Political Change in Britain*, Penguin, 1971, pp. 90–104.
3 R. Alford, *Party and Society*, Chicago, 1963.
4 J. Westergaard and H. Resler, *Class in a Capitalist Society*, Penguin, 1975, p. 362.
5 J. Gyford, *Local Politics in Britain*, Croom Helm, 1976, p. 129.
6 S. Lipset, *Political Man*, Heinemann, 1960; see also S. Lipset and S. Rokkan, *Party Systems and Voter Alignments*, Free Press, New York, 1967, pp. 1–64.
7 R. Rose, 'Social structure and party differences', in R. Rose, *Studies in British Politics*, 3rd edn, Macmillan, 1976; see also R. Rose, 'Britain: simple abstractions and complex realities', in R. Rose, *Electoral Behaviour: a comparative handbook*, Free Press, New York, 1974, pp. 481–542.
8 I. Crewe et al., 'Partisan dealignment in Britain, 1964–1974', *B.J. Political Science*, Vol. 7, 1977, especially pp. 129–31.
9 K. Roberts et al., *The Fragmentary Class Structure*, Heinemann, pp. 161–79.
10 P. Dunleavy, 'The urban bases of political alignment: 'social class', domestic property ownership, or state intervention in consumption processes', *B.J. Political Science*, Vol. 9, 1979, pp. 409–43.
11 Rose, op. cit., pp. 217–30.
12 J. Rex and R. Moore, *Race, Community and Conflict*, Oxford University Press, 1967; see also J. Rex and S. Tomlinson, *Colonial Immigrants in a British City*, Routledge, 1979, ch. 5.
13 R. Haddon, 'A Minority in a Welfare State Society', *New Atlantis*, Vol. 2, 1970, pp. 80–133.
14 P. Saunders, 'Domestic property and social class', *International Journal of Urban and Regional Research*, 1978, pp. 233–51, and P. Saunders, *Urban Politics*, Hutchinson, 1979, pp. 66–102.
15 R. King and N. Nugent, 'Ratepayers' associations in Newcastle and Wakefield', in J. Garrard et al., *The Middle Class in Politics*, Saxon House, 1978, p. 242.
16 W. Grant, *Independent Local Politics in England and Wales*, Saxon House, 1977, pp. 86–103.
17 M. Castells, 'Advanced capitalism, collective consumption and urban contradictions', in L. Lindberg et al., *Stress and Contradiction in Modern Capitalism*, Lexington Books, 1975, p. 185.
18 Saunders, op. cit., p. 92.
19 Castells, op. cit.; see also M. Castells, *The Urban Question*, Arnold, 1979; M. Castells, *City, Class and Power*, Macmillan, 1978.
20 Dunleavy, op. cit., especially pp. 418–20.
21 R. Pahl, 'Collective consumption and the state in capitalist and state socialist societies', in R. Scase, *Industrial Society: class, cleavage and control*, Tavistock, 1977.

22 Crewe et al., op. cit., p. 170.
23 D. Jary, 'A new significance for the middle-class Left?', in Garrard et al., op. cit., p. 136.
24 J. Goldthorpe et al., 'Trends in class mobility', *Sociology*, Vol. 12, 1978.
25 F. Parkin, *Middle-Class Radicalism*, Manchester University Press, 1968.
26 C. Rallings, 'Two types of Middle Class Labour Voter?', *B.J. Political Science*, Vol. 5, 1975, pp. 107–11.
27 K. Roberts et al., op. cit., p. 169.
28 Jary, op. cit., p. 138.
29 Crewe et al., op. cit., p. 166.
30 J. Habermas, *Legitimation Crisis*, Heinemann, 1976.
31 A. Gouldner, *The Intellectuals and the Rise of the New Middle Class*, Macmillan, 1979.
32 W. Guttsman, *The British Political Elite*, MacGibbon and Kee, 1963, p. 237.
33 W. Hampton, *Democracy and Community: a study of politics in Sheffield*, Oxford University Press, 1970.
34 G. Jones, *Borough Politics: a study of Wolverhampton Town Council 1888–1964*, Macmillan, 1969.
35 F. Bealey et al., *Constituency Politics: a study of Newcastle-under-Lyme*, Faber, 1965.
36 B. Elliott et al., 'Property and political power: Edinburgh 1875–1975', in Garrard et al., op. cit., p. 111.
37 B. Hindess, *The Decline of Working Class Politics*, MacGibbon and Kee, 1971, p. 163.
38 T. Forester, *The Labour Party and the Working Class*, Heinemann, 1976, p. 68.
39 R. Johnson, 'The political élite', *New Society*, January 1974; R. Johnson, 'The British political élite 1955–72', in *European Journal of Sociology*, 1973 pp. 35–77.
40 Hindess, op. cit., p. 19.
41 Forester, op. cit., p. 80.
42 J. Gould, 'Riverside', *Fabian Journal*, No. 54, 1954.
43 Bealey et al., op. cit.
44 Hampton, op. cit.
45 A. Birch, *Small Town Politics*, Oxford University Press, 1959.
46 G. Jones, op. cit.
47 E. Janosik, *Constituency Labour Parties in Britain*, Pall Mall, 1968.
48 Elliott et al., op. cit.
49 Hampton, op. cit.
50 L. Sharpe, 'Elected representatives in local government', *B.J. Sociology*, Vol. 13, 1962, pp. 189–208.
51 Saunders, op. cit., p. 213.
52 R. Baxter, 'The working class and labour politics', *Political Studies*, Vol. 20, 1972, p.105.
53 Forester, op. cit., p. 119.
54 Saunders, op. cit., pp. 279–80.
55 Forester, op. cit., p. 122.
56 M. Pinto-Duschinsky, 'Stratification and policy in the British Conservative Party', *American Behavioural Scientist*, Vol. 17, 1973, pp. 285–92.
57 Bealey et al., op. cit., p. 251.

58 M. Tappin, 'Conservative activists: the social structure, recruitment and role perceptions of Scottish party activists', paper presented to the BSA/PSA Political Sociology Study Group, University of Manchester, November 1979.
59 A. Gamble, *The Conservative Nation*, Routledge and Kegan Paul, 1974 p. 133.
60 N. Harris, *Competition and the Corporate Society*, Methuen, 1972, p. 261.
61 Pinto-Duschinsky, op. cit.
62 F. Bechhofer and B. Elliott, 'The politics of survival', in J. Garrard et al., op. cit., p. 315.
63 J. Curran and M. Stanworth, 'Worker involvement and social relations in the small firm', *Sociological Review*, May 1979, pp. 317–42.
64 H. Newby et al., *Power, Property and Paternalism*, Hutchinson, 1978, pp. 134–40.
65 N. Killingback, 'Retail traders and Cooperative Societies: the shopocracy and politics', paper distributed at the BSA/PSA Conference on 'The Middle Classes in Politics', held at the University of Salford, January 1977, p. 4.
66 See, for example, J. Blondel, 'The Conservative Association and the Labour Party in Reading', *Political Studies*, Vol. 2, 1958, p. 102; and D. Butler and M. Pinto-Duschinsky, *The British General Election of 1970*, Macmillan, 1971, p. 288; M. Parkinson, 'Central-local relations in British parties: a local view', *Political Studies*, Vol. 4, 1971, pp. 440–6.
67 Butler and Pinto-Duschinsky, op. cit., p. 293.
68 M. Wilson, 'Grass roots Conservatism: the motions to the Party Conference', in N. Nugent and R. King (eds), *The British Right*, Saxon House/Teakfield, 1977, pp. 64–98.
69 F. Bechhofer and B. Elliott, 'Resistance and change: the petite bourgeoisie in industrial society', *European Journal of Sociology*, Vol. 17, 1976.
70 Gamble, op. cit., p. 75.
71 W. Grant and D. Marsh, *The CBI*, Hodder & Stoughton, 1977, Ch. 5.
72 For a fuller discussion of NARAG see N. Nugent, 'The ratepayers', in King and Nugent, op. cit., pp. 23–45.; for a fuller discussion of NFSE see J. McHugh, 'The self-employed and the small independent entrepreneur', ibid., pp. 46–75.
73 Nugent, op. cit., p. 34.
74 Ibid., p. 38.
75 R. Dowse and J. Hughes, 'The sporadic interventionists', *Political Studies*, Vol. 25, 1977, pp. 84–92.
76 For a fuller account of the Middle Class Association see R. King, 'The middle class in revolt?', in King and Nugent, op. cit., pp. 1–22.
77 Ibid., p. 17.
78 Garrard et al., op. cit., Bechhofer and Elliott, op. cit.
79 C. Crouch (ed.), *British Political Sociology Yearbook: participation in politics*, Croom Helm, 1977, p. 2.
80 W. Grant, 'Insider groups and outsider groups', paper given at the European Consortium for Political Research Conference on 'Political Attitudes and Behaviour of the Middle Class in Europe', Berlin, 1977.
81 A. Barker and M. Keating, 'Public spirits: amenity societies and others', in Crouch, op. cit., p. 145; see also A. Barker, *The Local Amenity Movement*, Civic Trust, 1976.
82 F. Parkin, *Marxism: a bourgeoise critique*, Tavistock, 1979, p. 127.

83 R. Miliband, *The State in Capitalist Society*, Quartet, 1973, p. 55.
84 Guttsman, op. cit.
85 Johnson, op. cit.
86 M. Rush, *The Selection of Parliamentary Candidates*, Nelson, 1969, p. 203.
87 Johnson, op. cit., p. 71.
88 Ibid., p. 52.
89 N. Poulantzas, 'The problem of the capitalist state', in J. Urry and J. Wakeford, *Power in Britain*, Heinemann, 1973, pp. 291–305.
90 E. Hennock, *Fit and Proper Persons*, Arnold, 1973.
91 D. Morris and K. Newton, 'Profile of a local political élite: businessmen as community decision-makers in Birmingham, 1838–1966', *The New Atlantis*, Vol. 2, 1970, pp. 111–24.
92 Bealey et al., op. cit., p. 400.
93 Birch, op. cit., p. 117.
94 Jones, op. cit., p. 368.
95 J. Lee, *Social Leaders and Public Persons*, Oxford University Press, 1963.
96 Newton and Morris, op. cit., p. 116.
97 Elliott et al., op. cit.
98 Ibid., p. 114.
99 See, particularly, Saunders (1979), op. cit., pp. 297–324.

INDEX

THE ELDERLY IN MODERN SOCIETY
Anthea Tinker
First published 1981

Economic constraints combined with the projected large increase in the numbers of frail elderly pose difficult problems for families and policy makers in the next two or three decades. By taking into account a wide range of literature from medicine, architecture, sociology, psychology and social policy media, this book presents an account of the present situation and analyses some of the problems and options for the future. The author suggests that families and voluntary bodies will have to play an even greater part than they already do in family care and that realistic supportive services are necessary. In contrast it is also noted that many elderly people require little in the way of services and their contribution to society is greatly underestimated. The book also includes a summary of recent major surveys with views of the effect of recent changes in the organisation of the social services on the elderly.
This text is aimed at students studying degree and diploma courses in social policy. It also presents a reappraisal of society's responsibilities towards the elderly, and will stimulate great interest among social workers, trainee social workers, and the general public.

COMMUNICATION
Denis McQuail
First published 1975

This book offers a sociologist's view of some of the basic questions about communication as a social process. Theories and models of communication are reviewed, and a variety of relevant empirical researches are summarized. Professor McQuail takes the view that communication processes and outcomes reflect the distribution of power in society and between societies, and that an understanding of how communication works can contribute to defining and resolving some current human problems.

THE MASS MEDIA
Peter Golding
First published 1974

This book examines the media in contemporary Britain, and reviews attempts by social scientists to research into their structure and effects. It surveys the evolution of the mass media and the continuing process of change, the communicators themselves, and the role of the mass media as part of a wider complex of social institutions.

PERSONALITY AND HEREDITY
an introduction to psychogenetics
Brian W. P. Wells
First published 1980

Some of the most acrimonious and crucial scientific controversies of recent years have been concerned with the genetic transmission of human psychological characteristics, particularly in relation to sex differences, criminal and psychopathic behaviour, racial differences, intelligence and homosexuality.

In *Personality and Heredity* Dr Brian Wells has provided a reliable and clear introduction to the relatively new science of psychogenetics. The wide range of material includes evidence in support of the view that aspects of normal intellectual and temperamental development are not only differentially influenced by genetic mechanisms, but so too are many psychotic, neurotic and personality disorders. The author discusses in detail the question of the social significance of inherited psychological traits and its implications for education and psychiatry, race and sex relations, eugenics and genetic engineering.

This book provides a fascinating guide to inherited characteristics for a wide range of readers concerned, scientifically, practically and intellectually with human behaviour and adjustment.

POLITICS TODAY

Edited by Bernard Crick and Patrick Seyd

This paperback series introduces the general reader and the student to the main issues of modern British politics in such a way that the reader can gain a reliable account of how an issue arose, of its institutional context and then discuss what should be done.

THE POLITICS OF NATIONALISM AND DEVOLUTION
Henry Drucker and Gordon Brown

THE POLITICS OF THE INNER CITIES
Geoffrey Green

THE POLITICS OF POVERTY
Susanne MacGregor

THE POLITICS OF SEXUAL MORALITY
Cate Haste

THE POLITICS OF LOCAL GOVERNMENT
Alan Alexander

THE POLITICS OF WOMEN'S RIGHTS
April Carter

THE POLITICS OF TOWN PLANNING
Gordon Cherry

THE POLITICS OF PENAL REFORM
Mike Ryan

THE POLITICS OF TRANSPORT
Enid Wistrich

THE POLITICS OF ENERGY
Roger Williams